Modern Real Estate Investing
The Delaware Statutory Trust

tax rules for real estate under the TAX CUTS AND JOBS ACT

Build a Diversified Portfolio of Institutional Real Estate Using the DST & §1031 Exchange Tax Deferral.

- office
- retail
- multifamily
- senior
- hotel
- industrial

Institutional Real Estate for the Private Investor with Low Minimum Investment Amounts (DSTs are for Accredited Investors Only)

Section 1031:
No gain...
Shall be recognized...

CORNERSTONE
REAL ESTATE INVESTMENT SERVICES
COMBINING THE POWER OF §1031 & SECURITIZED REAL ESTATE

By John Harvey, CPA, MBT, Trawnegan Gall, and David Kangas

Copyright © 2018 John Harvey CPA, MBT,
Trawnegan Gall, and David Kangas
All rights reserved
First Edition

PAGE PUBLISHING, INC.
Conneaut Lake, PA

First originally published by Page Publishing 2018

ISBN 978-1-64298-342-5 (pbk)
ISBN 978-1-64298-343-2 (digital)

Printed in the United States of America

Modern Real Estate Investing

THE DELAWARE STATUTORY TRUST

John Harvey CPA, MBT, Trawnegan Gall,
and David Kangas

Author Contact Information:

Cornerstone Real Estate Investment Services
Address: 1 City Boulevard West, Suite 870 Orange, CA 92868
Website: www.dstproperties1031.com
Email: info@cornerstoneexchange.com
Telephone: (800) 781-1031

Reviewed by FINRA

Contents

Acknowledgments 7
Foreword 9
About the Authors 13

Introducing the DST
Chapter 1: The DST Vision 19
Chapter 2: DST Advantages 30
Chapter 3: The DST Structure 44
Chapter 4: DST Disadvantages, Risks, and Fees 60
Chapter 5: Who May Invest 66
Chapter 6: The 2017 Tax Cuts and Jobs Act 72
Chapter 7: Introduction to the 1031 Exchange 88

The DST Offering
Chapter 8: DST Industry Overview 107
Chapter 9: Choosing a Broker 120
Chapter 10: Choosing a Sponsor 129
Chapter 11: Choosing a DST Property 136
Chapter 12: The Closing Process 150
Chapter 13: The Hold Period and What to Expect 159
Chapter 14: The Final Disposition 167

Analyzing the DST Offering
Chapter 15: Due Diligence 175
Chapter 16: Analyzing the PPM Document 186
Chapter 17: Debt Structures 197
Chapter 18: Diversification Strategies 205
Chapter 19: Depreciation and Tax Matters 215
Chapter 20: Investment Risk Factors 223

Chapter 21: Why Not a TIC? 267
Chapter 22: The History of the TIC and DST Industry 277

Direct Investments (Non-1031)
Chapter 23: Private Real Estate Investment Trusts......................297
Chapter 24: Real Estate and Other Funds.................................303

Appendices
Chapter 25: Revenue Ruling 2004-86..311
Chapter 26: Revenue Procedure 2002-22..................................323
Endnotes 329

Acknowledgments

The goal of this book is to introduce the DST concept for real estate investing to the nation. To accomplish this objective, the publication must by necessity be representative of the industry and a collaborative effort between the authors and multiple individuals and organizations within the DST industry. At the outset of this publication, I would like to thank the many valuable contributions made by my brilliant and altruistic professional colleagues.

I would like to thank my coauthors and trusted business partners Trawnegan Gall and David Kangas. Their excellent and insightful chapters were forged from the immeasurably valuable time between client service and family devotion. In turn, I and my coauthors extend our heartfelt thanks to Susan Gall for her editing work on our countless revisions and her contributions to style and formatting.

Broadening the scope of our thanksgiving to contributions from the industry in various forms, we would like to thank Louis Rogers of Capital Square 1031 for the dialog on tax reform and its impact on DSTs; Darryl Steinhause of DLA Piper for his valuable insights on the history of the industry and due diligence; Matt Calabrese, Simon Brower, Bluerock and Baker & McKenzie for their contribution to DST risk disclosures; Stephen Decker of IPX1031 Exchange Services for his contribution to the ID rules for DSTs; Sean Hall and Nati Kiferbaum of Inland Private Capital for their contribution to the sponsor acquisition process; Andy Wang and Adriana Olsen of Passco Companies for their contribution to hold period issues; Geoff Flahardy of ExchangeRight for his contribution to the closing process; Taylor Garrett, Brandon Balkman, and Mountain Dell Consulting for their accurate reporting of industry statistics and their informative graphics. Speaking of graphics, I would like to thank my brother Peter Harvey for his artistic and creative cover and graphs, which bring a touch of color and artistry to a technical subject. Thank you all for your wisdom and participation!

I would like to thank my wonderful wife, Galina, and our beautiful children—John Paul, Joshua, and Simona—for their loving and faithful support. Kids, you are the best "investment" we have ever made! Sorry if we were late once or twice to football practice or dance class. No, Dad was not spending all that time at the computer playing video games, but rather struggling to present a new concept to the nation.

My coauthors and I dedicate this book to our clients—you are truly our inspiration!

Foreword

A wise politician once said that he did not run for public office when he was younger as he felt he did not have sufficient life experience to contribute to the nation. Similarly, we did not set out to write this book until we had nearly two decades of experience in the real estate private placement industry. Since we began in the industry in early 2004, we have assisted hundreds of 1031 exchange clients to acquire over half a billion dollars in fractional ownership real estate. This past decade we have also witnessed the impact that a period of hyper-CAP rate compression (rising prices), followed by the Great Recession, have had on fractional ownership real estate, and how the industry has evolved to cope with these economic and market forces.

We believe the past decade of significant economic cycles forced the fractional ownership structure to evolve from TICs to DSTs to provide the investor with a tried and tested investment vehicle that is best equipped to allow the private investor access to institutional real estate as never before, while employing the tremendous power of tax deferral under IRC §1031 exchange. The timing of this publication is especially suitable as we believe we are the first to present DST real estate investing under the new tax provisions of the 2017 Tax Cuts and Jobs Act. These new tax rules not only preserve §1031 exchange for generations to come but also help to significantly accentuate DST tax advantages.

We have endeavored to produce a publication that is far more than an advertisement for our firm and its services. We have asked several of our trusted colleagues from various real estate sponsors, attorneys, and qualified intermediaries to further enrich this book through their contributions in various forms. In doing so, we believe this book represents the entire industry as we seek to introduce DSTs and private placement real estate to the nation.

The material is divided into four sections. In the first section, we strive to provide a comprehensive introduction to alternative real estate investing using the DST offering. We hope this introduction will invite the private investor to test the waters of private placement investing. In the second section, we provide a roadmap to the DST offering, giving context and perspective, to an otherwise unfamiliar and uncharted industry. Along the way, we hope to provide insight into choosing trusted business partners (qualified intermediaries, brokerages, and sponsors) and help build investor confidence, ultimately empowering the private real estate investor to utilize the effectiveness of § 1031 exchange tax deferral to build a well-diversified personal portfolio of institutional-grade real estate.

The third section is what we term "analyzing the DST offering." In our view, real estate investing is more about data analysis than the art of the deal. Here we endeavor to provide even the more seasoned investor with greater insight into utilizing the abundance of data and information in the full-disclosure private placement memorandum, in order to select properties that minimize risks and meet investment objectives.

The final section of the work introduces the reader to other alternative real estate investment structures, namely publicly registered but privately traded REITs and limited partnerships (funds). While these structures do not qualify for § 1031 tax-deferred exchange, they do allow for even greater diversification, with limited exposure to the volatility of the financial markets, utilizing noncorrelated real estate investments.

To be true to our readers and our highly regulated industry, we strive throughout the book to offer a fair and balanced presentation. In doing so, we attempt to balance advantages with disadvantages and opportunities with associated risks. To this end, we have dedicated an entire chapter to potential risks.

We hope that this book helps open new doors of investment opportunity for the reader and, by implementing its insights, contributes to the reader's continued financial success. For more information and for any questions, our contact details are available at www.dstproperties1031.com.

John Harvey, CPA, MBT
President
Cornerstone Real Estate Investment Services

About the Authors

John Harvey CPA, MBT

John Harvey is the firm's owner and general securities principal. Mr. Harvey holds a master of business taxation and a bachelor of science in accounting from the University of Southern California (USC) Leventhal School of Accounting. He began his career in 1989 with the Beverly Hills office of Ernst & Young as a tax consultant to high net-worth celebrities. Mr. Harvey has been a licensed CPA since 1991 and has worked as a tax consultant for Price Waterhouse and as a senior manager with Deloitte & Touché in Los Angeles.

Mr. Harvey is a registered investment advisor, general securities representative, and general securities principal (FINRA series 24, 7, 66, and 63) and offers Delaware Statutory Trust properties for investment through WealthForge Securities LLC (member FINRA, SIPC). He is a licensed real estate broker in the state of California and a member of the Real Estate Investment Securities Association, National Association of Realtors, Apartment Owners Association, and the California Society of CPA's.

Mr. Harvey is an elite advisor for Cornerstone, assisting investors in the purchase of over $1 billion in tenants-in-common and Delaware Statutory Trust real estate. These credentials, together with his business knowledge and real-world experience, allow the firm to offer in-depth real estate advice on § 1031 exchange replacement properties with a view to the effects on income and estate taxation.

Trawnegan Gall

Trawnegan Gall is a licensed securities representative for Cornerstone. After graduating from Pomona College with a BA in history in 1990, he spent extensive time abroad working with non-profits, specializing in the areas of strategic planning of international operations, project management, personnel development, negotiations, and problem-solving. Strong in factual analysis, he also played an integral role in the areas of budgeting and financial planning. His passion has always been languages and linguistics. He is functionally fluent in four languages, and has studied languages from the European, Middle Eastern, Asian, and Pacific Islands groups.

In his practice at Cornerstone, Mr. Gall specializes in brokering Delaware statutory trust investments as replacement properties for 1031 exchange. He also brokers investments into real estate funds, private equity and private debt funds, private REITs and energy-based offerings. Mr. Gall has a regular working relationship with nearly all DST sponsors and has reviewed approximately 90% of all syndicated DSTs since the recession, brokering investments in excess of $160 million on behalf of 1031 exchange investors.

David Kangas

David Kangas is a licensed general securities representative (FINRA series 7 and 63) for Cornerstone. He spent many years managing technical sales within the construction industry, focusing on relationship management, new product development, and client services.

Mr. Kangas spent more than fifteen years managing nonprofit organizations, specializing in the areas of domestic and international affiliate relations, project management, asset management (commercial and residential), budgeting, social media marketing, and operations. In addition to his strong analytical and problem-solving skills, Mr. Kangas brings to Cornerstone his passion for working with people and providing them with the best in client service. Mr. Kangas graduated from Henderson State University with a BS in business administration and aviation science and holds a Commercial Pilots License and Certified Flight Instructor certificates (CFII, MEI).

Introducing the DST

Chapter 1

The DST Vision

The dream of building wealth and enjoying financial independence is alive again in America! Over a century of major US legislation has allowed real estate to effectively synthesize with protective securities regulation and beneficial tax law to produce a new investment concept known as the Delaware Statutory Trust, or simply the DST.

A DST is a trust formed under Delaware statutory law that essentially provides for a *fractionalized* real estate investment, and presents the opportunity, through a securities private placement offering, for an individual to join with other accredited investors to own investment-grade real estate that none of them could own individually. With DST minimum investments as low as $25,000 ($100,000 for exchanges), the private investor may own larger commercial institutional-grade real estate with values up to $100 million. A *fractional ownership* interest provides the investor with an undivided fractional ownership interest in the entire property or properties, including the projected cash flow, potential appreciation, and tax-deductible depreciation. Thus, a fractional ownership allows for coownership with other similarly qualified investors, but not the right to use or possess the property. Furthermore, the purchase and sale of a DST interest may qualify for capital gain nonrecognition under Section 1031 of the Internal Revenue Code.

Accordingly, what's new and exciting in real estate investing is not the partnership, the LLC, the S-Corporation, or even the TIC. It's the Delaware Statutory Trust! The advantages of a DST property offering include, but are not limited to, a low minimum investment amount, access to institutional-grade properties, national credit tenants, stabilized monthly income, greater diversification, full disclosure offering materials, professional due diligence, limited liability protection, more favorable financing terms, lower transaction and administrative costs, and tax-deferred capital gains. The DST vision is the cumulative realization of these numerous advantages.

Background and Perspective

America, with all its diversity and innovation, has traditionally provided the private investor with three core means for *passively* building wealth. These are commodities, securities, and real estate. Commodities, from gold to soybeans, are purely speculative and do not add value; they are disadvantaged because they provide the investor with no cash flow and no tax shelter. Securities markets have developed over the nation's history to provide investors with very regulated, highly liquid, and well-diversified markets for stocks, bonds, derivatives, and alternative investments. While marketable securities have a place in every income and growth portfolio, the two major headwinds to building wealth using securities have traditionally been *taxation* and market *volatility*. Although both commodities and securities may be held in qualified investment accounts such as an IRA or 401K, tax rules strictly delay any enjoyment of income until the investor's retirement years, and even then, with certain limitations.

Thankfully, nearly one hundred years of legislative and judicial landmarks have integrated to bring together in the DST some of the best features of these core markets. Chronologically, these legislative and judicial landmarks are:

- The 1921 adoption of Section 1031 into the Internal Revenue Code to allow for nonrecognition of capital gain for real estate,
- The 1933 Securities Act that provided for Regulation D private placement rules applicable to certain real estate offerings,

- The 1946 landmark case of *SEC v. W. J. Howey Company*, the US Supreme Court defined an investment contract,
- The 1988 Delaware Statutory Trust Act that provided a multi investor structure flexible enough to accommodate the requirements of IRC Section 1031,
- The 2004 IRS Revenue Ruling 2004-86 holding that real estate held in a properly structured Delaware Statutory Trust qualifies for IRC Section 1031 exchange, and
- The 2017 Tax Cuts and Jobs Act that preserved 1031 exchange for real property.

The cumulative effect of these real estate laws, securities laws, and tax laws has formulated a new ownership structure in the Delaware Statutory Trust. The DST has become a means for the private investor to build and preserve wealth within a regulated investment environment using institutional-grade real estate on a tax-deferred basis while enjoying tax sheltered passive income. In short, the modern private investor may now enjoy the best of both worlds—the tax benefits of real estate and the due diligence and full disclosure of securities.

Taxation

We will explore all the advantages of a DST, as well as the disadvantages, in chapter 2, chapter 4, and throughout the book. But first, let's address the elephant in the room. Why a trust? Aren't trusts used for estate planning and gifts to charity? Why not a traditional LLC or partnership? The answer is that one thing that is most often paired with death—taxes! As with every other kind of investment, the sale of an asset is met with a short-term or long-term capital gain tax.

With real estate, the tax bite out of an investor's wealth can be especially substantial, as any allowed or allowable depreciation that was deducted against the rental income over the hold period must first be recaptured at a rate of 25 percent—ouch! Then there is the tax on the long-term capital gain at 20 percent (in most cases), not to mention the Affordable Care Act tax at 3.8 percent, and finally the state and local taxes at 6 percent (on average). These taxes can add up to a third or more of all the gain realized from the investment. Considering this haircut to the investor's built-up equity, as well as the lost future income that could have been earned on that equity, we quickly realize that taxation, in addition to volatility, can be a major obstacle to building wealth in America.

Thank goodness for Internal Revenue Code Section 1031! About one hundred years ago, our forefathers realized that, unlike selling an investment interest in one business entity (such as the Coca-Cola Corporation) and then reinvesting in another business entity (such as the Pepsi Corporation), selling a real property and then immediately exchanging it for another like-kind real property was not a change in the actual investment at all, and should therefore not be taxed. Over the past decades, this "Cinderella" concept encoded in 1921 into IRS Section 1031 has allowed real estate to excel as a means of building wealth over its comparatively ugly step sisters—commodities and securities (at least from a tax point of view).

The tax advantages of gain nonrecognition with real estate have come at a heavy price—active management. The labor necessary to manage real estate can be time-consuming and exhausting. The private real estate investor knows all too well the burdens and stresses of rent collection, repairs, maintenance, bill payments, and accounting, just to name a few. How about local laws controlling eviction and—should I say it? Rent control! These troubles are often accentuated with smaller and older properties. And it is this menace of active management that has kept most private investors in the commodities and securities markets despite the disadvantage of taxation.

A DST effectively liberates the private real estate investor from the management obligations of individual ownership, commonly referred to as the "three Ts"—tenants, toilets (presumably leaky ones), and troubles—while providing a truly passive investment in institutional-grade properties. DST investments require no active participation on the part of the investor, as they are professionally managed to provide monthly cash distributions and positioned for potential appreciation.

So why a trust, and a Delaware Statutory Trust for that matter? What we need in order to solve the dual problem of taxation and active management is an entity to hold the real estate for us, provide liability protection, and be able to accommodate other coinvestors. The standard LLC, limited partnership, S corporation or trust will not do, as these would all constitute a business entity, and be excluded by the Section 1031 statute, due to the activities of the managing member, general partner, corporate officers, or trustees, respectively. However, the State of Delaware is unique in that it enacted in 1988 its Delaware Statutory Trust Act that provides for extreme flexibility in the trust to limit the powers of the trustee to such an extent that there is no business entity[1], but simply a direct interest in the real estate. Accordingly, the Delaware trustee is a mere agent for the holding and transfer of title to real property, and the investor beneficiary retains direct ownership of the real property for federal income tax purposes. Furthermore, to avoid being a business entity for federal tax purposes, the trust may not have the power to vary the investment of the investor beneficial owners for the entire life of the trust.[2]

Meeting these requirements, federal tax law considers the owner of the DST as the owner of an undivided fractional interest in the trust property.[3]

Accordingly, an exchange of real property for an interest in the trust is an exchange for the property in the trust and will qualify for nonrecognition of gain under Section 1031.[4]

The DST for Section 1031 exchange is not a "tax loophole," but rather a well-thought-out tax policy with the intent by the IRS to provide legitimate tax deferral as defined by Revenue Ruling 2004-86 (a full copy of the Revenue Ruling has been included in the appendices to this book). Accordingly, investors may defer capital gains tax and depreciation recapture on built-up equity in their relinquished properties and reinvest their full equity into DST replacement properties. When the DST investment property is ultimately sold, investors may exchange their gains into yet another DST property, or back into a single-ownership property, with no tax exposure. To date, thousands of DST exchanges have been successfully transacted. Furthermore, in the 2017 Tax Cuts and Jobs Act, Congress has confirmed its continued support for real estate by preserving tax deferral for gains on real property under IRC Section 1031.

Volatility

In addition to taxation, the other major obstacle to building wealth is volatility. This is especially true with the highly liquid securities market. It may be said that, just as the price to be paid for the beneficial tax treatment of real estate is active management, so the price to be paid for liquidity is volatility. Securities markets are so volatile that they may lose value on any negative political or economic news. The volatility is especially acute during periods of recession. Accordingly, success in the stock market has a lot to do with the timing of the buy-and-sell of the investment.

Real estate and DST investments are illiquid investments, meaning that they cannot be sold in a day by presenting your broker with a sell order. Sales for real estate are usually transacted over months, not hours, and finding a willing and able buyer without a market maker could take up to a year. The advantage to this illiquidity is that the markets are less sensitive to short-term volatility and are considered uncorrelated investments relative to the volatility risk of the securities markets.

In contrast to the short-term volatility of the securities markets, commercial real estate, including properties held in the DST, tends to have longer-term cycles that parallel the national economy. Historically, these cycles are on average over six to eighteen-year periods (see the data table below). The cycle may be graphed in a hyperbola curve with four quadrants, beginning with a period of recovery (the optimum time to buy), followed a period of expansion (near the top of which is the optimum time to sell before a period of oversupply), and ultimately a period of recession. While it is difficult to accurately predict the exact timing for the bottom of the hyperbolic curve for recession and the climax of the expansion curve, the timing of a real estate investment can typically be made with more precision than the securities markets, to buy at a lower price and sell at a higher price.

U.S. Commercial Real Estate Market Cycle

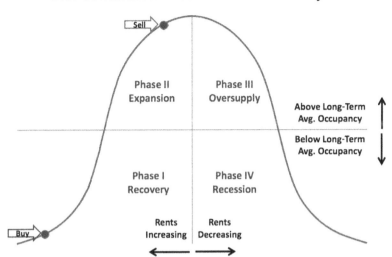

Peaks in Land Value Cycle	Interval (Years)	Peaks in Construction Cycle	Interval (Years)	Peaks in Business Cycle	Interval (Years)
1818	--	--	--	1819	--
1836	18	1836	--	1837	18
1854	18	1856	20	1857	20
1872	18	1871	15	1873	16
1890	18	1892	21	1893	20
1907	17	1909	17	1918	25
1925	18	1925	16	1929	11
1973	48	1972	47	1973	44
1979	6	1978	6	1980	7
1989	10	1986	8	1990	10
2006	17	2006	20	2008	18

Source: Fred E. Foldvary, "The Depression of 2008"

Please note the forty-seven-year real estate expansion cycle following the Great Depression. How long might the expansion cycle be following the Great Recession? Several factors including the 2017 tax cuts and tax reform, the immerging Millennial Generation at 75.4 million people (surpassing the number of Baby Boomers)[5], increased immigration, and American energy independence, have some economists pointing to a new American renaissance that may prolong the expansion of the real estate market.

A key strategy to hedge against volatility is to diversify over different geographic markets, industries, and asset classes. As the number of beneficial owners in a DST is virtually unlimited (although typically limited to 499), the minimum investment for most DST offerings is as low as $100,000 ($25,000 for a direct investment), yet the total value of the typical DST property ranges from $20 million to $100 million. With access to the various asset classes of commercial property at low minimum investment requirements, the private real estate investor now has the ability to build an extremely well-diversified personal portfolio of passive institutional-grade properties and build wealth on a tax-deferred basis using Section 1031 exchanges. Thus, the private investor is able to create and build what would be analogous to a personal real estate mutual fund, diversified over asset class, geographic location, and sponsor, with tax advantages similar to a qualified plan such as an IRA or 401K.

Heretofore, these investment-grade properties were only available to large REITs, pension funds, university endowments, and insurance companies, with their immense amounts of capital to invest. While private investors with lower investment amounts could access these larger properties through investments into REITs and funds, the Section 1031 statute expressly prohibits investments in these types of business entities from benefiting from tax-deferred exchanges. Thus, REIT and real estate fund investments do not have the advantage of maintaining and growing the investor's portfolio on a tax-deferred basis. Furthermore, public REITs are traded on the stock exchange and are exposed to the volatility of the stock market as a whole.

A Tried and True Investment

The DST is a tried-and-true structure for real estate investment. Beginning in 2002, thousands of private real estate investors have seen the vision of fractional ownership real estate, and have invested in aggregate over $35 billion dollars in hundreds of DST and TIC investments. Many of these DST properties have gone full cycle, from acquisition to management to disposition. Accordingly, there is a strong track record of performance for many DST sponsors.

The graph below represents DST and TIC equity sales over time. One can see how their popularity rocketed higher and higher each year until the prerecession peak in 2006 of $3.65 billion. They then plummeted during the Great Recession, as real estate values were decimated and 1031 exchange volume plunged throughout the nation. What might have been, if not for these external forces? However, as the national economy recovers, so does the demand for DSTs and their benefits. Accordingly, we have seen a recovery in DST equity sales to over $1.9 billion in 2017.

DST and TIC Market Since 2002 (in Thousands of Dollars)

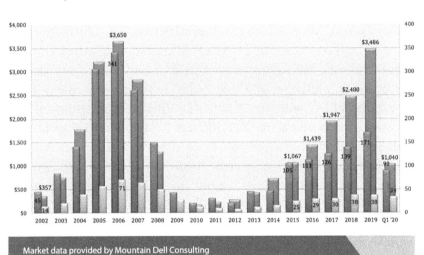

Market data provided by Mountain Dell Consulting

The industry that encompasses fractional ownership real estate has evolved since 2002 to be almost exclusively private placement syndications. In this context, syndicated may be defined as the pooling of capital for the purpose of carrying out a project requiring large resources of capital, as with the underwriting of an issue of stock or bond, to offer participation in the financial sharing of risk and returns.

Under the 1946 US Supreme Court landmark case *SEC v. W. J. Howey*, a DST will be deemed as an investment contract as income from the investment is derived from the efforts of others. Accordingly, the DST offering is a security and regulated as a private placement under the 1933 Securities Act. Therefore, a DST interest is offered by the issuing sponsor through a syndication of securities broker-dealers. Often a managing broker-dealer will manage the offering and invite other broker-dealers to join the selling group, broadening the likely pool of investors to include the client base of the member broker-dealers from around the nation. Accordingly, the equity raise for the typical DST offering will be sold out and completed within thirty to sixty days, accommodating investors with closings each week during the raise period.

These syndicated private placement offerings are regulated by FINRA (the Financial Industry Regulatory Authority), a self-regulatory organization authorized by the SEC (Securities and Exchange Commission). More will be developed later on this subject, but here we want to point out that DSTs are offered in a regulated environment, and that FINRA requires of its members a fair and balanced presentation, presented in a full disclosure private placement memorandum (PPM) with significant due diligence. In addition, it is important to note that a DST interest is offered under an exemption granted under Regulation D of the 1933 Securities Act and that only accredited investors may invest in these offerings. An individual accredited investor is simply any investor with a net worth of $1,000,000 or more, not including the equity in the investor's primary residence. Alternatively, the individual investor may qualify with an income level of $200,000 ($300,000 if married) for the prior two years, and an expectation of the same for the current year. Please refer to chapter 5 for the accreditation standards for entities.

Why Have I Not Heard about DSTs Before?

One may ask, why have I not heard of the DST for real estate investment before? The plain truth is that the industry is unable to do extensive advertising due to securities restrictions on general solicitation. It has been quietly referred by the very few CPAs, attorneys, and financial professionals in the know. General solicitation rules require the advisor to have a substantial business relationship with the client investor before a DST recommendation is proposed. The purpose for these rules is to be sure that the investor is not only accredited, but also that the investment is suitable for the client given his unique financial position, experience, and objectives. However, general education and information that is not related to a current DST offering is permitted, and the introduction of the DST industry to the nation is our goal with this book.

Chapter 2

DST Advantages

Having introduced the DST concept, we would now like to drill down and explore in more depth the various advantages of a DST. While shock and awe may not be the right words, we believe the reader will be impressed with the quantity and quality of the DST advantages. Given the relatively low minimum investment, the quality of the institutional-grade real estate, the possibilities for diversification, and the level of professional services inherent in the DST offering, the advantages are simply astounding. These are why Cornerstone entered the industry and why we have spent so many years in its service. To help prove this point, let's discuss the principal advantages of the DST, followed by a few real-world case studies.

Access to Institutional Grade Investment Properties

A major DST advantage is that a DST investment presents the opportunity for an individual to join together with other accredited investors, with minimum investments as low as $100,000 ($25,000 for nonexchange investments), to own commercial investment-grade real estate properties, often with syndicated values between $20 million to $100 million, which none of them could own individually.

Available asset classes for DST offerings may include:

- **Multifamily apartment complexes**. These properties are often large two-hundred- to five-hundred-unit class A apartment complexes with all the latest accommodations including a fitness gymnasium, business center, swimming pools, pet parks, common cooking facilities, and common lounges. These properties are professionally managed and are stabilized with 90 percent to 95 percent occupancy. Class B multifamily properties are sometimes offered with a capital improvement plan to add value to both common areas and individual units in a campaign to raise rents on a per-unit basis over the hold period and grow net operating income (NOI).

- **NNN Retail Properties.** These properties range from single tenant buildings to large shopping malls. The trend with the retail DST offering is to combine multiple properties, with as many as twenty individual single-tenant properties under one DST offering with a combined property value to over $100 million, to provide the investor with greater diversification.
- **Senior Care Properties.** These properties include everything from senior assisted living centers to Alzheimer's centers. With the Baby Boomers reaching their retirement years, the senior care asset class has increased in popularity with DST investors, to the extent that some sponsors are specializing in this single asset class.
- **Student Housing.** With millennials and generation Z of college age, and with many colleges underfunded, private student housing located near major universities is a growing asset class.
- **Industrial Complexes and Warehouses.** Industrial complexes and warehouses are less glamorous but can be cash cows if the fundamentals are right. Included in this class are self-storage and parking lots.
- **Office Buildings.** Over the past decade, the office building as a DST asset class has included the downtown high-rise skyscraper, medical office buildings, and single-tenant headquarters for large corporations. Some of the past trophy TIC and DST office buildings have included One World Trade Center, a 573,000 foot, twenty-seven-story class A

office building in Long Beach, California; Emerald Plaza, a 355,000, thirty-story class A office building in downtown San Diego; and 123 North Wacker Drive, a 540,700, thirty-story class A office building in Chicago, Illinois. Corporate headquarters have included the headquarter buildings for Verizon and Dunkin' Donuts.

- **Hotels**. Hotels are often considered the most glamorous, and past DST offerings have included national operators such as Marriott and Hilton. With a lease term for not years, but for a single day, rents per unit can be increased almost instantaneously due to increase RevPAR (revenue per available room), and cash flows are typically higher than other asset classes to compensate for the downside vacancy risk, which can be immediate and substantial.

2020 DST Asset Equity Placement

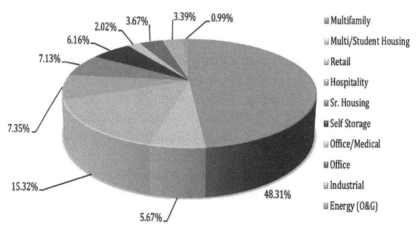

Data provided by Mountain Dell Consulting

National Credit Tenants

DST properties typically have more financially secure, creditworthy tenants, and include some of the best companies in America.

Accordingly, an investor may exchange a rental home with a tenant struggling to make rent to a tenant with a billion-dollar balance sheet. These tenants mostly have credit ratings from the major credit agencies such as Moody's, Standard & Poor's, and Fitch. Most due diligence officers look for a minimum long-term, investment-grade credit rating, which for Moody's is Baa3 and for Standard & Poor's and Fitch is BBB-.

Diversification

With minimum investment requirements as low as $100,000 for an exchange (or $25,000 for direct investment), investors can now hedge risk by diversifying their real estate portfolio to include multiple properties in different geographic locations as well as different sectors such as residential apartment complexes, retail shopping centers, office buildings, industrial parks, senior care centers, student housing, and others.

Many DST investors have chosen to diversify over multiple asset classes, industries, sponsors, and geographic locations. For example, an investor with $200,000 in equity could diversify with an investment of $100,000 into a DST with a five-hundred-unit class A multifamily apartment building, and another investment of $100,000 into a DST with as many as nineteen separate retail stores all with investment-grade tenants. By doing so, the investor would diversify from the concentration risk of a single rent payer to as many as 519 rent payers. In this scenario, half of the portfolio would have relatively flat cash flow with recession-resistant, more stable, long-term retail leases with a major credit tenant. The other half of the portfolio would have more dramatic cash flow escalations with the short-term annual residential leases and greater potential for NOI growth. We discuss diversification strategies, property selection, and due diligence in later chapters.

A Truly Passive Investment

Rental real estate ownership is typically associated with the burdens of property management and oversight. The investments that DSTs offer are fully managed and overseen by the sponsor and/or property manager, so the investor enjoys a truly passive investment, responsible only for cashing the net rental payment check each month (or arranging for direct deposit).

With a securitized real estate offering, the investor enjoys the service of nationally reputed real estate management companies (called sponsors) that structure the property acquisition, lease and maintain the property, collect rent, service the mortgage, and eventually sell the property. These management companies have a vested interest in the performance of the property, and typically have strong historical track records with many past DST properties.

A securitized real estate investment eliminates the headaches and time-consuming burdens of active property management, specifically designed to be a solution for rental property investors who wish to retire from the daily burdens and liabilities that come with being a landlord. Such an investment is also perfect for professionals who are dedicated to their career, but still desire to build a well-diversified real estate portfolio with current income and strong appreciation potential. Combined with the 1031 exchange process, such a portfolio can grow tax-deferred through the course of the investor's career.

Potential Income, Pay-Down of Loan Principal as a Percent of Equity Invested, and Appreciation

Investment-grade properties typically enjoy stable cash flow from rental income, which can be paid monthly or, in rare cases, quarterly. In addition, if the mortgage debt is amortizing as the debt is serviced, the investor equity in the property increases, even if the actual value of the property remains constant. Finally, there is the potential for appreciation in the value of the property, realized at the time of sale.

Most DSTs utilize a master lease structure, which contractually obligates the master lessee to pay a monthly base rent that covers the debt service plus a cash flow. In addition, if the property out-performs the projections, then a portion of the additional rents received by the master lessee will be paid out to the investors as bonus rents. In recent years, cash flows have averaged 5–6 percent for multifamily, 6–7 percent for retail and office, and 7–8 percent for senior care and hospitality.

It may be helpful to consider DST investment income in the context of the bond market. Many novice investors consider a securitized real estate offering to be like a bond, as they misunderstand the monthly cash flow to be similar to the coupon rate of a bond investment. As alluded to above, the cash flow of a DST investment is essentially the flow-through cash flow from the leased real estate, and it does have the potential to fluctuate, unlike a bond interest payment. Nonetheless, much care is taken, in the form of reserves and master lease rent projections, to stabilize and flatten the rent to meet investor expectations.

The bond comparison is interesting, however, as many of the retail and office tenants for DST properties also issue public bonds. Unlike the bond holder, who must pay income tax on the full amount of interest income, the lease holder may deduct the applicable depreciation on the property to shelter a portion of the rental income. Once the bond matures, the bond holder only realizes a return of capital in the principal amount of the bond, while the lease holder has the hope that his capital (which is often leveraged) will appreciate. Finally, in the event of bankruptcy, the bond holder is superior only to common and preferred stock holders, in the middle of the capital stack, while the lease holder is superior to the bond holder.

Tax-Sheltered Cash Flow

Unlike income from nonreal estate investments, a significant portion of the cash flow from DST investments can be tax sheltered due to depreciation pass-through and interest deductions. And if an investor has held a property for so long that their depreciation deductions have either run out, or will do so soon, a 1031 exchange offers the opportunity to restore these deductions in a replacement property. This opportunity arises when the DST offers a greater amount of debt than the debt on the investor's relinquished property. The additional nonrecourse debt becomes new tax basis to the investor, which can provide for greater depreciation expense to shelter rental income from federal and state taxes. Many DST properties are leveraged with 45 percent to 65 percent nonrecourse debt financing.

Deduction for Qualified Business Income

The 2017 Tax Cuts and Jobs Act provides for a 20 percent deduction for qualified business income. The net rental income from a DST *may* possibly qualify for this above the line (nonitemized) deduction. Consequently, the cash flow from a DST *may* potentially be sheltered not only by a depreciation deduction but also by the qualified business income deduction. Please see chapter 6 for a more detailed discussion.

Nonrecourse Debt

The lender on a conventional single-ownership commercial property will typically require a personal guarantee from any owner with a 20 percent interest or greater. In cases where the single tenant has a strong credit rating, the lender may offer a nonrecourse loan, but the owner would be required to sign various carve-outs for fraud and other "bad boy" acts which could expose the investor to personal liability. However, with a DST the loan is not only always nonrecourse, but the trustee, not the investors, signs the recourse carve-outs. Thus, the DST debt is an absolute nonrecourse loan. Consequently, it is not necessary for the investor to be qualified and approved by the lender. While the loan is assumed by the investor for tax basis and ownership purposes, the loan is serviced by the asset manager and does not appear on the investor's credit report.

Limited Liability

The DST is a bankruptcy-remote entity that limits the liability of the investor to only the invested capital. Like many real estate LLCs and per its name, the DST is registered in the State of Delaware. Delaware has one of the strongest case precedents for protecting investor rights and preserving the corporate veil to limit investor liability. Accordingly, only the investor's invested equity is exposed to risk and not his personal assets. Delaware law provides the beneficial owners of a DST with the same limitation on personal liability extended to shareholders of Delaware corporations.

Regulated Environment

These syndicated private placements are regulated by FINRA (the Financial Industry Regulatory Authority) which is a self-regulatory organization (SRO) authorized by the SEC. The SEC and FINRA are much more active in enforcement than the applicable state department of real estate. Broker-dealers are typically audited on an annual basis for compliance. Investors are also provided with a pro-investor arbitration process, as well as SIPC insurance with certain limits.

Due Diligence

As DST offerings are considered securities and regulated by FINRA, the 1933 Securities Act requires the issuer, its council, and the broker-dealer to perform due diligence. DST offerings pass through four layers of due diligence before being offered to investors. The first three layers of due diligence are performed by the sponsor, the lender, and legal counsel, while the broker-dealer performs a fourth layer. The broker-dealer due diligence is done at both the sponsor level and the property level.

The broker-dealer due diligence at the sponsor level includes examination of the sponsor's financial statements and financial position. In most cases, audited financial statements are required and analyzed to determine the depth of financial resources and liquidity. Furthermore, the broker-dealer will examine the sponsor's organizational capabilities, including depth of real estate expertise, customer service capacity, and operational manpower, as well as review of the track record of the sponsor for both full-cycle and currently operating properties, with respect to estimated projections and actual performance. Annual background checks are done on the principals of the sponsor, including the search for any criminal records, bankruptcy, and judgments, as well as their track record in the field of syndicated real estate.

The property-level due diligence includes analysis of the properties themselves from a real estate perspective, including but not limited to property tours (site visits), tenant interviews, lease agreement review, review of loan covenants and recourse carve-outs, appraisal assessment, environmental issues, and the adequacy of tenant improvement, loan, and other reserves.

Full Disclosure

All DSTs are structured and offered as securities under the Securities Act of 1933, which requires the investor to be provided with a private placement memorandum (PPM) created out of significant due diligence from the real estate company, the lender, and the securities industry. The PPM discloses all possible risks and material facts about the investment. In comparison, for traditional real estate, in most cases, the standard "caveat emptor" or buyer beware essentially makes it the buyer's responsibility to inspect the property and discover whether there are any unacceptable conditions or defects before closing the deal, with some states imposing a requirement for the seller to disclose only known material items.

The combination of due diligence and full disclosure is a powerful advantage for the DST investor. When contemplating the purchase of a traditional single-ownership property, the investor would have to pay in advance and out of his own pocket for appraisals, environmental studies, and loan application fees, all before removing contingencies on a possible purchase. If the investor performs similar due diligence on multiple properties, these significant expenses would increase proportionately. However, with a DST investment, an investor can compare and contrast many DST offerings at no expense, simply by requesting and reviewing the PPM documents. All the pertinent information such as appraisals, environmental studies, leases, tenant agreements, and loan documents are presented in the full disclosure PPM at no cost to the investor. Similar formatting between PPMs allows the investor to easily compare and contrast multiple DST offerings and make an informed investment decision with no upfront costs. This is especially advantageous given the forty-five-day identification and other time constraints of the 1031 exchange.

Real-World Case Studies

We have selected three real-world clients as case studies from our database of clients from the past fifteen years. These case studies represent the array of diversification opportunities available to the DST investor. These investors had a wide range of equity amounts to invest from a single investor with $430,000 to a partnership with $9.4 million.

Robert with $430,000 in Equity

In 2014, Robert came to us with an exchange with $430,000. He was in his seventies and retired. He and his late wife had originally purchased the relinquished property as a cherished first residence that the family soon grew out of once their children were born and experienced several growths spurts. They kept the home as a rental property, and after many years of depreciation had very little tax basis remaining. The year before the exchange, the property in Virginia was rented to a single family for $1,700 per month, or a 2.9 percent annual cash flow return on equity after accounting for expenses such as property tax and insurance.

Robert exchanged his $430,000 equity into 4 DST offerings, thereby deferring the tax on the gain from the sale of the rental property. By reinvesting the full $430,000 in equity, he more than doubled his monthly and annual cash flow, from 2.9 percent to 6.22 percent. He diversified over four sponsors, three asset classes, and four geographical areas. His new portfolio included two residential apartment complexes in Colorado and North Carolina with a total of 822 units, a CVS Pharmacy retail store on the Las Vegas strip with a twenty-two-year lease guaranteed by an investment-grade tenant, and a sixty-one-bed senior care center in his home state of Virginia. We think that is pretty good!

See graphic on the following page.

MODERN REAL ESTATE INVESTING

Michael with $4 Million in Equity

In 2015, Michael called us with a $4 million exchange. Michael's top objective was to diversify into as many DSTs as possible. After several proposals by Cornerstone, Michael settled on a portfolio of 10 DSTs with an average of $400,000 per DST. Several of the DSTs had multiple properties within a single DST, so Michael was able to diversify into 21 separate properties, including nine multifamily complexes with a total of 2,505 rental units, four medical office buildings, and eight Walgreens Pharmacy NNN retail stores. Michael is a busy professional with little time to manage rental properties. Now he has a well-diversified personal, institutional-grade real estate portfolio that he can continue to exchange through his lifetime. He has also supplemented his professional earnings with an additional DST income of $206,860 or a 5.17 percent first year cash-on-cash return. Not too bad, Michael!

Paul with $9.4 Million in Equity

Lest one might think that larger investors are not attracted to the benefits that DSTs have to offer, in 2015 we went to visit Paul and his partners at their office in New Jersey. They were retiring after building a successful business in the Meadowlands. They did not want additional exposure to the stock market, and wanted a truly passive income stream so that they might travel and enjoy their retirement years. The partnership ultimately decided on four DSTs, wanting to keep larger equity amounts in each investment so that, when the properties were ultimately sold at different times in the future, they would have sufficient equity to exchange into larger replacement property opportunities. Accordingly, the partnership invested in 4 DST interests ranging from $1.5 million to $4 million per DST. The overall portfolio included a DST with a portfolio of pharmacy stores, a DST with a national net lease retail store portfolio, a DST with a portfolio of medical office buildings, and a DST with a class A multifamily apartment complex. Paul and his partners had extensive experience in business and real estate, and carried out extensive due diligence on the sponsors and the properties. It speaks volumes that they chose the DST structure to finance their hard-earned retirement.

Have You Seen the Vision?

Have you seen the DST vision? Succinctly put, the DST vision is the opportunity to build a world-class personal portfolio of institutional-grade real estate diversified over geographic location, sponsor, and asset classes such as multifamily, retail, office, industrial properties, senior housing, and others. A portfolio that will not only provide potentially tax-sheltered monthly cash flow but also continue to grow and build wealth by preserving potential gains over the years using Section 1031 tax deferred exchanges. All this in a regulated environment of due diligence and full disclosure as mandated under the investor protection provisions of the securities industry.

While the disadvantages of loss of control, illiquidity, and other risks may make a DST not a suitable investment for every investor, including those investors willing and able to actively manage their real estate investments, we believe the DST advantages of institutional-grade commercial real estate, national credit tenants, diversification, limited liability, and potential monthly tax-sheltered income make the DST an intriguing and attractive option for the passive real estate investor.

These advantages are especially suited for busy professionals who desire to build a diverse real estate investment portfolio and those investors looking to retire from the active management of real estate. Moreover, the core advantages of access to institutional-grade real estate, diversification over multiple asset classes, and gain non-recognition under Section 1031 exchange may be so compelling as to attract even the active real estate investor to supplement existing active management real estate with a more passive DST portfolio.

Chapter 3

The DST Structure

The 1988 Delaware Statutory Trust Act
The 2004 IRS Revenue Ruling 2004-86

A Delaware Statutory Trust (DST) is a separate legal entity created as a trust under the Delaware Statutory Trust Act of 1988. The DST, like an LLC, is a bankruptcy-remote entity created as a special-purpose entity to hold title to real estate. Investors are granted a beneficial ownership interest in the DST, and the trustee is given powers per a trust agreement to manage the property, thus creating a passive ownership interest in the real estate for the investor. If the DST is structured in accordance with IRS Ruling 2004-86, the investor may utilize a tax-deferred IRC § 1031 exchange into and out of the DST investment.

> The DST is essentially the TIC version 2.0 with a new and improved structure.

Readers may be more familiar with the LLC and the limited partnership (LP), many of which are incorporated in the state of Delaware as special purpose entities for holding title to real estate but may be less familiar with the statutory trust. To provide some assurances as to its viability, we want to cover the history and structure of the Delaware statutory trust.

The History of the DST

The concept of the business trust for property ownership goes back to English Common Law developed in the sixteenth century.[6] The trust was used for approximately four hundred years by English landowners, granting fiduciary powers to family attorneys to hold property title for the purpose of passing asset ownership from generation to generation, minimizing taxation and rendering a great degree of security in the process.

The Kings' Chapel in feudal England assumed the role of issuing official documents, such as royal writs initiating common law proceedings. This evolved into the Court of the Chancery which, among other things, provided judicial remedies due to the dishonesty and rigidity of the common law courts. The English Chancellor, while relying upon common law, more resembled the ecclesiastical courts in its simplicity and adaptability, being able to decide according to common sense and conscience where the rigid application of common law could cause adversity or inequality in a particular case.[7]

In the formation of the American State of Delaware in 1792, the Second Delaware Constitution, Article VI made provision for the equity jurisdiction (previously exercised by the Court of Common Pleas) to be detached from the jurisdiction of common law and vested in the Chancellor and the Courts of Chancery throughout the State.[8] The common law of Delaware did not begin to recognize the statutory trust, however, until 1947. In due course, the Delaware Statutory Trust Act (originally the "Delaware Business Trust Act"), 12. Del. C. 3801 et. Seq, was passed into law in 1988.

The act was written by a committee of the Delaware State Bar Association, mainly composed of lawyers practicing in corporate finance. The key aim of the commission was to restructure the legal framework to increase the usefulness of the business trust in contemporary financing transactions. The act, therefore, essentially replaced the prejudicial concepts of the common law of trusts, establishing new provisions to legally enable a greater range for negotiations and contracts between the trustee and the trustor regarding liabilities and trust management.[9]

Accordingly, Delaware's statutory trust framework is second to none due to its flexibility, predictability, and permissiveness that provide a distinct advantage to our syndicated DSTs for holding real estate under the Business Trust Act as opposed to a common law trust. For example, the act allows for limiting the powers that would normally be afforded to the trustee under the common law. As we will discuss later in this chapter, the IRS Revenue Ruling requires a limitation of the trustee powers to prevent it from acting as a deemed general partner and being disqualified for purposes of IRC § 1031 tax-deferred exchanges. Another prime example is that the Delaware Trust law provides comprehensive statutory provisions as to rights of creditors in trust property and trustee liability to third parties. This allows the trustee in our syndicated real estate DSTs to sign the various nonrecourse carve-outs, providing the DST investors with truly nonrecourse debt (assuming the subject property is leveraged).

Furthermore, the Delaware Court of Chancery is recognized as a preeminent court for resolving complex corporate law disputes and brings an equivalent degree of proficiency and sophistication to disagreements involving common law trusts. The Court of Chancery has jurisdiction over a DST interest, the rights and responsibilities of its trustee(s) and beneficial owners, and the interpretation of its contractual agreements[10]. These factors combine to make Delaware an ideal jurisdiction for the formation of common law trusts for syndicated real estate offerings as well as other commercial transactions. Since 2000, Delaware statutory trusts have been used for thousands of common law business trusts, but also as a replacement for other business entities for such activities as holding real estate, mutual funds, mezzanine financing, real estate investment trusts (REITs) and securitizations.

Given the history of the Delaware statutory trust, it was not only the advantageous Delaware case law that made the DST the preferable vehicle for our 1031 exchange investments but also the flexibility of the design and operation of the trust under the Delaware Statutory Trust Act which allows the structure to bend and stretch to conform to the requirements of its intended purpose. This flexibility allows for a trust structure that provides for a direct real estate interest without creating a business entity, and thereby qualifies for preferential tax treatment under § 1031 of the Internal Revenue Code as formalized in Revenue Ruling 2004-86.

Structural Limitations of the Delaware Statutory Trust

The central objective of the DST structure is to prevent the DST from becoming a business entity that would not qualify for tax deferral under Section 1031. Essentially, any form of business activity, such as a partnership interest, are prohibited from enjoying nonrecognition of gain under Section 1031. Accordingly, to avoid the DST being deemed a limited partnership, with the investors being deemed as limited partners and the trustee being deemed as a general partner, the DST structure limits the activities of the trustee (or the trust manager) and creates a direct interest in the underlying real estate.

In accordance with Revenue Ruling 2004-86, the DST must be a fixed income trust and is immutable. Accordingly, the trust and its trustee may not react to market conditions. These trust restrictions are built into the DST trust agreement and have become known as the "seven deadly sins."[11] These seven limitations are as follows:

1. *Once the offering is closed, there can be no future contributions to the DST by either current or new beneficiaries.*
2. *The trustee cannot renegotiate the terms of the existing loans, and cannot borrow any new funds from any party, unless a loan default exists as a result of a tenant bankruptcy or insolvency.*
3. *The trustee cannot reinvest the proceeds from the sale of its real estate.*
4. *The trustee is limited to making capital expenditures with respect to the property for normal repair and maintenance, minor nonstructural capital improvements, and those required by law.*

5. Any reserves or cash held between distribution dates can only be invested in short-term debt obligations.
6. All cash, other than necessary reserves, must be distributed on a current basis.
7. The trustee cannot enter into new leases, or renegotiate the current leases, unless there is a need due to a tenant bankruptcy or insolvency.

In accordance with an earlier IRS Private Letter Ruling,[12] these seven powers listed above may effectively be transferred to a master tenant, whereby the master tenant takes on all the operating responsibilities of managing the DST property under a master lease agreement. We will discuss the transfer of these powers to the master tenant, the master tenant, and the master lease agreement later in this chapter.

We would like to point out here that with respect to item four above, on the limitation to make capital expenditures to maintain the property, the question may be raised as to how much activity by the trust would raise to the level of a trade or business and violate the Revenue Ruling? While there is no bright line test, REIT rules may allow for expenses up to 30 percent of the property for nonstructural improvements and repairs. Furthermore, based on UBTI and Subchapter S rulings, the trustee may be able to act to conserve and protect the trust's corpus property but may not modify the corpus.

The Structure of the DST

The sponsor of a DST offering will create the Delaware Statutory Trust and formulate its governing instrument in conformity to IRS Revenue Ruling 2004-86. The DST investor has only to review the private placement memorandum (PPM) and accompanying tax opinion that present the DST previously created by the sponsor. While the investor does not participate in these formation activities, it may be helpful and insightful for the reader to understand and be informed regarding the requirements of the Delaware Statutory

Trust Act for a valid Delaware Statutory Trust. The formation of a Delaware Statutory Trust (pursuant to Delaware Code Ann. title 12, §§ 3801–3824) is somewhat straightforward. The act provides for the following requirements for a Delaware Statutory Trust to exist:

1. *A certificate of trust filed with the Office of the Secretary of State of Delaware,*
2. *One or more trustee(s),*
3. *A governing instrument (usually a trust agreement), and*
4. *One or more beneficial owners.*

In addition to the statutory requirements, a syndicated DST offering will also include the following provisions to be able to acquire and manage real estate:

5. *A depositor*
6. *A property manager*
7. *A master tenant*
8. *A master lease agreement*

Certificate of Trust

A certificate of trust must be filed with the Delaware Secretary of State. The certificate is actually the only document that must be filed with the Secretary of State in order to be constituted as a separate legal entity. A statutory trust may be organized to carry on any lawful business or activity including for the purpose of holding or otherwise taking title to real property.

At a minimum, the certificate of trust is required to contain the name of the trust and the name and address of one trustee in the State of Delaware. Additional matters may be included in the certificate of trust, though most parties choose to include such matters in the governing instrument instead. With our syndicated real estate DST, nearly all governing matters are relegated to the trust agreement.

Trustee and Trust Manager

The trustee is named in the certificate of trust and will have a Delaware resident address. As a default rule, the trustees of a Delaware Statutory Trust manage the business and affairs of the trust. However, management of a Delaware Statutory Trust can be completely or partially divested from the trustees and placed with other persons. Management can be vested in officers, employees, managers or other persons, either as agents or independent contractors of the Delaware Statutory Trust. Such parties may have such relative rights, powers and duties as the governing instrument provides.

Our syndicated real estate DST will limit the sole purpose of the trustee to simply fulfill the requirements of the Delaware Statutory Trust Act. Most sponsors will either retain a person or an entity already domiciled in Delaware to act as the trustee, or they will create a special purpose entity LLC with an office address in Delaware to act as trustee. The trustee is reimbursed for any expenses and held harmless except for cases of willful misconduct, bad faith, fraud or gross negligence. The DST trust agreement, will relegate all actual trust management to a trust manager. The trust manager is a single member LLC with the sponsor as the sole member.

Trust Agreement

The trust agreement is the working instrument of the trust that governs the affairs of the trust. The act is intended to give great flexibility to parties in structuring their trust, and maximum effect to the principle of freedom of contract. The Delaware Statutory Trust Act allows unparalleled flexibility in structuring the trust agreement that is not found in common law. While it cannot contradict the certificate of trust, it can make any other legal provisions. This flexibility allows the trust to define the powers of the trustee and the trust manager, who must manage the trust in the manner provided in the trust agreement, and comply with the provisions of IRS Revenue Ruling 2004-86. Finally, the trust agreement determines, in conformity with the Revenue Ruling, the amount for reasonable reserves and the ultimate amount of cash flow distributions from the trust to its beneficial owners from the funds paid to the trust from the master tenant under the master lease agreement.

Depositor

In addition to the trustee and the trust manager, there is a third party to the trust agreement, called the depositor. The depositor is also an LLC, with the sponsor as the sole member. The depositor and the trustee are the creators of the trust. The sponsor, who contracted to acquire the real estate, will make an assignment of the purchase agreement to the depositor as consideration for the acquisition fee. Per the trust agreement, the depositor will agree to contribute the real estate to the trust in exchange for 100 percent of the class B beneficial intertest in the trust. The trust will then sell a newly issued class A beneficial interest in the trust to the investors for cash. Lastly, the depositor will return its class B beneficial interest in the trust back to the trust in exchange for the cash remaining after the acquisition of the real estate and associated costs and expenses (i.e., the acquisition fee).

Beneficial Owners

The term "beneficial owner" means any owner of a beneficial interest in a statutory trust, the fact of ownership to be determined and evidenced (whether by means of registration, the issuance of certificates or otherwise) in conformity to the applicable provisions of the governing instrument of the statutory trust. The investors (called holders in the PPM), as holders of the Class A beneficial interests, collectively own 100 percent of the Delaware Statutory Trust, and the trust will have 100 percent fee simple ownership of the real estate. The aforementioned Class B beneficial interest are only initially used to contribute the real estate to the trust by the depositor and are fully retired once that objective is accomplished.

The Delaware Statutory Act provides that a beneficial owner shall have an undivided beneficial interest in the property of the statutory trust and shall share in the profits and losses of the statutory trust in the proportion (expressed as a percentage) of the entire undivided beneficial interest in the statutory trust owned by such beneficial owner. The beneficiaries have no voting rights and no power to direct the actions of the trust. The sole right of the beneficiary is to receive distributions from the trust as a result of its ownership or sale of the interest in the property.

Per the act, except to the extent otherwise provided in the governing instrument of the statutory trust, the beneficial owners shall be entitled to the same limitation of personal liability extended to stockholders of private corporations for profit organized under the general corporation law of the State. No creditor of the beneficial owner shall have any right to obtain possession of, or otherwise exercise legal or equitable remedies with respect to, the property of the statutory trust. A beneficial owner's beneficial interest in the statutory trust is freely transferable.

The Master Tenant

The master tenant and the master lease is an ingenious and elegant element of the overall DST structure as it cleverly allows the trustee (and trust manager) to be limited in its powers to constitute a direct interest in the real estate while effectively allowing the sponsor to manage the property without creating a business entity under Section 1031.

In a DST, the master tenant is a special purpose entity (SPE) created by the sponsor, is controlled by the sponsor, and is considered an affiliate of the sponsor. Therefore, the trust manager, the depositor, and the master tenant are all related and affiliated entities of the sponsor. Simultaneously with the acquisition of the real estate, the trust will enter into a master lease with the master tenant. Under the master lease, the trust leases the properties to the master tenant for an original term of ten years; typically, the master tenant has the right, at its sole discretion, to renew the master lease for three additional terms of five years each.

The master tenant will in turn enter into leases of the property with residential or commercial subtenants, handle maintenance and repairs, contract with the management agent (also often an affiliate of the sponsor) and, generally, be empowered to do everything that an owner of the mortgaged property would otherwise do. The duties of the master tenant generally include, but are not limited to, the operation, repair, replacement, maintenance and management of the property, except that, generally, the master tenant is not responsible for "capital expenses" as defined in the master lease, or for the costs of repair following a condemnation or casualty. The master tenant may engage the property manager to perform some or all its duties. The main objective of the master tenant will be to generate cash flow for the payment of the rent to the trust by maintaining the current subtenant occupancy level, and by maintaining and increasing rental rates upon termination of any sublease. Any property manager may be hired or terminated, including a property manager affiliated with the sponsor, solely at the discretion of the master tenant, without consultation with or notice given to the trust or beneficial owners. The beneficial owners will not be involved in the management of the Properties.

Rent from the master lease will be distributed to the beneficial owners net of any reserves and payment of debt service and property expenses incurred by the trust. Any cash from the properties in excess of the rent obligations of the master tenant under the master lease will be retained by the master tenant.

Three Master Tenant Rent Payment Structures

Now that we know how a DST is structured, "How do I get paid?" As mentioned above, the master lease will generally provide for rent to be paid monthly by the master tenant to the DST and its beneficiaries in a set amount. The master lease rent agreement should be structured in a way to align the interest of the master tenant with that of the investors (DST beneficiaries) in order to economically incentivize the master tenant to maximize the mortgaged property's net operating income. This may be done by allowing the master tenant to retain an amount of the net operating income over and above debt service and contracted rent payments under the master lease, thereby incentivizing the master tenant to cover short-term operating deficits in order to protect its desired return and its valuable investor reputation in the industry. A best practice by the leading sponsors is to reserve from net operating income (over and above typical lender replacement reserves) for unanticipated repairs and uninsured losses, because there is no real ability to raise additional capital after the initial capitalization of the DST.

There are three possible methods for the master tenant to structure the monthly rent payments to the DST and its beneficiaries. The structure that would be most advantageous to the investors (DST beneficiaries) is a cash flow master lease. Here all the available cash flow would be paid to the investor owners of the DST property. However, a lease agreement that does not allow for any income or economic benefit to the master lessee could be deemed by the IRS as not a lease at all, and could be disallowed. If the master lease is disallowed, then the 1031 tax benefits of the DST structure could be jeopardized.

The second possible rent payment structure is called a base rent master lease. Under a base rent master lease, the net operating income after debt service is divided between the master tenant and the DST beneficiaries. While this method would seem amicable, there is a danger that the structure could be considered by the IRS, under the REIT rules and the step transaction doctrine,[13] as an effective partnership between the master tenant and the DST. As mentioned above, if the DST property was deemed to be owned by a partnership, then it would not qualify by statute for the 1031 exchange.

For DST intents and purposes, a third master lease payment structure is the only practical solution. This structure is called a bonus rent master lease payment structure. The bonus master lease serves both the purpose of incentivizing the master lessee and providing upside cash flow to the investors. While the details of the bonus rent master lease may vary from sponsor to sponsor, the basic structure requires the master tenant to pay to the trust as "rent" on a monthly basis as follows:

1. *a "base rent" amount equal to the debt service payments, including principal and interest payments and necessary deposits into all lender-required reserve funds;*
2. *an "additional rent" amount when the gross revenues from the property exceed the additional rent breakpoint after deducting the asset management fee (defined by the master lease and typically 3 percent of gross revenue). The asset management fee may be deferred if gross revenues are below the breakpoint; and*
3. *a "bonus rent" when the base rent and additional rent have been fully paid, an amount equal to 90 percent (typically) of the amount by which the annual gross revenues exceed the supplemental rent breakpoint, with the master tenant retaining the amount equal to 10 percent (typically) by which the annual gross revenues exceed the supplemental rent breakpoint. Again, the percentage split of the bonus rent between the investors (the trust) and the master tenant may vary from sponsor to sponsor.*

The annual cash-on-cash return, or cash flow, as a percentage of invested capital for a DST typically ranges between 5 percent and 8 percent. Cash flow will often escalate each year over the hold period. In addition to the cash flow, the annual return may also include the principal payments on an amortizing loan, which may add 1 percent to 2 percent to the overall annual return. With loan amortization there may be exposure to "phantom income," income allocated to reduce the principal loan balance and subject to income tax yet not received by the investor.

The actual cash flow depends on a host of variables including asset class, tenant credit worthiness, location, purchase price, and rent and expense projections, to name a few. The sponsor of the DST offering will take these variables and other assumptions into a formal "Argus spreadsheet" to calculate cash flow projections using their master lease payment structure. The cash flow projections are presented in the private placement memorandum, as well as a description of the master lease and the payment structure for the particular offering. There is certainly a correlation between risk and return, discussed in more detail in a later chapter. The cash flow is paid monthly to parallel the cash stream of the property and the monthly rent payments from the tenant(s) and master lessee.

Master Tenant Capitalization

The master tenant will be a newly formed limited liability company and an affiliate of the sponsor. The master tenant is typically capitalized with a noninterest-bearing demand note from the sponsor's sole member, in an amount equal to the greater of (1) approximately three months' base rent or (2) $250,000, for example. This is a typical dollar amount, but the actual amount may vary from sponsor to sponsor. One of the larger and more prolific sponsors typically capitalizes its master tenants for larger multifamily residential complexes with several hundred thousand dollars in cash plus reserves. If the sponsor choses to capitalize the master tenant with a demand note rather than cash, and if they have syndicated multiple offerings over the years, then there is a risk that an economic downturn that affects the performance of multiple properties may place severe financial stress on the sponsor, which may not then be able to fund all its demand note obligations. This is a major point of investigation in the due diligence process at the sponsor level. Furthermore, it is important that the master tenant is well capitalized to have economic substance, as there is a risk that an undercapitalized master tenant could be deemed by the IRS to be sponsor, and the master tenant activities could be deemed to be those of the sponsor, in violation of Revenue Ruling 2004-86.

The Springing LLC

In most cases the trustee (sponsor) will reserve and make adequate provisions to hold the property in the DST for the full length of the hold period. The trust may also act to modify a lease in the event of a tenant insolvency, including the master tenant due to nonpayment of a demand note, without having to spring into an LLC. Nevertheless, to build in an ultimate fail-safe and provide lenders with additional comfort against the DST's inability to act in the event that the loan is endangered, the sponsor should place an operative provision in the trust agreement. This provision provides that, if the trustee determines that the DST is in danger of losing the mortgaged property due to an actual or imminent default on the loan, and tax-related restrictions are preventing the trustee's ability to act (the seven deadly sins), the DST can convert into a limited liability company (the springing LLC) with a lender preapproved operating agreement.

Delaware law permits the conversion by what is basically a simple election, which does not constitute a transfer under Delaware law. The "springing LLC" will contain the same SPE and bankruptcy remoteness provisions as the DST (for the lender's benefit), but it will permit the raising of additional funds, the raising of new financing or renegotiation of the terms of the existing financing, and entering into new leases. In addition, it will provide that the trustee (or sponsor) will become the manager of the LLC with full operating control.[14] During the period that the springing LLC is in place, the master tenant would continue to be required to pay to the trust rent on a monthly basis per the master lease agreement.

Once the property has again been stabilized and there is no longer a risk of loan default, the LLC may spring back into a DST structure once again. While the leading attorneys in the industry have always assured us that springing back into a DST was theoretically possible, at the time of this writing, there had been one successful precedence where a leading DST sponsor successfully sprang into an LLC to manage an ACE Hardware property and service the debt. The LLC ultimately sprang back into a DST and the investor members were able to enjoy IRC Section 1031 exchange out of the DST and into other like-kind property.

There are also other less elegant alternatives to springing back into a DST. Assuming that the measures taken after springing into the LLC are successful, the property could simply continue as an LLC and refinance as the property appreciates over time, to return the investors' capital or a significant amount of capital. Distribution of refinance proceeds would be tax free, and the small amount of equity remaining in the LLC would have relatively low tax if the property is ultimately sold, or the investors' heirs could enjoy a step-up-in basis and never have to pay tax on the built-up gain. If the sponsor is the issuer of a REIT offering or arranges with a REIT, there is also the possibility for the investors to conduct an IRC Section 721 exchange, commonly called an "up-REIT."

Final Disposition of the DST Property

The DST trust agreement will dictate that the trust will terminate, dissolve, and distribute all its assets to the beneficial owners, on the first of three possible events: (1) the tenth year after acquisition of the property by the trust, (2) a transfer disposition, or (3) the sale of the trust property. In most cases, the DST property will be marketed and sold within five to nine years from the date of acquisition. The beneficial owners will not be entitled to approve a sale of a property or properties.

While the DST trustee has the power to act unilaterally to sell the property, marketing and offer information will be communicated in advance to the beneficial owners. Nevertheless, before the trust enters into a binding contract to sell or convey a property or properties, the signatory trustee will canvass the beneficial owners regarding their views on the potential transaction. The signatory trustee will consider the beneficial owners' views and opinions in good faith, but will not be bound by their opinions, and the decision to sell or convey a property or the properties will rest solely with the signatory trustee.

Factors that interact to affect the length of the hold period include loan term, lease terms, market conditions, and total average annual return. The standard commercial loan term is 10 years with a requirement of a balloon payment by the end of the tenth year. This is standard for all commercial real estate loans. Given the restrictions on the trustee that prevent refinancing, the sponsor will want to market and sell the property several years before the loan is due and payable.

In the case of a retail or office lease situation, the sponsor will want to preserve a meaningful lease term for the new buyer to maintain or improve property value. Accordingly, if there are, for instance, twenty years remaining in a NNN retail lease, then the trustee would want to sell after burning off only five to seven years, thus preserving twelve to fifteen years for the new buyer looking for dependable cash flow.

We have seen market conditions dramatically effect projected hold periods over the years. In a growing economy, we have seen DST properties sell in as little as 3 years after receiving a nonsolicited offer that was too good to refuse. On the other hand, a recessionary economy may stretch a hold period out to the year ten, until real estate values can recover, and investor capital can be preserved. Typically, the sponsor is looking to maximize returns for the investors, with a target of between 9 percent to 14 percent average annual return. For example, an average total return of 12 percent might break down to approximately 7 percent from cash flow, 2 percent from amortization, and 3 percent from appreciation (one hundred basis points above 2 percent inflation would be typical in most cases).

The old adage that pigs (presumably greedy ones) get slaughtered is applicable here. Sponsors will not try to maximize returns by attempting to sell at the top of the market, but will look to sell once the overall return approaches a reasonable return. In the effort to fund investor cash flow and build wealth, DSTs are structured, to use a sports analogy, to be single and double base hits and not home runs.

Chapter 4

DST Disadvantages, Risks, and Fees

The 2004 IRS Revenue Ruling 2004-86

To present the reader with a fair and balances presentation and in the spirit of full disclosure, we wanted to devote a chapter early in the publication to consider some of the disadvantages, risks, and fees associated with a DST interest. In addition to pointing out various disadvantages, risks, and fees in our regular discourse throughout the book, we also dedicated chapter 20 to a lengthy presentation of typical DST risk disclosures. As with any investment, risks may be researched, identified, disclosed, and mitigated but they ultimately still exist.

The entire chapter is not altogether on the "dark side." One man's disadvantage may be another man's advantage. For example, loss of control for one investor may translate to passive peace of mind for another investor. Risks are best known in advance so that logical steps may be taken to allay or avoid them altogether. Moreover, fees may be fair compensation for value added or services rendered and deemed reasonable and equitable when compared with industry standards.

Disadvantages of the DST

Disadvantages are not the same as risks. The DST disadvantages are limitations due to its structure, which have been compromised or conceded in exchange for the ability to qualify for the larger advantage of tax deferral under IRS Section 1031 and the applicable Revenue Ruling. The three basic disadvantages are presented below but should not be considered as comprehensive.

Loss of Control

Per Revenue Ruling 2004-86, for a DST interest not to not be classified as a business entity, either a corporation or a partnership, an interest in which is prohibited from tax deferral under Section 1031, the beneficiaries may not have a voting or controlling interest. The trustee must have the power to unilaterally make all decisions regarding the properties or assets of the trust.

While most sponsor trustees will solicit the will of the investor beneficiaries on major decisions, they are not bound by that will, and may make any decision they deem necessary to safeguard the assets, including the sale of the property. The lack of control may be a positive for investors looking for a totally passive investment who are happy to yield control to an experienced commercial real estate operator. This disadvantage may also be a positive in preventing one rogue investor from prohibiting or retarding an important and timely decision, as was the case with many TIC properties when faced with critical decisions during the past recession.

Illiquid Investment

A DST interest is considered an illiquid investment, and there is no developed secondary market for DST interests. Therefore, a DST investor will typically hold the investment until the property is itself sold. DSTs are not long-term investments, with the average hold period for the property being between five and ten years. A main limitation on the hold period is the standard ten-year term debt financing. Therefore, the sponsor will look to sell after any loads are effectively burnt off, a year or so before the balloon payment on the ten-year note is due and payable, and the investors would receive their full capital back plus some appreciation (not to mention the cash flow along the way).

However, if a willing buyer is found during the hold period before the property is sold, the actual transfer of a DST interest is very straightforward, as the new buyer does not have to be approved by the lender. Most successful DST sales before the hold period have been at a discount, although in an interest rate-rising environment, a case may be made for a premium if the DST is cash flowing better than the current market.

May Not Raise Additional Capital

Per the IRS requirements, no new capital or cash contributions may be made once the DST equity raise is closed. This prohibition includes new investors, additional debt financing, and capital calls—although no possibility of additional capital calls may appear to some to be an advantage. Accordingly, adequate reserves must be in place upon closing, either from debt, equity or both, and the funding of reserves from cash flows must be structured into the deal. These reserves should not be misinterpreted as part of the fee load. It should also be noted that, if the property is in imminent peril, there is the possibility to raise additional capital or obtain additional financing through a springing LLC. For more on the springing LLC see chapter 3 on the DST structure.

Risk Overview of a Delaware Statutory Trust

As with most investment, an investment in a DST interest is highly speculative and involves substantial risks. Preeminently, it should be noted by every investor that an investment in a DST interest is highly speculative and involves substantial risks. Below is an overview of the most common, but not all, of these risks.

- A "best-efforts" offering with no minimum raise or minimum escrow requirements;
- The holding of a beneficial interest in the trust with no voting rights with respect to the management or operations of the trust or in connection with the sale of the property;

- Risks associated with owning, financing, operating and leasing a multifamily apartment complex and real estate;
- Performance of the master tenant under the master lease, including the potential for the master tenant to defer a portion of rent payable under the master lease;
- Reliance on the master tenant (and the property manager (defined below) engaged by the master tenant, and the property submanager (defined below) subcontracted by the property manager) to manage the property;
- Risks associated with sponsor funding the demand note that capitalizes the master tenant;
- Risks relating to the terms of the financing for the property, including the use of leverage;
- Lack of diversity of investment;
- The existence of various conflicts of interest among the sponsor, the trust, the master tenant, the property manager, and their affiliates;
- Material tax risks, including treatment of the interests for purposes of Code Section 1031 and the use of exchange funds to pay acquisition costs, which may result in taxable boot'
- The lack of a public market for the interests;
- The interests not being registered with the Securities and Exchange Commission (SEC) or any state securities commissions;
- Risks relating to the costs of compliance with laws, rules and regulations applicable to the property;
- Risks related to competition from properties similar to and near the property;
- The possibility of environmental risks related to the property.

Again, for a more detailed discussion of DST risks, please refer to chapter 20 on risk disclosures. There we discuss risks related to the trust structure, operating risks, risks related to the master lease, real estate risks, financing risks, risks related to private offerings, and tax risks.

Fees and Expenses

With all the benefits and advantages of a passive DST real estate investment, the investor may ask, "What will all this cost me?" The DST has essentially what is known as a front-end load. This means that the majority of the fees and expenses are charged at the beginning of the investment rather than at the end. Unlike a partnership or fund, which would typically compensate the general partner or sponsor with a back-end split of the profits from property appreciation, in a DST the profits must go to the investors.

The fees and expenses for the acquisition phase of a DST offering (i.e., the front-ended load) include, but are not limited to, fees for acquisition of the property, debt structuring fee, commissions, marketing fees, environmental reports, closing costs, and appraisals. In aggregate, these fees may amount to between 9 percent and 14 percent of the total value of the property. Therefore, care should be taken to evaluate the total load for a DST in comparison to the tax savings in utilizing the DST for a 1031 exchange. Cornerstone will typically approve a DST only if 89 percent or more of the investor funds are used to acquire and finance the property.

During the operational phase of the DST, the sponsor may only participate in monthly cash flows in line with market rates for asset management services and as a master tenant. The asset management fee and property management fee are disclosed up front in the PPM. The asset management fee typically ranges from 1 percent to 3 percent of gross rents, depending on the asset class and the labor intensity required. The management fee would apply to services such as cash flow distributions, debt servicing, and investor relations. The

> Cornerstone typically will not approve a DST if less than 89% of the investors' funds go "into the ground", i.e., are used to acquire and finance the property.

property management fee may be passed on to the onsite property manager if applicable. The sponsor will also participate to a limited extent in the bonus rent income from the master tenant per the master lease agreement as discussed earlier.

Lastly, at the disposition phase of the DST, the sponsor may charge a disposition fee of between 3 percent or 4 percent of the sales price. As stated earlier, the DST sponsor is not permitted to share in the back-end profits from the sale of the property as is the case with real estate funds structured as partnerships. The disposition fee is split with the procuring real estate broker who brings the willing and able buyer and is therefore competitive with most real estate commissions on single-ownership commercial real estate paid by the seller. In the event that the property is sold at a price that does not return all the investors' capital, the acquisition fee is often forfeited by the sponsor. On this issue, the IRS rules allow the fee, contingent on the return of capital but not a participation on the return on capital.

It should be noted that many of the costs associated with the DST would also be incurred when acquiring a single ownership direct real estate interest. For example, the investor in a direct real estate investment would still need to pay for appraisals, environmental reports, loan fees, real estate broker's commissions, and property management services. As a rule of thumb, the DST investor may be paying between 2 percent to 4 percent more in fees for a DST, but this is often more than justified by the extreme degree of due diligence that a DST is put through, and by the fact that the investor is acquiring a truly passive investment based on the efforts of others.

In summary, the investor must weigh all the advantages against the disadvantages of a specific DST investment, as well as account for the risks and fees associated with that investment. These considerations should be viewed from the perspective of the investor's unique cash flow requirements, tax exposure, financial objectives, portfolio diversification, and risk tolerance. A DST investment may not be suitable for every investor.

Chapter 5

Who May Invest

The 1933 Securities Act
The 1946 US Supreme Court case of SEC v. W. J. Howey Company

In order to purchase an equity interest in a DST investment, the investor must be an "accredited investor" as defined by the Securities and Exchange Commission. An individual accredited investor is simply any investor with a net worth (assets minus liabilities) of $1,000,000 or more, not including the equity in the investor's primary residence. Alternatively, the investor may qualify with an income level of $200,000 ($300,000 if married) for the prior two years, and an expectation of the same income for the current year.

Over the years we have encountered many investors who were sold on the passive real estate opportunity that a DST could offer as an alternative for their 1031 exchange, but who did not meet the definition of an accredited investor. These investors were accordingly prohibited from investing, even though they were already invested in single-ownership real estate assets and were willing to accept the potential risks. Understandably, this prohibition was extremely frustrating to these unaccredited investors. An understanding of the applicable securities law may help to assuage this frustration.

So why are DST and TIC investments marketed as securities and subject to the investor accreditation rules? Generally, the Securities Act of 1933 § 2 contains definitions of the term "security." In the subsection, there is a catch-all category known as an "investment contract" which constitutes a security. In the 1946 landmark case of *SEC v. W.J. Howey Company*, the US Supreme Court defined an "investment contract" as any transaction in which

1. a person invests money
2. in a common enterprise and is
3. led to expect profits
4. solely from the efforts of others.

DSTs and most other real estate syndications are considered "securities" because they involve the selling of fractional interests coupled with some type of promised return and a management contract based solely from the efforts of others. The term "investment contract" was previously undefined by the Securities Act or by relevant legislative reports, but was common in many state "blue sky" laws in existence prior to the adoption of the federal statute.

In the 1946 Supreme Court case, the Howey Company owned large tracts of citrus acreage in Lake County, Florida. The company planted about five hundred acres annually, keeping half of the groves for itself and offering the other half to the public "to help finance additional development." Each prospective customer was offered both a land sales contract and a service contract, after having been told that it is not feasible to invest in a grove unless service arrangements are made. While the purchaser was free to make arrangements with other service companies, the superiority of Howey-in-the-Hills Service, Inc., was stressed, and 85 percent of the acreage sold during the 3-year period ending May 31, 1943, was covered by service contracts with Howey. Justice Murphey delivered the opinion of the Court stating that the case involved the application of § 2(1) of the Securities Act of 1933 to an offering of units of a citrus grove development, coupled with an investment contract for cultivating, marketing and remitting the net proceeds to the investor.

The Howey case spread a broad net for the definition of a security as an investment contract, which has been followed in many circuit-level court and Supreme Court cases, applying the investment contract concept to a wide range of investments. Accordingly, from the point of view of the SEC, the pooling of funds to attain a return on those funds, based solely on the efforts of others, should be classified as a security for regulatory purposes and subject to their jurisdiction.

Under the Securities Act of 1933, a company that offers or sells its securities must register the securities with the SEC or find an exemption from the registration requirements. To register a DST property offering as a security under the 1933 Securities ACT would be immensely prohibitive, due to both time and cost constraints. To register the offering would require a lengthy SEC filing process that could take several months or more, well beyond the opportunity window for identifying and closing on a property priced at or below market. When in competition with institutional buyers such as REITs and pension funds, a buyer with a contingency to wait many months to complete an SEC registration before closing would not be considered a competitive offer and would not be practical. In addition, the legal fees for an SEC registration, required financial statement audit, quarterly Q10 filing, and annual K10 filing would further stress the offering with excessive costs and loads. Fortunately, the act provides companies with a number of exemptions from SEC filings if certain criteria are satisfied. For some of the exemptions, such as rules 505 and 506 of Regulation D, a company may qualify for the exemption from registration only if it sell its securities to those who are known as "accredited investors."

As a security, the DST offering must be presented in a private placement memorandum (PPM) under Reg. D of the Securities Act of 1933, and have all the appropriate disclosures, disclaimers and information to allow an investor to make an informed decision. As far as the IRS is concerned, if the sponsor has syndicated the property offering following either Revenue Ruling 2004-86, they will consider the offering as real estate available for 1031 exchange.

Accreditation

Individual

As stated above, the term "accredited investor" is defined in Rule 501 of Regulation D and is applied to any individual with a net worth of at least $1 million, not including the value of his or her primary residence, or an individual with income exceeding $200,000 in each of the two most recent calendar years, or joint income with a spouse exceeding $300,000 for those years, and a reasonable expectation of the same income level in the current year.

Other accredited investors under Rule 501 are the following:

- an enterprise in which all the equity owners are accredited investors;
- a trust with assets of at least $5 million, not formed solely to acquire the securities offered, and whose purchases are directed by a person who meets the legal standard of having sufficient knowledge and experience in financial and business matters to be capable of evaluating the merits and risks of the prospective investment;
- a bank, insurance company, registered investment company, business development company, or small business investment company;
- an employee benefit plan (within the meaning of the Employee Retirement Income Security Act) if a bank, insurance company, or registered investment advisor makes the investment decisions, or if the plan has total assets in excess of $5 million;
- a tax-exempt charitable organization, corporation or partnership with assets in excess of $5 million; or
- a director, executive officer, or general partner of the company selling the securities.

Family Trust

A common practice is for the investor to register title to the DST interest under the investor's family trust. In most cases, the trust is a revocable living trust, which would be accredited as an enterprise in which all the equity owners are accredited investors. Therefore, a revocable trust will be deemed accredited if the trustees are themselves accredited under the individual standard. Alternatively, if the trust is irrevocable, then the trust itself would need to have trust assets of at least $5 million to meet the accreditation requirement for an entity. The $5 million of assets would be the aggregate fair market value of all the trust assets and would not be reduced by the trust's liabilities.

Pass-Through Entities

Another common entity used by investors to register their DST interest is a previously registered pass-through entity such as an LLC, S-Corporation, or LLP. While these types of entities are not necessary to limit the investor's liability, as the Delaware trust is itself a bankruptcy remote entity that limits the investor's liability to the member's investment, many investors chose to have a continuity of the holding entity for 1031 exchange purposes. For a valid 1031 exchange, the relinquished property must be held by the same entity that is taking the ownership interest in the replacement property. For these pass-through entities, the accreditation requirement would look to all the individual members to meet the individual definition of accreditation.

Corporations

With respect to regular C corporations (corporations that have not made the IRS subchapter S election) and LLCs that have made an election to be taxed as a corporation, the entity would need to meet the definition of accreditation at the entity level, with total assets of at least $5 million (not accounting for liabilities).

So why must an investor be accredited? Essentially, the answer is Big Brother looking out for the investor. Government oversight of the individual investor, and by extension the safeguarding of the national economy, was the resolve of the 1933 Securities Act following the stock market crash of 1929 and the Great Depression of the 1930s. While less true today, at that time in 1933, a millionaire was a person with significant business experience and/or financial resources. The government considered a millionaire as having the financial experience necessary to evaluate the risks of the investment such as illiquidity, suitability, and concentration, to name a few. If the accredited investor did not have the experience necessary to evaluate the offering's investment risks, then he would have the financial resources necessary to retain a financial or legal advisor to evaluate the investment risks for him.

Up until 2010, the $1 million net worth definition for accreditation of an individual included the equity in the investor's primary residence. However, with the dramatic inflation in home prices over the years, many unsophisticated investors were meeting the accreditation standards simply by the built-up equity in their home. In an effort to increase the accreditation standards to meet the original intent of the exemption, Rule 501 of Regulation D was amended by the Dodd-Frank Wall Street Reform and Consumer Protection Act to not account for the investor's home equity in determining the $1 million net worth.

If the reader does not currently meet the definition for accreditation, he may not invest in a DST or any other private placement offering, such as a real estate fund, that has not been registered with the SEC. A nonaccredited investor may, however, invest in a private or public REIT that has an SEC registration. These REITs have investment minimums as low as $2,500, and some may have much lower accreditation requirements, such as $70,000 in income or $250,000 in net worth. We invite the unaccredited reader to learn more about private REITs in chapter 23.

Chapter 6

The 2017 Tax Cuts and Jobs Act

Major tax reform has historically been a once-in-a-generation event. While a full discussion of all the new tax rules is beyond the scope of this book, given the significant impact on investor after-tax income, it is important to address the provisions affecting commercial real estate and DST investments. Accordingly, a basic understanding of the new tax rules is foundational to a discussion of the tax benefits of a DST investment and Section 1031 like-kind exchanges.

As discussed in chapter 1, taxation has a major impact on every type of investment. Tax law is especially impactful on real estate, and by extension on the DST investment. To find evidence for this assertion, one may look to Ronald Regan's Tax Reform Act of 1986 to see the significant negative impact that the passive loss rules had on real estate tax shelter partnerships, and its extended negative impact on commercial real estate values. With this understanding of history, Cornerstone closely followed the current tax reform efforts, from the presidential candidate's tax plan, to the House Republican Blueprint on tax reform by Chairman Kevin Brady (R-Texas Eighth District), to the House and Senate tax bills, and ultimately to the reconciliation process that resulted in the Tax Cuts and Jobs Act of 2017 signed by the President.

Throughout the process, Cornerstone lobbied congressmen and senators on Capitol Hill in coordination with the Federation of Exchange Accommodators, supported lobbying efforts of the DST industry, and provided clients with access to petition their congressional representatives in support of Section 1031 exchanges. We are happy to report that all these efforts were immensely successful, and resulted in an Act that is beneficial to DST and real estate investing on many levels. The act not only has preserved Section 1031 like-kind exchanges for real estate, but should also have a significantly positive affect on the after-tax income for most DST real estate investors. We feel that these beneficial results were not simply an accommodation to the voice of a relatively broad coalition of real estate industry lobbyists, but rather testify to true congressional intent to support real estate as a means to build wealth in America, and as an underpinning to the stability and growth of the national economy.

New Income Tax Rate Reductions

Single Filer Tax Brackets for Ordinary Income (2018 Tax Year)

10%	$0–$9,525
12%	$9,525–$38,700
22%	$38,700–$82,500
24%	$82,500–$157,500
32%	$157,500–$200,000
35%	$200,000–$500,000
37%	$500,000+

Married Filing Jointly Tax Brackets for Ordinary Income (2018 Tax Year)

10%	$0–$19,050
12%	$19,050–$77,400
22%	$77,400–$165,000
24%	$165,000–$315,000
32%	$315,000–$400,000
35%	$400,000–$600,000
37%	$600,000+

Corporate Tax Rate Reduction

The ACT reduces the income tax rate for corporations (C corps) from 35 percent down to 21 percent.

Capital Gain Rates

The act did not change the preexisting maximum capital gain rates. The long-term capital gain rate continues to be generally 15 percent. However, for most real estate investors with gains that elevate total taxable income above $418,400 for single filers, the capital gains rate continues at 20 percent ($470,700 for married filing jointly or qualifying widow(er); $444,550 for head of household, and $235,350 for married filing separately). Recaptured depreciation is basically a capital gain (Section 1250 gain) taxed at an ordinary income rate. The recapture of all allowed or allowable depreciation during the hold period remains at 25 percent. Taxpayers earning income above certain thresholds ($200,000 for singles and heads of household, $250,000 for married couples filing jointly and qualifying widow(er)s with dependent children, and $125,000 for married couples filing separately) pay an additional 3.8 percent tax on all investment income. Therefore, the top federal tax rate on long-term capital gains is 23.8 percent.

Alternative Minimum Tax

The Alternative Minimum Tax (AMT) was one of the most reviled aspects of the tax code. It was originally put into place in 1969 to create an alternative tax system to force the wealthy to pay some level of tax, given numerous tax loopholes and tax deductions. However, over time and due to inflation, many in the middle class were beginning to be subject to the AMT. The House bill eliminated the AMT altogether, but the final Act only eliminated the AMT for corporations, retaining the AMT for individual taxpayers.

Fortunately, the act did significantly increase the exemption amount for the AMT to $70,300 for single filers and $109,400 for joint filers, with the AMT phase-out threshold increasing to $500,000 for single filers and $1,000,000 for joint filers.

Standard Deduction

The act eliminates the earlier personal exemptions and doubles the standard deduction to $12,000 for single filers and $24,000 for joint filers. For future years the new standard deduction is indexed to inflation.

The National Association of Realtors (NAR) lobbied hard against the doubling of the standard deduction, as it greatly reduces the value of the mortgage interest deduction and the tax incentives for homeownership. Per Congressional estimates, only 5–8 percent of taxpayers will be able to benefit from home mortgage and other itemized deductions by itemizing expenses. In other words, there will be no tax differential between renting and owning a home for more than 90 percent of taxpayers.

State and Local Tax Deduction

States and local tax deductions are now limited under the act to only $10,000. The deduction limitation also includes property taxes as well as income and sales taxes. The $10,000 limit is applicable to both single and joint filers and is not indexed for inflation.

Exclusion of Gain on Sale of a Principal Residence

Representing a major victory for the NAR, the ACT did not change the rules governing the exclusion on the sale of a principal residence. The House bill would have phased out the exclusion for taxpayers with income above $250,000 single and $500,000 married filing jointly; while the Senate version of the bill would have changed the timing to require living in the home for 5 out of the past 8 years. Fortunately, the rules remain unchanged, requiring the taxpayer to live in the home for 2 out of the past 5 years, and with no phase-out provisions.

Mortgage Interest Deduction

The act further reduces the limit on deductible home mortgage debt from $1 million to $750,000 for new loans funded after December 14, 2017. Home loans taken out prior to December 14, 2017, up to $1 million, are grandfathered and not subject to the new $750,000 limitation. Mortgage interest on second homes is still deductible, subject to the $750,000 limitation, and preexisting loans up to $1 million on a second home are likewise grandfathered.

The act repealed the deduction for home equity debt interest, effective until December 31, 2025. However, the interest on home equity loans is still deductible (i.e., second mortgages) as long as the loan proceeds are used to substantially improve the residence.

Business Interest Expense Deduction Limitation

The act provides that, for tax years 2018–2022, businesses will be able to deduct business interest up to a limit of 30 percent of the business's earnings before interest, taxes, depreciation, and amortization ("EBITDA"). For tax years after 2022, the limit changes to 30 percent of the business's earnings before interest and taxes ("EBIT"). However, the limitation has the following exemptions:

1. *The real estate industry is excluded from the limits and can fully deduct their interest expenses if they meet certain conditions.*
2. *The farming industry is excluded from the limits and can fully deduct their interest expenses if they meet certain conditions.*

3. Businesses with average gross revenues of $25 million or less over the prior three years are excluded from the limit and can fully deduct their interest expenses.
4. Taxpayers will be able to carry forward any business interest that is not deductible in the current tax year due to the application of these limitations.

Cost Recovery (Depreciation)

The rules for depreciation remain unchanged under the act. Residential properties, including multifamily properties held in a DST, continue to be depreciable on a straight-line basis over a recovery period of 27.5 years. Commercial nonresidential properties, including retail, office, industrial and other nonresidential properties held in a DST, continue to be depreciated on a straight-line basis over a recovery period of 39 years. The act replaces separate classifications for qualified restaurant, leasehold, and retail improvements with one classification of "qualified improvement property" (QIP), with a general 15-year recovery period.

However, under the act a real property trade or business must use the Alternative Depreciation System (ADS) if the taxpayer elects out of the limitation on interest deduction. Making the election would require a forty-year recovery period for nonresidential properties, a thirty-year recovery period for residential real property, and a twenty-year recovery period for qualified improvement property.

Carried Interest

A "carried interest" (also known as a "promoted interest" or a "promote" in the real estate industry) is a financial interest in the long-term capital gain of a development. The "carried interest" is given to a general partner, usually the developer, by the limited partners, the investors in the partnership. Many in Congress wanted to change the tax treatment of carried interest compensation from capital gains to ordinary income. Carried interest was highlighted as a prime example of an industry-specific tax break that needed reform. The act, with original language in both the House and Senate bills, requires a three-year holding period to qualify for capital gain treatment.

Rehabilitation Credit

The act repealed the 10 percent credit for pre-1936 buildings, but retained the 20 percent credit for certified historic structures, allowable over a five-year period (20 percent per year allocation).

Deduction for Qualified Business Income

Many members of Congress felt that, because corporations greatly benefited from the decrease in the corporate tax rate from 35 percent to 21 percent, sole proprietors, independent contractors, and pass-through businesses such as partnerships, limited liability corporations (LLCs) taxed as partnerships, and subchapter S corporations (S-corps) should likewise enjoy a tax reduction. To compensate, the final ACT provides a 20 percent deduction for qualified business income under a new section of the Internal Revenue Code, Section 199A.

In general, the section provides that, in the case of a taxpayer other than a corporation, there shall be allowed as a deduction for any taxable year an amount equal to the sum of 20 percent of the combined qualified business income with respect to a qualified trade or business. The act provides for certain "guardrails" to limit the 20 percent deduction to nonpersonal service businesses. Accordingly, income from a personal service business will generally not qualify for the deduction. A specified service trade or business includes accounting, law, health, consulting, athletics, financial services, non–real estate brokerage services, and any business where the main asset of the business is the reputation or skill of one or more of the employees or owners.[15]

The National Association of Realtors, through its lobbying efforts, was able to secure a limited exemption for sole proprietors (independent contractors) and pass-through business owners with personal service income. The exemption allows for a business owner with taxable income of less than $157,000 for single filers or $315,000 for joint filers to deduct 20 percent of noncapital gain net income from the business. Over these income levels, the benefit of the 20 percent deduction is phased out over an income range of $50,000 for single filers and $100,000 for joint filers.

For nonpersonal service income above these thresholds, the 20 percent deduction is also subject to a series of complicated limitations based on the wages and capital of the pass-through entity. The wage and capital limitation exception limit the deduction by the greater of:

- 50 percent of the W-2 wages paid by the qualified trade or business, or
- The total of 25 percent of the W-2 wages paid by the qualified trade or business plus 2.5 percent of the cost basis of the tangible depreciable property of the business at the end of the tax year.

In short, sole proprietors and pass-through business owners with personal service income and total taxable income below $157,000 for single filers or $315,000 for joint filers may generally claim the full 20 percent deduction under the personal service income exemption. Sole proprietors and pass-through business owners with nonpersonal service income and total taxable income above these thresholds may also be able to claim the 20 percent deduction, limited by the wage and capital limit exception outlined above.

The sixty-four-thousand-dollar question is whether rental income from a DST interest will qualify for the 20 percent deduction of qualified business income? To qualify for the annual above-the-line (nonitemized) deduction of 20 percent of the DST's net annual income, it appears from that three basic test criteria need to be met:

1. *The DST must not be a corporation;*
2. *The DST must have qualified business income; and*
3. *The DST must be a qualified trade or business.*

The DST, structured in accordance with Revenue Ruling 2004-86, is a separate trust entity for federal tax purposes, and is not a business entity classified as a corporation or a partnership. Therefore, the DST passes the first test, as it is not a corporation.

The second test is whether the qualified business income is related to a service business. The section defines qualified business income to mean income from *any* trade or business other than:

1. *A specified service trade or business, or*
2. *A trade or business performing services as an employee, or*
3. *A trade or business which involves the performance of services that consist of investing and investment management, trading or dealing in securities, partnership interests or commodities.*

A DST structured in accordance with Revenue Ruling 2004-86 does not provide services. In addition, a DST does not meet the definition of any of the service-related activities described as a specified service trade or business.[16] Therefore, DST income is not service-related income, and should be considered qualified business income.

However, the third test still remains: is a DST a qualified trade or business? Generally, the term *trade or business* is considered any activity carried on for the production of income from selling goods or performing services. In the Internal Revenue Code[17], a taxpayer's adjusted gross income is computed by deducting all ordinary and necessary expenses incurred in carrying on a trade or business. Interestingly, the term "trade or business" in this context has not been defined in the Code, the regulations, or in any IRS guidance. Accordingly, there are no uniform standards, and the determination as to whether a taxpayer's activities qualify as a trade or business is based on the unique facts and circumstances of each individual case.

The Supreme Court has historically acknowledged regularity (i.e., activity over a certain period) and a profit motive as key factors that the courts have generally accepted as indicating the existence of a trade or business. In 1987, the Court in the Groetzinger case[18] stated, "We accept the fact that to be engaged in a trade or business, the taxpayer must be involved in the activity with continuity and regularity and that the taxpayer's primary purpose for engaging in the activity must be for income or profit."[19]

Nevertheless, assessing the degree of activity necessary for the rent and management of real property to reach the level of a trade or business is challenging. Formulating the question in another way, when is a taxpayer owning rental properties considered to be in the trade or business of renting real estate? The IRS discussed the concept of real estate trades or businesses in Letter Ruling 9840026 in the context of excluding cancellation-of-debt income if the debt is incurred or assumed in connection with, and is secured by, real property used in a trade or business.[20] In the letter ruling, the IRS acknowledged that there are no uniform gauges and concluded:

The issue of whether the rental of property is a trade or business of a taxpayer is ultimately one of fact, in which the scope of a taxpayer's activities, either personally or through agents, in connection with the property, are so extensive as to rise to the stature of a trade or business.

Per Revenue Ruling 2004-86, a DST is an entity separate from its owners and is formed for investment purposes. Furthermore, the Ruling states that a DST is classified for federal tax purposes as a trust[21] by virtue of the fact that the DST's trustee has none of the powers to carry on a profit-making business.[22] If the DST trustee did have the powers to carry on a profit-making business, then the DST would be a "business entity,"[23] defined as an entity recognized for federal tax purposes as either a corporation or a partnership. Therefore, the DST is a separate trust entity for federal tax purposes, formed for investment motives, and is not a business entity classified as a corporation or a partnership. Furthermore, the investor beneficiaries have no voting rights and no power to direct the actions of the trust. The sole right of the beneficiary is to receive distributions from the trust due to its ownership or sale of the interest in the property.

Given that the DST in not a business entity and not a profit-making business, an argument could be made that the DST is not a trade or business and should not qualify for the 20 percent deduction for qualified business income. It may be that the DST investor cannot have the proverbial cake (no business activity for 1031 exchange purposes) and eat it too (business activity for the 20 percent qualitied business income deduction). Ultimately, we may have to wait for a new IRS Revenue Ruling or Treasury guidance on the issue to know with more certainty.

Notwithstanding the above discussion on the meaning of a trade or business, the authors believe that the 20 percent deduction should apply to the income of a DST investment. Here is our reasoning that the investor and his or her tax adviser may follow to reach their own conclusion:

1. *The Congressional intent seems to be to provide the deduction for any nonservice business income other than a corporation.*
2. *The DST, per Revenue Ruling 2004-86, is a trust entity formed for investment purposes, and while not a business entity, the investors clearly have a motive to derive profit over a certain period, which seems to be in line with the Supreme Court's historic definition of a trade or business.*
3. *While the House version of the bill discussed trade or business activity in terms of the passive loss rules, the Senate version of the bill defines a qualified trade or business to mean "any trade or business other than a specified service trade or business and other than the trade or business of being an employee." Ultimately, the final Conference Agreement follows the Senate version of the bill and not the House version*[24].
4. *The Senate version of the bill defines all the types of investment income that do* not *qualify, including dividends, interest, and currency gains, but it does* not *mention rental income.*

5. *The Senate version specifically provides that the deduction is allowed for qualified REIT dividends. Generally, a REIT must derive at least 75 percent of its gross income from rents, mortgage interest, or gains from the sale of real property.*
6. *The Conference Agreement and the final Act provide that trusts and estates are eligible for the 20 percent deduction under the provision. It states that rules similar to the rules under present-law Section 199 (as in effect on December 1, 2017) apply for apportioning between fiduciaries and beneficiaries any W-2 wages and unadjusted basis of qualified property under the limitation based on W-2 wages and capital.*

Although there is some uncertainty with the language of a "trade or business," it appears to the authors that the Conference Agreement rejected the House language using the passive loss rules, and specifically included trusts in the final Act. We believe that DST income should qualify, as rental income is not mentioned in the Senate bill which clearly lists all other possible types of investment income that do not qualify, and it provides that rental income included in dividend income from a REIT will qualify.

DSTs are within the spirit of the provision intended to benefit owners of pass-through entities and sole proprietorships. While a DST is different (a grantor trust, disregarded entity), it functions in the same manner as a pass-through or sole proprietorship, because all the income passes through the DST as an entity to the beneficial owners. If REIT stockholders qualify, it would be unfair to treat owners of DSTs differently.

If the position is taken that the DST is a qualified trade or business, then the annual income from a DST is nonpersonal service income. For investors with taxable income above the threshold amounts, the amount of the deduction would be subject to the wage and capital limitation. The capital limitation would be calculated at 2.5 percent of the unadjusted basis immediately after acquisition of all the qualified property allocated to the DST investor.

Cash Method of Accounting

The act allows taxpayers with average gross revenues of $25 million or less over the prior three years to use the cash method of accounting.

Immediate Expensing (Section 179) and Bonus Deprecation

The act significantly increased the amount of qualified property eligible each year for immediate expensing under Section 179, from $500,000 to $1 million. The phase-out limitations are likewise increased from $2 million to $2.5 million. Under prior law, businesses exceeding a total of $2 million of purchases in qualifying equipment have Section 179 deduction phase-out dollar-for-dollar, and completely eliminated above $2.5 million. The general definition of qualified real property eligible for Section 179 expensing was expanded to include improvements to nonresidential real property after the property was placed into service, including roofs, heating, ventilation, air-conditioning, fire protection, alarm systems, and security systems.

Beginning in 2018 until 2022, the act will allow businesses to take immediate 100 percent bonus depreciation (increased from the current 50 percent bonus depreciation limit) with respect to certain short-lived assets such as machinery and equipment. The act therefore provides full expensing for most tangible personal property, providing a marginal effective tax rate of 0 percent to fully expensed property, equating to the deferral that like-kind exchanges provided under prior law. Again, the expensing provision is temporary, sunsetting after five years.

Like-Kind Exchanges

The preservation of like-kind exchanges for real property under IRC Section 1031 was a major victory for the real estate industry. Cornerstone, together with the Federation of Exchange Accommodators (FEA), the Alternative & Direct Investment Securities Association (ADISA), the National Association of Realtors, and the REALTORS Land Institute, all lobbied on Capitol Hill to protect and defend like-kind exchanges for real estate.

The alarm bell was first sounded early in 2017, when the House Blueprint for tax reform proposed 100 percent immediate expensing of all investments in tangible property (such as equipment and buildings) and intangible assets (such as intellectual property). According to the Blueprint, the immediate expensing deduction could be netted against other capital gains and passive income in the year of acquisition. The authors of the Blueprint commented in early 2017 that, given the Blueprint's lower capital gain tax rates and the provision for immediate expensing, they did not think that §1031 would be necessary.

Our broad coalition of industry associations and organizations firstly lobbied that the Section 1031 like-kind exchange was essential to defer capital gain tax on land which would not have qualified for immediate expensing. The Federal Reserve's Flow of Funds report contains enough data to calculate the value of privately held land in the US at $14.488 trillion[25]. Furthermore, land comprises much of the savings for farmers and ranchers. If immediate expensing had replaced Section 1031, all this savings would be penalized by being taxed. In most cases, land savings are ultimately exchanged using Section 1031 into income-producing property to fund retirement as the landowner ages. These savings are therefore indispensable to fund a large segment of the population's retirement, especially given the challenges to funding Social Security.

Secondly, the industry lobbied that like-kind exchanges are a key component to the vibrancy and growth of the national economy, as real property changes hands at a greater rate when sellers are not penalized by the taxation of their gains. New buyers often improve the property and "make it their own" by painting, improving, and buying furniture and other fixtures, all of which benefit local industries such as real estate agencies, contractors, title insurers, lenders, equipment dealers, manufacturers, transportation, energy, and agriculture. In addition, city budgets and local schools also benefit from the turnover of real estate through new property value assessments. Immediate expensing, on the contrary, would discourage turnover and produce a lock-in or buy-and-hold culture, as a sale would generate significant taxes from capital gain, depreciation recapture, and state taxes. The Tax Foundation in 2016 reported that GDP growth would shrink by $18 billion dollars each year if §1031 like-kind exchanges were repealed. An earlier study by Ernst and Young reported a $13 billion yearly GDP contraction if §1031 were repealed.

While the act retains the Section 1031 like-kind exchange for real property, it repeals like-kind exchanges for all personal property such as machinery, equipment, vehicles, artwork, collectibles, and other intangible business assets. Formerly, large corporations such as airlines and rental car companies were using Section 1031 to exchange these personal property assets. Section 1031 like-kind exchanges for real estate will continue to its hundredth-year anniversary and beyond. Section 1031 was legislated into the tax code in 1921 and has grown over the century to be a major cornerstone of today's real estate market and national economy. We will fully develop the Section 1031 like-kind rules applicable to real estate and DST investments in the next chapter.

Estate Tax

The House bill provided for a full repeal of the estate tax as a form of double taxation. The final ACT, however, preserved the estate tax, but the amount for the unified estate and gift tax exemption has been doubled to approximately $11 million per person, which will be indexed to inflation. It remains to be seen if the states will adapt to the new federal exclusion amount, as was typically the case in the past, or adopt their own unique levels for the unified exemption.

A major victory for Section 1031 exchange real estate is that the step-up provisions have also been preserved. Accordingly, real estate that has continued to defer capital gain taxes through successive exchanges over the investor's lifetime may pass to heirs at a stepped-up basis in the inherited property to the fair market value at the date of death, or at an alternative election date no more than 6 months later. Accordingly, the heirs' basis would then be the new assessed value or stepped-up basis, and they would only pay capital gains tax from that point forward upon an ultimate sale. Interestingly, per a study by Ling and Petrova[26], 88 percent of the real estate replacement properties acquired in a §1031 exchange are ultimately disposed of through a taxable sale, so for federal and state budget purposes, in most cases the tax does eventually get paid.

Please note that Cornerstone is not licensed to provide tax advice. Tax information is provided for information and discussion purposes only and should not be relied upon, as every investor taxpayer has a unique tax and financial situation. However, the firm's owner (and one of the authors of this book) is a licensed CPA, manages a licensed tax practice, has a master's degree in business taxation, and was a tax consultant and senior manager with Ernst & Young and Deloitte & Touché, respectively. NONETHELESS, EACH PROSPECTIVE PURCHASER SHOULD SEEK ADVICE FROM AN INDEPENDENT TAX ADVISOR, BASED ON THEIR PARTICULAR CIRCUMSTANCES, CONCERNING THE INCOME AND OTHER TAX CONSEQUENCES OF PARTICIPATION IN ANY INVESTMENT.

Chapter 7

Introduction to the 1031 Exchange

The 1921 adoption of Section 1031 into the Internal Revenue Code.
The 2017 Tax Cuts and Jobs Act

The United States Internal Revenue Code Section 1031(a) reads as follows:

1. *In General—No gain or loss shall be recognized on the exchange of property held for productive use in a trade or business or for investment if such property is exchanged solely for property of like kind which is to be held either for productive use in a trade or business or for investment.*
2. *Exception—this subsection shall not apply to any exchange of—*
3. *Stock in trade or other property held primarily for sale,*
4. *Stock, bonds, or notes,*
5. *Other securities or evidence of indebtedness or interest,*
6. *Interest in a partnership,*
7. *Certificates of trust or beneficial interests, or*
8. *Choses in action.*

(Please note that final wording for this code section may change once the 2017 Act is written into the code.)

According to Internal Revenue Code § 1031, an investor can defer capital gains tax and depreciation recapture by reinvesting the proceeds from the sale of real property into replacement property, thus preserving significant wealth in their estate.

Section 1031 has been a vital economic stimulant and part of the tax code since 1921. A study of the early tax court cases clearly shows that the two key purposes for the provision were (1) to avoid unfair taxation of ongoing investments in property and (2) to encourage active reinvestment.[27] The use and dependence on § 1031 exchanges have grown over the past nearly one hundred years to be a major cornerstone of today's real estate market and national economy. Without the possibility of tax deferral on capital  gains, a buy-and-hold mentality would pervade the real estate industry, resulting in significantly less sales transaction volume and lower values. Furthermore, the ripple effect of fewer real estate transactions would significantly retard the national economy, as businesses associated with real estate such as real estate brokers, appraisers, architects, painters, building contractors, and furniture retailers would all have less revenue. Even public schools and local governments would feel the effect of real estate values not being regularly reassessed. Accordingly, over the decades, Section 1031 has survived multiple tax reforms, including the 2017 Tax Cuts and Jobs Act. Cornerstone, as an associate member of the Federation of Exchange Accommodators (FEA), has lobbed on Capitol Hill to protect and preserve Section 1031 exchanges.

Section 1031 Case Study

In chapter 1, we began discussing the DST vision by extoling the "tremendous advantage" of a Section 1031 exchange for building wealth. We think it fitting to begin our introduction to the Section 1031 exchange with a sample case study, to quantify this advantage in terms of investment preservation, income tax savings, and increased annual income. We will take some average numbers from our experience over the years to provide an average case study tax scenario for our example.

In our example, we will use a single taxpayer with ordinary annual wage income of $200,000. The taxpayer originally acquired a multifamily property in 1992 at a price of $900,000. The taxpayer had no prior 1031 exchanges and purchased the property with no debt financing. The taxpayer held the property for 25 years and, after taking the allowable straight-line depreciation over a tax-useful life of 27.5 years, sold the property with only an $81,818 remaining tax basis. The property was sold in 2016 to a cash buyer for $4,000,000 representing a pure capital gain of $3,100,000 and a tax gain of $3,918,182 including $818,182 of depreciation recapture.

Below, we present the computations for the taxpayer, in accordance with the 2017 Tax Cuts and Jobs Act, with and without a Section 1031 exchange.

See graphic on next page.

Multifamily Building Purchased in 1992

Depreciation from 1992 to 2016: 818,182
Adjusted tax basis: 81,818
Property sold in 2017: 4,000,000
Adjusted tax basis: 81,818

Original purchase price: 900,000

Gain on the sale: 3,918,182

Assuming $200,000 of earned income and $2,000 of rental income the total tax for the seller would be as follows:

	Without a 1031 Exchange	With a 1031 Exchange
Wages:	200,000	200,000
Rental income:	2,000	500
Capital gain (Schedule D):	3,100,000	-
Depreciation recapture (Form 4797):	818,182	-
Standard Deduction:	12,000	12,000
Taxable income (1040):	4,108,182	185,500
Tax (1040):	837,804	33,819
Tax from Form 8960 (1040 line 62):	148,891	17
Total tax (1040):	986,695	33,836
Plus state tax (average state rate of 5%):	205,409	9,425
Total tax liability:	1,192,104	43,261
Effective tax rate:	29%	23%
Total increase in tax:	1,148,843	
Total sales price:	4,000,000	
Percentage of sales price lost to taxes:	29%	

Income Pre and Post Tax

Reinvested:	2,851,575	4,000,000:
Cash Flow:	5%	5%
Annual Income:	142,579	200,000
Hold Period:	7	7
Total Income:	998,051	1,400,000

	Capital Gain	Depreciation Recapture	Form 8960 (ACA)	State tax
Portion of gain:	3,100,000	818,182	3,918,182	3,918,912
Rate:	20%	25%	3.8%	5%
Tax:	599,080	204,545	148,891	195,909
Total federal tax:			952,516	
Total federal and state taxes:				

Note: Capital gain tax rate goes from 15% to 20% when adjusted gross income (AGI) exceeds $418,400

The amounts highlighted in red in the example demonstrate the tremendous advantage of a Section 1031 exchange. Without an exchange, the taxpayer would have paid $1,148,425 in tax on the gain and depreciation recapture. This amount represents 32 percent of the investment's value that would have been lost to federal and state income taxes.

Even more advantageous is the income that could be generated from the entire $4,000,000 investment carried over to the DST investment by utilizing the exchange. With an average 5 percent cash-on-cash return, the taxpayer enjoys an annual income of $200,000, contrasted with only $142,579 on income if the after-tax amount is reinvested. Over a seven-year hold period, the annual income aggregates to $1,400,000 with the exchange, contrasted with only $998,051 without an exchange. Thus, not utilizing a 1031 exchange would have cost the taxpayer $401,949 in income before tax over 7 years. The loss in income divergence would be even greater on an after-tax basis if the after-tax sale proceeds were reinvested in the stock or bond market without the advantage of a tax shelter due to depreciation.

A final lesson to be gleaned from the example is the principle of employing built-up equity. If the taxpayer had made an astute real estate investment back in 1992 and was enjoying a 10 percent cash-on-cash return which escalated to 15 percent over the years, the original investment would only still represent a 3.4 percent return-on-equity ($135,000/$4,000,000) with an annual income of $135,000 ($900,000 × 15 percent). However, by conducting a Section 1031 exchange into a new DST property, the built-up equity of $3,100,000 is now being utilized to produce an income of $200,000 per year. The $200,000 per year cash flow would translate into a cash-on-cash return of 22 percent from the original investment of $900,000. This principle should be employed every seven to ten years in an appreciating market, and DSTs with a five- to ten-year hold period and accessibility are the perfect vehicle.

Swap until You Drop

Section 1031 exchange deferrals can be continued from exchange to exchange, deferring tax liability until sale without a 1031 exchange or until the tax liability passes into that investor's estate. This is often referred to as "swap until you drop." The investor's heirs are then entitled to a step-up in basis to the fair market value at the date of death, or an alternative election date no more than six months later. The heir's basis would then be the new assessed value or stepped-up basis, and they would only pay capital gains tax from that point forward until an ultimate sale.

Increasing Cost Basis by Assuming Greater Debt

A significant number of investors have owned their relinquished property for many years and have little or no remaining debt. In this case, it is worth considering increasing basis through investment in a higher leveraged property. If an investor assumes greater debt with the replacement property than they had with the relinquished property, the additional amount of debt may be added to the tax basis of the investment. This additional tax basis can then be depreciated over a new useful life on a straight-line basis. This additional basis can provide increased tax shelter due to a larger deduction for depreciation expenses. (Please note that depreciation is an accounting concept and is allowed even if the property is appreciating in value.) The additional depreciation, in many cases, can shelter as much as 50 percent to 60 percent of the investor's rental income cash flow from income taxation.

1031 Exchange Requirements

As outlined above, a 1031 tax-deferred exchange can be a powerful wealth-building tool, allowing an investor to defer capital gains tax by reinvesting the proceeds from the sale of investment property into qualified replacement property. However, a set of strict identification and timeline rules must be followed to the letter. A professional tax advisor should be utilized to ensure that every requirement of § 1031 is met. Failure to do so can result in immediate tax liabilities plus associated penalties.

Some of the most important requirements for an IRS-approved 1031 exchange are the following:

1. *The replacement property must be of equal or greater value than the relinquished property.*
2. *The equity of the replacement property must be of equal or greater value than the equity of the relinquished property.*
3. *The debt held by the replacement property must be of equal or greater value than the debt held by the relinquished property, unless the investor offsets lower debt on the replacement property by adding cash to the exchange.*
4. *All net profit from the relinquished property must be used in the purchase of the replacement property.*

If one or multiple of the above requirements are not met, the exchange is not entirely invalidated. However, the amount by which the equity, debt or property value falls short of the stipulated requirement is considered "boot" and subject to taxation. Unfortunately, the boot is first taxed a deprecation recapture at the higher federal tax rate of 25 percent. Once all prior allowed or allowable deprecation is recaptured, then the long-term federal capital gain rates would apply. This principle is true for all forms of taxable boot—value, cash or mortgage boot.

The Equal or Greater Value Rule

It should be noted that the replacement value is not strictly the sales price of the relinquished property. The sales price may be reduced by any and all costs associated with the sale, including the cost of the Qualified Intermediary.[28] Accordingly, the value of the replacement property (which is effectively the purchase price between unrelated parties) must be equal to or greater than the net sales price after closing costs of the relinquished property. The dollar amount of any decrease would be considered taxable boot. Any increase in value would be due to adding cash or increasing the amount of leverage, both of which would increase the investor's tax basis in the property. (See chapter 19 for a discussion on deprecation of new basis.)

The Use of All Equity Rule

In most cases, the requirement that all the equity in the relinquished property be invested in the replacement property (less any sales and closing costs as outlined above) is automatically met if the investor does not take cash out of the transaction. Any cash taken out of the exchange would always be considered cash boot and is always subject to taxation.

> Cornerstone has a useful DST diversification tool for calculating the blended leverage on multiple DST offerings and calculating additional tax basis.

The Equal or Greater Debt Rule

To avoid mortgage boot, the dollar amount of the debt on the replacement property must be equal to or greater than the debt that was secured by the relinquished property and paid off at the sale closing. Any reduction in debt is considered by the Service as if cash was received by the taxpayer and used to reduce the debt, and thus constitutes constructive receipt. The tax theory behind the rule is that incurred liabilities by the taxpayer in the context of a Section 1031 exchange may offset liability relief of the taxpayer in that tax-deferred exchange.[29]

The DST to Eliminate Mortgage Boot

A DST investment can be a significant advantage when the taxpayer is attempting to match replacement debt with relinquished debt in order to avoid taxable mortgage boot. Cornerstone typically offers fifteen to twenty-five DST offerings with various levels of debt or loan-to-value (LTV). DST LTVs can range from 0 percent all cash offerings to a historic maximum of 84 percent for zero coupon highly leveraged offerings. The taxpayer may either select a single DST offering with an appropriate level of leverage for his exchange, or blend the leverage levels for multiple DSTs to achieve an aggregate level that is equal to or greater than the relinquished debt.

The zero-coupon DST is often used as a tool if the investor requires higher leverage for his exchange. This tool may be necessary if the relinquished debt is significantly above the level of leverage offered by available DSTs with cash flow. A surprisingly small amount of equity may be allocated to the highly leveraged zero coupon to reach the required debt level to eliminate mortgage boot. Cornerstone has a DST diversification tool that is very useful for calculating the blended leverage on multiple DST offerings and calculating additional tax basis.

The zero-coupon DST offering typically has no cash flow, as the lender will sweep the cash flow in order to hyper-amortize the debt. The lender will lend to such a high LTV (typically as high at 84 percent) only if the tenant is of institutional credit grade, such as a Walgreens store, with the national company guaranteeing the lease. While these offerings have no cash flow, the amortization can potentially provide a significant return once the property is sold. These highly leveraged zero-coupon DST investments may help the investor to effectively de-lever the debt level on the reminder of the investor's real estate portfolio, while reducing the debt on the highly leveraged DST over the hold period due to hyper-amortization. The zero-coupon sponsor will try to mitigate the effects of phantom income on the loan principal paydown with interest expense and depreciation expense. However, there may be some phantom income exposure to the taxpayer each year.

The 45 Day, 180 Day, and Identification Rules

The strict identification and timeline rules for a 1031 exchange must be followed to the letter:

1. *The investor must identify, in writing, the exchange properties within forty-five days of the closure for the relinquished property in accordance with one of the following rules:*

    o   **Three-property rule**: *Identification of up to three properties regardless of the total value of property identified;*
    o   **200 percent rule**: *Identification of any number of properties wherein the combined FMV (fair market value) does not exceed 200 percent of the relinquished properties' FMV;*
    o   **95 percent rule**: *Identification of any number of properties regardless of the aggregate FMV, as long as at least 95 percent of the property is ultimately acquired.*

2. *The investor must also close on the replacement property or properties within 180 days of the closure for the relinquished property.*

Identifying Multiple DST Offerings

As discussed in earlier chapters, an advantage of the DST offering with lower minimum investment level is the ability to diversify. However, when identifying multiple DST properties, much care must be taken to comply with the identification rules.

DST Application of the Three-Property Safe Harbor

The most straightforward identification is one utilizing the three-property rule as a safe harbor. In this scenario, any three single-property DSTs may be identified, and the investor has the option to invest all the exchange equity into one, two, or all three identified DSTs. If the investor wishes to diversify into more than three properties, then either the 200 percent rule or the 95 percent rule must be used.

DST Application of the 200 Percent Rule

The 200 percent rule may be used to identify any number of DST properties as long as the total value of all DST properties identified is not greater than 200 percent of the value of the property relinquished (sales price less deductible selling expenses). Do not make the mistake of aggregating only the equity to be placed in the DSTs. The number to target is the total value or sales price of the replacement DST properties. This is quite easily achieved if the relinquished property has significant debt, or a debt level in line with the blended leverage of the identified DSTs. However, if the investor is increasing the level of debt from the relinquished property to the replacement properties, then the 200 percent rule may not be able to be utilized, and the investor must default to the 95 percent rule.

DST Application of the 95 Percent Rule

The 95 percent rule is very rarely used when identifying traditional single-ownership properties. This is due to the fact there are so many variables and contingencies that could prevent the investor from closing on the acquisition of the identified replacement properties. However, DST properties are, in most every case, already acquired by the sponsor, with very little risk, if any, of the investor not being able to close. Sponsors typically have closings on a weekly basis to accommodate all the equity investors for that week.

The one case where the 95 percent rule must be used is in the case of a debt free exchanger who would like to identify and acquire replacement properties which are both more than 3 in number and also whose total acquisition value exceeds 200 percent of the sale price of their relinquished property. This will be an issue for exchangers with either no debt or low leveraged relinquished property that will be acquiring moderate to higher leveraged properties. This is true as the value of the aggregate replacement properties could easily exceed 200 percent of the value of the relinquished property. Of course, exchangers should only use the 95 percent rule when their decisions are firm and when they have near certainty of close on all the identified properties.

As a practical matter, most DST investments will close before the exchanger's forty-five-day identification period is over. The closing is a de facto identification and makes the ID matter moot. If, however, the investor needs to close on the DST investments beyond the forty-five-day window, this is typically not a problem as long as only DST properties have been identified. Cornerstone recommends the exchanger identify all properties (including DSTs) with their qualified intermediary prior to day forty-five even if the replacement properties have already been acquired.

Multiple Properties in One DST Offering

A trend with DST offerings, particularly with retail offerings, is to offer multiple properties in a single DST. Some sponsors have included as many as twenty single-tenant retail properties in one DST offering, to provide greater diversity over tenant credit and geographic locations. Occasionally, multiple multifamily properties that are not contiguous (i.e., adjoining) are also offered in a single DST offering. It should be noted that these offerings may require an ID for each property in the DST. Accordingly, a single DST with four noncontiguous properties would require four IDs and not qualify for the three-property safe-harbor. Consequently, either the 200 percent rule or the 95 percent rule would need to be applied.

When employing either the 200 percent rule or the 95 percent rule, the investor must be careful to identify not only the address of the property, but also the total value of the DST that the investor will be acquiring. Please note that this is the total value, including both debt and equity, that the investor will be assuming or acquiring, and not the total value of the entire DST.

DSTs as a Backup ID

Some investors chose to use DSTs as a backup ID for their 1031 exchange in the event that the targeted properties are not closed on for various reasons. DSTs are ideally suited for this purpose, as an equity position may be reserved by the investor with no commitment on the investor's part, and because there is little risk that the property can be closed successfully in a short time period. However, the investor should be careful to satisfy one of the three ID rules if the DST contains multiple noncontiguous properties.

The Like-Kind Property Requirement

Paragraph 1031(a)(1) of the code section has the requirement that the exchanged properties must be like-kind. This requirement is liberally construed, and virtually all real estate properties, whether raw land or those with substantial improvements, qualify as like-kind. However, REITs, real estate funds, or other securities do not qualify for 1031 exchange. Types of like-kind properties may include:

- Raw land
- Multifamily rentals
- Single-family rentals
- Retail shopping centers
- Office buildings
- Industrial facilities
- Storage facilities

While the scope of like-kind is quite broad, even to the inclusion of oil and gas and other mineral rights, the tax code restricts like-kind based on geographic location. It is interesting to note that real property located within the United States and its territories is considered like-kind with other real property located in the United States and its territories, while real property located in foreign countries is considered like-kind with real property in other foreign countries. So properties as described above may be freely exchanged with other properties located in the United States, but not with similar properties located in foreign countries. Likewise, foreign properties may not be exchanged for properties in the United States but may be freely exchanged with other properties outside the United States. (For example, a rental apartment in Paris may be exchanged for a rental villa in Italy, but may not be exchanged for a rental home in Los Angeles.)

The Role of the Qualified Intermediary

The exchange process must be facilitated by a Qualified Intermediary (QI). The QI is the professional executor of the mechanics of an exchange. They hold the proceeds from the relinquished property until they are reinvested in the exchange property. An "exchange agreement" must exist in writing between the QI and the investor in order to prevent the investor from having "constructive receipt" of the funds during the exchange period.

The use of a qualified intermediary as an independent party to facilitate a tax-deferred exchange is a safe harbor established by Treasury Regulations. It is very important that the investor select a qualified intermediary before they close on the relinquished property, and notify the escrow company in advance that he or she will be executing a 1031 exchange. Cornerstone can work with any authorized QI the client choses, or we can suggest a nationally reputed, bonded QI to the client.

Qualitied intermediary fees are relatively nominal. For more than a decade the flat fee has been around $750 but has increased recently to approximately $1,000 per transaction. Interest on the funds while in the QI account are usually passed through to the investor. Due to the short-term deposit and recent market interest rates, interest income on the funds is typically a nominal benefit.

Risks of a 1031 Exchange

If the strict timeline and procedural rules are not followed, the 1031 exchange may be disqualified. Also, there is no guarantee that the IRS will approve each individual exchange, nor that tax law will not be altered in the future, nor that the IRS will not change their application of present law to future cases. Finally, the full scope of tax-related risks can only be determined in counsel with the client's personal tax advisor, taking into account all the facts and circumstances of that client's tax situation and the specific laws of the state where they reside.

At a minimum, a "should level" tax opinion will be provided in the PPM document for each DST offering. The opinion basically reviews the details of the offering in relation to Revenue Ruling 2004-86 and concludes that the DST offering "should" qualify for a Section 1031 exchange. However, each investor's facts and circumstances are unique to their exchange, and care must be taken that all the applicable rules are followed, including the ones outlined in this chapter. A professional tax advisor or CPA familiar with the Section 1031 exchange rules is highly recommended for anyone contemplating an exchange.

1031 Exchange Dos and Don'ts

Do plan in advance.

Advance planning is key to success in any exchange. Particular attention must be given to the timing of the sale of the relinquished property, estimating equity and debt replacement objectives to avoid boot, and retaining an expert qualified intermediary.

Do Not be tardy on your deadlines.

The IRS will not honor the exchange if either the forty-five-day identification period is missed, or replacement property is not acquired within the 180-day exchange period.

Do make every effort to sell before you purchase.

If you identify an ideal replacement property before your relinquished property is sold, then you may have to negotiate a reverse exchange (i.e., buying before selling). The IRS has provided guidance on this type of reverse exchange in Revenue Procedure 2000-37, but a reverse exchange is considered a more aggressive type of exchange, as either the replacement property or the relinquished property must be parked with an Exchange Accommodator Titleholder for 180 days, pending the successful completion of the exchange.

Do Not change how title is held during the exchange.

Changing how title to your property is being held, or dissolving partnerships during the exchange, may cause the exchange to be dishonored due to holding-period issues.

Do be mindful of the "napkin test" in a balanced exchange.

The two components of the napkin test are the following:

- if you are trading down in total value, you are potentially taxable to the extent of the trade-down;
- if you are trading down in equity, you are potentially taxable to the extent of the trade-down.

The DST Offering

Chapter 8

DST Industry Overview

An impressive characteristic of the DST industry is the high level of professionalism and the high quality of individuals and organizations that together comprise the industry. Most individuals involved in the industry are highly educated real estate, tax, or legal professionals with advanced university degrees. Many have resumes with many years in national real estate, law and accounting firms. Many of the organizations in the industry are prestigious well-known firms such as Cantor Fitzgerald, Baker McKenzie, and DLA Piper to name a few.

In addition to the qualified intermediary who facilitates the 1031 exchange for the investor, four parties in the industry are strategically involved to bring forth a DST offering:

1. *The sponsor,*
2. *The lender,*
3. *The attorney, and*
4. *The broker-dealer.*

These four parties work together in separate but interdependent roles to produce a DST offering and bring it to the marketplace. Furthermore, these four parties work to syndicate a DST offering in a four-step process.

The Sponsor

The sponsor is the major player in the industry and initiates the first step in a DST property syndication. The sponsor is a national real estate firm with a track record of acquiring, managing and divesting commercial properties. FINRA Rule 2310 defines a "sponsor" as a person or legal entity who directly or indirectly provides management services for a direct participation program, whether as a general partner, pursuant to contract, or otherwise. So the sponsor, in securities terminology, is the issuer of the DST offering. The sponsor, or one of its special purpose entities, sources the real estate, structures the DST offering, arranges the financing, syndicates the offering, manages the asset, services the debt (if any), distributes cash flow, provides periodic and annual reports, provides investor communications, and ultimately facilitates the sale of the property.

Below is a list of DST sponsors and their respective market share as a percentage of equity raised in the industry for 2020.

Inland Private Capital Corp.	21%	Flatirons Asset Management	1%
Black Creek Group	12%	CAI Investments	1%
ExchangeRight Real Estate	8%	Resource Royalty	1%
Passco Companies	8%	Starboard Realty Advisors	1%
NexPoint Real Estate Advisors	8%	Go Store It	1%
Capital Square Realty Advisors	7%	1031 CF Properties	1%
Cantor Fitzgerald	6%	Hartman Investment	1%
BlueRock Real Estate	4%	Platform Ventures	<1%
AEI Real Estate	2%	Livingston Street Capital	<1%
Nelson Partners	2%	Griffin Capital	<1%
Kingsbarn Realty Trust	2%	Cunat Inc.	<1%
JLL Exchange	2%	Moody National	<1%
RK Properties	2%	Croatan Investments	<1%

Net Lease Capital Advisors	2%	Carter Exchange	<1%
Syndicated Equities Group	1%	Senior Living Fund	<1%
NB Private Capital	1%	American Capital Group	<1%
CORE Pacific Advisor	1%	Arrimus Capital Partners	<1%

Mountain Dell Consulting, LLC is an affiliate of Orchard Securities, LLC, Member FINRA/SiPC

Most sponsors were commercial real estate owners and managers for years or even decades before entering the DST industry. Some of the larger sponsors are subsidiaries or branches of large real estate firms that continue to own and manage other institutional real estate outside of the DST industry. Several sponsors manage public REITs with hundreds of millions or even billions of dollars in property value. Still others were organized and incorporated solely for the purpose of syndicating DSTs. DST sponsors, therefore, range dramatically in size and financial strength, with Cantor Fitzgerald, Inland Private Capital, Passco and ExchangeRight being among the largest. These first tier sponsors currently comprise approximately 70 percent of market share for the industry in 2020.

The second tier, if you will, of sponsors is currently composed of approximately seven sponsors that constitute approximately 16 percent of the DST market share, with each sponsor claiming between 2 percent and 5 percent market share. The third tier of sponsors is approximately seventeen sponsors comprising the remaining 14 percent of market share, with 1 percent or less each. Altogether, there are presently around thirty-four sponsors actively syndicating DST offerings. This number is up from the post-recession low of sixteen sponsors and is continuing to grow as the national economy grows.

Even the smaller sponsors are somewhat substantial organizations. The average cost to put together an offering with a properly prepared private placement memorandum is about $500,000, including marketing and syndication costs. Furthermore, most due diligence firms require audited financial statements to verify the financial strength of a sponsor. In addition, the sponsor will have to maintain adequate staffing to source properties and provide investors services and accounting. Due to these factors, it is prohibitive for a new sponsor to enter the market and to offer a single one-off DST offering. With the high barriers to entry, a new sponsor will have to have significant success in prior non-DST real estate management and be dedicated to offering multiple DST offerings over many years. Consequently, most sponsors, even those with lower market share, have built up a large portfolio of properties under management over the years.

Several sponsors have developed a specific niche or asset class specialization over the years. Passco Companies, for example, began with syndicating retail, office, and residential properties, but has strictly focused on multifamily residential for the past several years. Others, like Cantor Fitzgerald and ExchangeRight, have almost exclusively syndicated single-tenant retail properties, with an exception for multifamily now and again. Still others have focused on more management-intensive assets, like Madison Realty with senior care facilities and MVP Parking with parking lot properties.

The sponsor initiates *the first step in a DST offering* through its acquisition process, by identifying a stabilized commercial property with a competitive market CAP rate. (Similar to a price earnings ratio for stock, a CAP rate is used for commercial real estate as a measure of the price of the property in relation to the annual income it can produce—net operating income divided by sales price.) The chief criterion for a DST sponsor is whether a property will provide constant cash flow for passive investors and provide some upside appreciation potential to safeguard and grow investor capital. As may be expected, the sponsor may review a multitude of properties before identifying a property that meets its due diligence standards and acquisition objectives. Most sponsors have built an acquisition department employing numerous real estate professionals. The acquisition department may also work with associated commercial real estate brokerages and developers to review dozens to hundreds of properties per month.

There is a valuable service component and a strategic advantage to the DST investor to effectively have an army of acquisition professionals searching the country to locate stabilized, cash flowing properties at below-market prices. Compare this to an investor having to search database after database or use LoopNet to find properties, with prices being bid up in the process, all with unverified disclosures and CAP rate estimates on a buyer-beware basis. The best values often come from off-market properties. One example is a sponsor contracting with a real estate developer to acquire a property once the developer has fully leased and stabilized the property. The sponsor benefits by contracting to acquire the property below market, and the developer benefits from reduced risk exposure to uncertain future markets. In some cases, sponsors may acquire a large portfolio of properties at a volume discount from an institutional seller such as a REIT or pension fund. Regardless of the method, the best DST sponsors make their profits by acquiring the DST property below market and offering the property to DST investors at or below market.

During the sponsor's due diligence process, the sponsor will perform various procedures to review the property as a candidate for acquisition. To support the sponsor's acquisition criteria, a detailed review of appraisals, environmental studies, condition reports, lease agreements, population demographics, traffic counts, historical occupancy reports, economic vacancy records, rent rolls, leases and their early termination clauses, and other documents are necessary and prudent. The sponsor may also conduct several site visits and tenant interviews. Most sponsors truly do earn their acquisition fee, given these activities and expenses.

Of those properties approved for acquisition for a potential DST offering, the sponsor may only win or be successful in the bidding process on a small set of properties. Many qualified properties are lost to other purchasers that have lower cash flow requirements and can bid at higher prices and lower CAP rates. While the sponsor may invest significant time and expense in the acquisition process, the investor is often served by a selective acquisition process that brings the best possible DST properties to the marketplace. Larger DST sponsors have a reputation for being able to perform and close on the acquisition of large commercial properties. This often allows the DST sponsor to win a bid on a property at a price lower than a competing bid at a higher price, as the seller trusts the sponsor from its track record to be able to close the escrow with certainty and on a timely basis.

The Lenders

Once the sponsor identifies and contracts to acquire a property or properties, *the second step in the syndication process* is for the sponsor to arrange nonrecourse debt financing with a lender. Most sponsors have a select number of lenders that they frequently utilize, and with whom they have long-term relationships. DST lenders include CMBS lenders, national banks, regional banks, and residential HUD lenders. To date, four of the twelve major CMBS lenders are providing loans to DST sponsor borrowers and their properties. National banks that are DST lenders include well-known banks such as Wells Fargo and Bank of America. Due to the size and stability of many of the sponsors, the quality of the property, and the credit-worthiness of the tenant, DST loans typically boast competitively low interest rates, currently between 3.5 percent and 4.5 percent. The loan is characteristically for an amount equal to 50 percent to 60 percent of the fair market value of the property.

The lender will also perform due diligence on the property before lending the majority of the purchase price. The lender's main due diligence objective is to ensure loan repayment. The lender will review the operating history for occupancy levels and examine rent revenue to be sure that the debt may be serviced at a conservative debt service ratio. The lender will also require adequate reserves for tenant improvements, leasing commissions, and designated capital improvements. Further, the lender will require independent professional appraisals to assess loan-to-value parameters and ensure loan principal recovery in case of foreclosure and resale. The loan is made in whole to the DST trustee, and ultimately assigned to the DST investor according to his or her proportionate membership interest in the trust.

After a loan is structured, and before the equity is raised from investors, the sponsor may complete the capital stack, either with a mezzanine loan at higher interest rates or from its own funds. Many sponsors have a separately managed fund that serves to provide bridge capital to the DST until the equity is raised. Alternatively, the sponsor may contract to acquire the property contingent on raising a minimum amount of equity. Such DST offerings have some risk that the sponsor will not be able to close, and investors should inquire whether the minimum equity has been raised and the initial closing has transpired before identifying the DST for 1031 exchange.

The Attorney

The third step in the DST syndication process is the creation of the Delaware Statutory Trust and the accompanying private placement memorandum (PPM). The sponsor's legal counsel is retained to compose the PPM and other offering materials. These law firms are often national or international law firms such as DLA Piper, Baker & McKenzie, Luce Forward, Hirschler Fleischer, and others. The attorney will create the trust's governing instrument (i.e., the trust agreement), and file a certificate of trust with the office of the Secretary of State of the State of Delaware. The attorney will present the sponsor, the DST, the property, and all related documents in the PPM to meet the requirements of full disclosure for a direct participation program (DPP). The PPM is prepared by the sponsor's independent law firm and includes all the information used in the underwriting of the offering.

In the process of composing the PPM, the attorney is required by professional standards[30] to disclose any and all material facts revealed in the discovery process. In addition to standard risk disclosures required in a direct participation program, the attorney must disclose all material facts and risks discovered in reviewing for presentation of the documents related to the sponsor, the property, its tenants, and the loan. This may be considered a third level of due diligence in addition to the due diligence of the sponsor and the lender. It should be noted that the attorney has a client-attorney privilege relationship with the sponsor.

As an integral part of the PPM, the attorney will also prepare a tax opinion as to whether the DST offering will qualify for an IRC Section 1031 exchange. Per the Alternative and Direct Investment Securities Association (ADISA), best practice standards require the tax opinion to be at a "should" or "will" level. The tax opinion does not apply to the unique facts and circumstances of the individual investor's exchange and whether it will qualify for tax deferral, but rather that the DST itself is structured in accordance with IRS Revenue Ruling 2004-86 and accordingly should or will qualify for Section 1031 exchange.

The Broker-Dealer

A broker-dealer is a natural person, company or other organization that engages in the business of trading securities for its own account or on behalf of its customers. Broker-dealers are at the heart of the securities and derivatives trading process. When executing trade orders on behalf of a customer, the institution is said to be acting as a broker. When executing trades for its own account, the institution is said to be acting as a dealer. The broker-dealer, as a member of FINRA, is subject to all SEC and FINRA laws, rules, regulations, and oversight, including numerous FINRA Notices to Members.

The larger broker-dealers, which are typically business units or subsidiaries of commercial banks, investment banks or investment companies, typically focus on conventional investments such as stocks, bonds, mutual funds, and derivatives. While these larger broker-dealers do offer publicly traded REIT investments and a few alternative investments such as SEC registered private REIT investments, it is not cost effective for them to offer smaller alternative real estate investments for 1031 exchange such as TIC and DST investments. Consequently, nearly all broker-dealers offering DST investments are independent firms solely involved in broker-dealer services. Of these independent broker-dealers, there is an even smaller set of broker-dealers that specialize in DST investment and have a large inventory of offerings, such as Cornerstone's broker-dealer.

The Financial Industry Regulatory Authority (FINRA) is the largest nongovernmental regulator for securities firms doing business in the US. FINRA oversees brokerage firms, branch offices, and registered securities representatives, and regulates the conduct of its broker-dealer member firms. The requirements for FINRA registration are set out under the Rule 1010 Series, and include the following:

- FINRA Principal Registration. Principal registration is required for persons associated with a member who are actively involved in the management of the member's investment banking securities business.
- State Securities Regulatory Agency Registration Requirements. For purposes of FINRA membership admission, the broker-dealer and its principals must be registered in the state in which the firm's home office is located. However, under state law the broker-dealer, principals, and each registered representative must be registered in each and every state in which a securities business will be conducted.
- Applicant's Capability to Comply with Industry Rules, Regulations, and Laws.
- Adequacy of Communications and Operational Systems.
- Applicant will be required to review its communications and operational systems and certify to the FINRA District Office that these systems are adequate for the proposed business.
- Determining the Adequacy of an Applicant's Capital. To be approved for FINRA membership, Applicants must meet the provisions of SEC Rules 15c3-1 and 17a-11, the SEC's net capital rule and early warning rule, respectively.
- Compliance with Net Capital Rule. The SEC's net capital rule requires a minimum amount of net capital, dictated by the type or method of business to be conducted, the securities products involved, and considerations of customer exposure. The statutory minimum amounts of net capital range from as low as $5,000 to over $1,000,000.

The broker-dealer may have branch offices and individual registered representatives throughout the country, known as associated persons. To be permitted to sell DST offerings, an associated person must be licensed to sell by passing the appropriate qualifying examinations, namely either the Series 7 (General Securities Representative) or the Series 22 (Limited Representative – Direct Participation Program Securities). In addition, they must pass the state required Series 63 (State Agents License). These representatives must be supervised by a General Securities Principal (Series 24) under a system of comprehensive written supervisory procedures designed to ensure compliance with applicable rules for suitability and sales practices.

While the attorney has a privity relationship to the sponsor, the broker-dealer has a special relationship to the investor. In *the fourth step of the syndication process*, the broker-dealer performs due diligence on the DST offering to be sure that its recommendations to the client investor rest on conclusions from a reasonable investigation, as well as assess whether the specific DST investment is suitable for the specific client investor.

A DST interest is classified as a nonconventional interest, and according to the Notice is subject to NASD Notice to Members 03-71. Specifically, that FINRA members are responsible to

- conduct appropriate due diligence;
- perform reasonable-basis suitability analysis;
- perform customer-specific suitability analysis for recommended transactions;
- ensure the promotional materials used by the members are fair, accurate, and balanced;
- implement appropriate internal controls; and
- provide appropriate training to registered persons involved in the sale of these products.

In addition to provision in NASD Rule 2310, with respect to suitability and due diligence, the Notice states that, before recommending an exchange, members must have a clear understanding of the investment goals and current financial status of the investor and consider asset concentrations and the risk of overconcentration against the benefits of tax deferral.

The foundations of the broker-dealer responsibility for due diligence starts with FINRA Regulatory Notice 10-22 (NTM 10-22), which depends heavily, in turn, on the anti-fraud provisions of the federal securities laws. The anti-fraud provisions impose a duty on broker-dealers who recommend a security to conduct a reasonable investigation into the security and the issuers' representations. Furthermore, under Notice to Members 05-18, the member should make reasonable investigations to ensure that the offering document does not contain false or misleading information. Such investigation should include background checks of sponsor's principals, review of agreements (e.g., property management, purchase and sale, lease and loan agreements), property inspection, and understanding the degree of likelihood that projections will occur. These procedures comprise a fourth level of due diligence.

While the broker-dealer may not rely entirely on the third-party due diligence, most broker dealers receive due diligence reports from third party due diligence firms. These are typically law firms that specialize in performing due diligence on DST sponsors and their properties. Some of the more active due diligence firms are Mick Law, Snyder Kearney and Fact Right. These firms provide independent, confidential due diligence reports to their broker-dealers and registered investment advisor clients. The due diligence report is based on in-depth, multidisciplinary due diligence review and analysis of the target properties and their sponsors.

Per Regulation D of the 1933 Securities Act, each accredited investor must be provided with the PPM in advance of a decision to invest in the offering. Once the selling agreement is signed by the broker-dealer, the offering may then be presented to prospective accredited investors (in the form of the PPM) by licensed registered representatives of the broker-dealer. The representatives of the broker-dealer must have a preexisting substantive business relationship with the investor before the DST investment may be presented. Furthermore, no DST that was previously available before the business relationship was established with the investor may be offered to the investor per the rules on general solicitation. Based on the representative's knowledge of the investor's financial situation, the registered representative, and the broker-dealer principals supervising the representative, must assess both accreditation of the investor and the suitability of the investment for the specific investor.

In addition to accreditation, the investment must be determined by the registered representative and broker-dealer to be suitable for the investor. Suitability is determined by assessing the investor's income level, net worth, risk tolerance, investment experience, tax rates, liquidity needs and time horizon objectives. It may be argued that an investor conducting a 1031 exchange is trading like-kind real property for DST real property (real estate for real estate), and that the DST investment would be suitable as a replacement for other rental real estate. While this is a viable argument, there are other factors, such as asset class, cash flow stability, hold period, and the level of leverage, that may make one DST property more suitable than others.

The Alternative and Direct Investment Securities Association

The DST sponsor, the lender, the attorney, and the broker-dealer are all come together to form the industry association known as the Alternative & Direct Investment Securities Association or ADISA. ADISA is a national trade association of decision makers who influence over thirty thousand professionals involved in alternative investments, primarily nontraded alternatives. These typically include nontraded Real Estate Investment Trusts (REITs), Business Development Companies (BDCs), Master Limited Partnerships (MLPs) and private and public funds (LPs/LLCs), 1031 exchange programs (DSTs/TICs), energy and oil and gas interests, equipment leasing programs, and other alternative and direct investment offerings. The association was founded in 2003 and has approximately 4,500 members who represent more than 220,000 professionals throughout the nation, including sponsor members that have raised in excess of $200 billion in equity and serve more than 1 million investors. ADISA works to maintain the integrity and reputation of this industry by promoting the highest ethical standards, providing education and networking opportunities, and in representing the industry in the public and political arena. ADISA connects members directly to key industry experts through exemplary events forums providing timely trends and education.

The Power and Beauty of the Process

The offering of a DST investment is an amazing convergence of real estate, securities, tax, and legal professionals. When all parties do their job, it is truly a beautiful thing to witness. Quality properties with value are sourced and bundled with the proper amount of leverage to maximize the investment potential, all material information is disclosed for an informed investment decision, and investors participate in a truly suitable investment on a tax deterred basis. The union of securities regulation on disclosure and due diligence, together with the tax advantages of real estate, have the power to provide sustainable cash flow while preserving capital and building wealth, thereby satisfying real current needs and achieving sustainable investment objectives and attainable long-term financial goals.

Chapter 9

Choosing a Broker

Due to the fact that Delaware Statutory Trust properties are sold as a security, an investment into this type of property must be made through a licensed securities broker-dealer and a registered representative. We want to begin the conversation on selecting a broker-dealer by pointing out that the selection of a broker is not an isolated decision. Rather, the selection goes hand-in-hand with the selection of the registered representative representing the broker-dealer, the selection of the sponsors with whom that broker has selling agreements, and the selection of the properties (or DST offerings) approved by the broker. Accordingly, this chapter should be integrated with the other chapters in this section on the DST Offering and viewed in whole as well as in part.

Selecting a Broker-Dealer

When selecting a broker-dealer to work with as part of a 1031 exchange, several factors should be considered. A broker-dealer can greatly broaden the scope of available DST investments to choose from, while eliminating less desirable DST offerings through competent due diligence. Therefore, who an investor works with can be just as important as the DST properties they purchase, so it is important to choose wisely. As the registered representative is licensed through a FINRA member broker-dealer, the selection of a broker-dealer and a registered representative go hand-in-hand. The registered representative may not "sell away" from the broker-dealer and may only sell the DST offerings and other investment products offered by the broker-dealer. Consequently, no matter how gifted the registered representative may be in sales presentation and technical analysis, they are restricted to the inventory of offerings available through the broker-dealer. Accordingly, the first step is for the investor to identify the optimum broker-dealer in order to establish a relationship for the investment.

A Broker-Dealer Should Specialize in DST Investments

For any investment into a private placement security such as a DST, it is not only a requirement, but also simple common sense that the broker who will handle such an investment be one who has a direct relationship with the investor, possessing a thorough understanding of their financial situation and investment objectives. Without establishing this type of relationship, it would be difficult for any broker to ensure that they are providing an investor with advice suitable for their specific needs. Does this mean that an investor should automatically turn to the financial advisor who has managed their assets for years? In many cases, the answer to this question is a resounding *no*. Just as a medical patient would not turn to their primary care physician for specialized medical treatment such as heart surgery, an investor should not work with a broker who lacks the specialized knowledge for these particular types of investments. All broker-dealers fit into one of three primary categories:

Large National Wire House broker-dealers such as Morgan Stanley and Charles Schwab focus primarily on managing stocks, bonds, mutual funds, and other traditional investment offerings. This concentrated focus provides them sufficient profit that they do not tend to expand out to 1031 exchange products. In addition, the errs and omission insurance policies required for an alternative investment in 1031 exchange real estate would be too costly for a large national brokerage to implement over its massive number of representatives and advisors.

Midsize broker-dealers mainly offer traditional investments to investors; some, however, may include a limited selection of DST offerings. The registered representatives for this type of broker-dealer, however, typically specialize in traditional securities investments and possess limited knowledge of DST investments. They can usually offer only a limited selection of DSTs from one or two of the larger DST sponsors. While these representatives may be experts at choosing the best mutual fund, they often have just enough DST knowledge to be dangerous. These representatives may dismiss a particular DST offering without having conducted any due diligence, simply on the basis that it is not on their platform. Unfortunately, on many occasions their initial instinct may be to steer their investor back to the limited choices they can offer in order to collect a commission on the sale.

Small broker-dealers specializing in DST investments and other securitized alternative real estate offerings typically provide the widest selection of DST products from all the major sponsors in the industry. Representatives who work with these specialized broker-dealers have access to a much broader spectrum of DST properties, and often focus all or most of their professional time working with these products.

While many representatives may work for a broker-dealer offering DST investments, not all representatives work with these specialized investment structures to the same degree. As part of their personal business model, some representatives may only handle a DST investment once or twice a year. Representatives specializing in these types of investments, however, can offer greater insight into the differences between various sponsors in the industry, as well as the differences between each individual DST offering. It is natural for an investor to initially consider using a financial advisor who is already managing their investment portfolio; however, depending upon how much direct experience a financial advisor has with DST offerings, they may or may not be the ideal choice to handle a 1031 exchange into a DST. In summary, the optimum arrangement is a registered representative specializing in DSTs and backed by a broker-dealer with a rich diversity of approved DST offerings.

A Broker-Dealer Should Have Deep Due Diligence Experience

Broker-dealers focusing on Alternatives and 1031 exchange products must have adequate experience in conducting due diligence on these types of offerings. When reviewing new offerings prior to approval for their registered representatives to present to investors, the broker-dealer needs to have both a broad and a detailed understanding of the real estate markets, including CAP rates, asset classes, and the various geographic markets. Additionally, broker-dealers need the ability to review, evaluate, and quantify the findings and recommendations from third-party due diligence reports.

This level of due diligence, as critical as it is, only pertains to the specific offering; a higher level of due diligence must also be performed regarding the sponsor putting forth the offering. For this level of due diligence, a thorough knowledge of the industry and its players is of utmost importance, since it provides perspective and context. For example, does the sponsor have a track record of paying distributions late, or of not providing timely tax documents? Does a principal have a disclosable item from their past that may not have been disclosed in the PPM? Does a sponsor have a track record of funding capital reserves for the master tenant, even though not required to do so, in a difficult economic or market situation? Broker-dealers that specialize in the alternative and DST markets should have a higher level of knowledge and skill related to these types of offerings and should be well equipped to weigh in on any offerings available across the industry.

Selecting a Registered Representative

The registered representative who manages a 1031 exchange into a DST functions somewhat like the quarterback of a football team who calls the plays and distributes the ball to various players in order to drive his team towards the end zone. The representative works with all the players involved in a DST investment, such as the investor, the broker-dealer, the DST sponsor, the qualified intermediary (QI), as well as CPAs and attorneys, to ensure that a successful DST investment reaches the goal line of a successful 1031 exchange. Just as football teams spend much time considering who to use as their starting quarterback, investors should take some time to consider who to use to broker their DST investment.

A Registered Representative Should Have an Understanding of Tax and 1031 Issues

The rules established by the IRS for Section 1031 exchanges are both specific and rigid, and it is of utmost importance that a broker advising investors possess a thorough understanding of these rules. In addition to brokering the investment into the DST, a registered representative also must be able to advise the investor through the entire 1031 exchange procedure, ensuring that each step of the process is completed according to the rules set forth in the Internal Revenue Code, and that the investor has met each of the exchange requirements. Even though registered representative and broker-dealer are not authorized to provide tax advice, a registered representative should have a thorough understanding of all the provisions of Section 1031.

A prime example is the forty-fifth day identification of the DST offering or offerings. There is a complex set of rules that will need to be navigated including the three-property safe harbor rule, the 200 percent rule, and the 95 percent rule. There are nuances to knowing which rule to employee that are based on the level of leverage from both the relinquished property and the replacement properties, as well as a DST offering with multiple assets and property addresses. One well-known story in the industry is the DST investor who blew an exchange because his registered representative advised him to identify the amount of equity placed in the various DSTs and not the total value invested in each DST. The satisfaction of completing an exchange into a replacement property can be erased if at a later date the IRS determines that an investor failed to comply with all the provisions of Section 1031, thus invaliding their exchange and triggering the necessity to pay the tax obligation. This is an experience that no real estate investor wants to pass through, and that can be easily avoided by working with an experienced and knowledge 1031 exchange broker.

A Registered Representative Should Have Detailed Knowledge of Each DST Offering

Beyond having a working relationship with the DST sponsors, a registered representative who works with DSTs should be able to clearly explain the details of each offering they are putting before an investor for consideration. It is very important that the broker have a personal relationship with each investor, be completely aware of their investment needs and objectives, and only present offerings that are suitable for that particular investor's situation. This requires that the representative have a detailed understanding of both the investor and all available DST offerings so that they can eliminate any offering that may not be suitable for any particular reason. Different sponsors have different investment strategies that they are seeking to execute in their specific DST offerings, and a representative should be aware of these different strategies and guide the investor through the selection process by explaining all the key differences that exist in each and every offering. This requires that a representative spend time to study the details of each DST property to become an expert on every detail.

This knowledge should go beyond the basic disclosures of cash flow, debt leverage levels, and hold period. How is the master lease payment structured? Is the master tenant properly capitalized? What is the appraised value compared to syndication price? What is the backstory for the sponsor's decision to acquire the property? What is the exit strategy? These are a few of the questions that a representative should be able to answer regarding any DST they would recommend as a suitable investment.

A Registered Representative Should Have Expertise in Real Estate

An investment into a DST is fundamentally an investment into the real estate that is owned by the trust. Because of this reality, a representative should have a thorough understanding of the real estate fundamentals that relate to any particular offering and be ready to address issues related to cap rates, master leases, loan terms, appraisals, and geographic real estate markets. To this point, Cornerstone is a licensed real estate brokerage and focuses on continued real estate education.

A knowledgeable representative should be able to speak immediately to the questions about: "Why should I buy this particular property, in this particular location, at this particular price, and at this particular time?" A valid review of any offering will delve much deeper than just the name of the sponsor or the type of asset that is contained in the offering. Being able to present a thorough understanding of the details of the real estate itself will be critical to an investor achieving peace of mind in their DST investments. For this, the representative must be completely familiar with the risks specific to each of the various asset classes, the levels of acceptable leverage, financial models that engineer cash flow, as well as the potential impact of debt defeasance and early payment penalties. Having this level of expertise will ensure that a registered representative is able to make a thorough presentation regarding any DST offering for an investor's consideration. Cornerstone representatives are required to take an exam to prove competency on the offering documents of each DST offering that they sell.

A Registered Representative Should Have Strong Working Relationships with the Sponsors

Many financial advisors in the securities industry focus their business on managing the assets of their clients. With this focus, they simply may not have the exposure to the breadth of 1031-viable investment products that exist across the industry. As an example, some brokers will limit themselves—and by extension their investors—to only working with one particular sponsor, and will only recommend the DST offerings from that sponsor exclusively. While this limited approach may work well for some investors, most prefer to have access to all the options in the market that are available for their consideration. With this in view, it is advisable for investors to be aware if the broker they are working with is working under an exclusive agreement with one sponsor or if he has access to all offerings that are being put forth across the entire industry. This is not to suggest that employing an exclusive agreement is inappropriate, but simply serves to ensure that the investor has all the available information they need to make an informed decision regarding their DST investment.

When an investor commits to any DST investment, their representative will work with an internal wholesaler of the sponsor to reserve an equity position in the amount required by the investor. Establishing a reservation becomes extremely important when a DST is reaching the end of its equity raise and available equity has become limited. Obtaining a reservation in a DST that is at this point of its equity raise is especially important if the investor is reaching the end of their forty-five-day window, because once this deadline is passed, an investor loses the option of locating other replacement properties. Working with a representative who has this close working relationship with the internal wholesalers at the different DST sponsors can make all the difference between getting into a closing DST or being required to pay a capital gains tax obligation if their DST ship sails while they are still on the docks.

Look for a Long-Term Relationship

Lastly, when selecting a broker-dealer and a registered representative, in addition to everything that has already been stated, investors would do well to work with a broker that they are comfortable working with for the long-term. Because DST properties are long-term investments, the broker-investor relationship will continue for the entire hold period. Choosing a knowledgeable broker who provides in-depth industry insights, 1031 exchange expertise, key sponsor relationships, and a comfortable working relationship will help ensure that investors receive the maximum benefit that a DST investment can provide.

Many broker-dealers and registered representatives either went out of business or left for other industries after the Great Recession of 2008. Specialized brokers such as Cornerstone, however, have remained committed to the DST industry and to combining the power of securitized real estate with 1031 exchange.

Chapter 10

Choosing a Sponsor

DST sponsors are national real estate companies that put together DST offerings and make them available to retail investors. By the time a DST is available in the syndicated market, it is prepackaged and ready for immediate investment. However, a great deal of labor is involved in bringing a DST to market, and the sponsor is responsible for completing that work. DST sponsors spend countless hours, days, weeks, and months, searching for suitable properties that will fit their business objectives. By way of review, sponsors take on the responsibility in their due diligence process for the following:

- studying the local submarkets for job and population growth, demographics, competition, and barriers to entry;
- producing financial models on the property to determine its viability as a DST-held asset;
- ordering environmental and engineering reports and property appraisals in order to have a thorough understanding of the condition and valuation of the property;
- negotiating the financing and terms with lenders to obtain a nonrecourse loan (for those DSTs that contain leverage); and
- marketing the DST property through a syndicate of broker/dealers and their registered representatives; and
- most sponsors will also function as the asset and property managers throughout the entire hold period.

An industry encompassing a wide-ranging group of sponsors ensures that the DST market has a regular and diverse supply of new offerings that investors may choose from in order to meet their specific 1031 exchange requirements and investments goals. Sponsors bring their own experience and specific market focus to the DST industry by focusing on specific asset classes. For example, one sponsor may focus exclusively on multifamily properties, while others may focus on triple-net portfolios, senior care facilities, or gas and oil royalty programs. Additionally, one sponsor in particular focuses exclusively on putting forth only all-cash DST offerings with no debt, to meet the needs of those exchangers that desire to maintain an all-cash position.

Sponsor Specialization

When considering any DST property for investment, many investors tend to focus solely on the asset class and the projected cash flow, without giving much consideration to the bigger picture of the offering, including who sponsored the DST itself. As mentioned previously, DST sponsors tend to focus on specific asset classes when creating their offerings. Thus, when investors are considering investing into any DST, there is value in considering which of the DST sponsors has more focus and experience with the specific asset class of properties that they are wanting to purchase.

Just as you might prefer a specialty restaurant for a specific cuisine, considering which DST sponsors specialize in the type of asset an investor may want to purchase will ensure that they are reviewing offerings that are prepared by experts in that specific type of real estate. In addition to the expertise of a sponsor with respect to asset class, the three main criteria useful in evaluating the sponsor of a DST investment are the following:

1. *the sponsor's prior performance (track record) in successfully offering, managing, and divesting DST investments;*

2. the sponsor's financial strength to provide continuous support to the DST investment through the entire duration of the hold period; and
3. the sponsor's capacity for investor relations and client services.

The Sponsor's Track Record

A sponsor's track record may reflect on its investment philosophy, underwriting skill, management ability, real estate experience, and marketing expertise. The sponsor's prior performance will be detailed in the full-disclosure private placement memorandum (PPM). As discussed in chapter 16 on analyzing the PPM, the sponsor's track record may be presented in both table and narrative form. The disclosures will allow the investor to compare actual yield with initial projections and discuss any discrepancies.

The key here is that the sponsor should only have a limited number of prior DSTs that did not meet projections. If too many deals fell short of initial projections, then this may indicate a deficiency in the sponsor's investment strategy, technical underwriting, management ability, or all of the above. So while the sponsor should have a clear history of success in consistently providing cash flow, preserving capital, and positioning the properties for appreciation, the old adage that no one is perfect may apply also to DST sponsors.

In most cases, the DST investment should perform as anticipated based on operating history, analytical and conservative cash flow projections, and other due diligence performed by the lender. However, the reality is that nobody has a crystal ball that can predict what will happen over a hold period that may span a decade. As such, the best of plans can fail to be realized when an uncontrollable event occurs that has a negative impact on the investment.

It is said that passing through hard times builds character. Passing through hard times also has the benefit of *revealing* one's character. Who we are as a person and as an institution are laid bare the moment we are thrust into a stressful environment. Because of this reality, an investor can learn a great deal about a sponsor by reviewing their behavior when prior programs fell into distress. In the unfortunate event that any offering would fall into distress, looking into a sponsor's prior history can be a productive exercise to learn what to expect from them if a future program were to suffer the same fate. A few questions to consider include:

- How early did the sponsor recognize that a property was beginning to fall into distress?
- What steps did they take to attempt to correct the issue?
- How did the sponsor interact with the investors who were involved in that investment throughout the entire process?
- Did the sponsor actions mitigate the problem successfully?

Those sponsors who were operating at the time of the financial crisis of 2008 all suffered loss as a result of the national crisis to one degree or another. It would be unreasonable to expect that these companies have a perfect record with every prior program, and they should not be evaluated merely on that that basis. What is of more value is understanding is the response of the sponsors to mitigate the external forces of the Great Recession and successfully lead the property back on the road to recovery. These actions speak volumes about a sponsor's true ability. While past performance is no guarantee of future results, it does help to shed some light onto the institutional knowledge, character, and integrity of the sponsor that an investor might select for a DST investment.

Lastly, the very few sponsors that use their own captive broker-dealer to sell their own DST offerings directly to the investor should be viewed with extreme caution. This is because there is no independent third-party review by a broker-dealer of either the sponsor or the property. With no independent review items may go undisclosed and undiscovered and projections may be more aggressive than historic performance and market trends indicate.

The Sponsor's Financial Strength

Another key criterion in evaluating a sponsor is the sponsor's financial strength to provide continuous support to the DST investment through the entire duration of the hold period. The first question may be, Will the sponsor be able to keep the lights on at the home office for the duration of the hold period? A new sponsor may have to continue to offer new DSTs in order to generate enough revenue to stay in business. If an economic or market cycle limited the sponsor's ability to offer new DSTs, then a going concern issue could arise. An older sponsor, having syndicated a larger number of offerings, will not only have revenue from new offerings, but will have a significant amount of revenue and resources from the ongoing management fees and master lease rents from multiple DSTs. Some of the older sponsors that survived the Great Recession were able to consolidate many of the troubled TIC properties of less agile sponsors. These "battle hardened" sponsors not only gained valuable experience in recovering failing TIC properties, but as the properties were brought back into profitability, enjoyed a significant amount of management fee income. While it is critically important that each DST offering be able to stand on its own financially, having significant revenue from other profitable DSTs in the sponsor's management portfolio may help to fund operations if one or two become challenged.

The golden rule of DST due diligence is that each individual DST property should provide sufficient cash flow on its own to fund debt service, reserves, and investor distributions, as well as, the management fee to fund the various client services required for monthly, quarterly, and annual reporting and other investor services. Furthermore, it is important to understand that a DST is a legal entity separate from the sponsor, and that there is a firewall that exists between them. In the event that any DST were to fall into distress, beyond funding the demand note to add additional capital to the master tenant, the sponsor does not necessarily have a legal obligation to intervene in order to rescue the project.

However, even with this understanding, the financial strength of the sponsor has been a vital factor in the success of past challenged TIC and DST properties. This is truer with more management intensive properties such as multifamily and multitenant retail. In this light, a critical part of broker-dealer level due diligence is to analyze the audited financial statements of the sponsor and to evaluate the sponsor's financial strength. Stronger sponsors will not only have the capacity to fund demand notes to the master tenant, but to willingly elect to increase the capitalization of the master tenant in the event of any shortfall. Furthermore, while under no legal obligation to do so, we have seen a more financially secure sponsor be willing to waive management fees and disposition fees to recover investor cash flow and preserve capital.

The Sponsor's Investor Services Capability

The sponsor's capacity for investor relations and client services is also key for a smooth and successful investment experience. With lower minimum investments, one can imagine the large number of investors from not only a single offering but from a large number of DST syndications. In addition to generating monthly, quarterly, and annual reports, there is also the need for the sponsor to address individual investor questions, concerns, and requests. For example, changing the title registration for the member certificate to a family trust, an heir, or an ex-spouse in case of divorce, not to mention changing investor bank accounts for monthly distributions and lost tax report documents. With all these investor service demands, Cornerstone also recommends sponsors with significant client relations support staffing and capabilities.

Conclusion

When considering making a DST purchase, investors should understand the important role that a sponsor plays in creating the

DST offerings and managing the assets during the hold period. Because a DST investment creates a long-term relationship between the sponsor and the investor, investors should take some time to get to know the sponsor, their specific area of focus, and their operating history. Doing so will not only help them to make a more suitable DST investment selection but will also provide greater peace of mind that their 1031 exchange investment is resting in good hands.

Chapter 11

Choosing a DST Property

Choosing one or more DSTs as replacement properties for a 1031 exchange is where the rubber meets the road, and whether an investor will work through several options together with their broker. Whether they are only reviewing the offerings of one sponsor, or whether they are reviewing DSTs on their own, there are a number of important criteria that must be reviewed and balanced in order to make an informed choice which aligns with the goals of the investor. Over the last several years leading up to this publication, on average there have been between ten and twenty syndicated DSTs available at any given time on the market. This selection of DSTs typically covers the major real estate asset classes of multifamily, net leased retail both single tenant and multitenant, and office, but often also smaller subsets such as assisted living, student housing, and self-storage.

Leverage

One of the first issues to be considered in selecting a DST property as replacement property for a 1031 exchange is the matter of debt or the loan-to-value of the DST. Debt is the initial factor in selecting a DST property because for full nonrecognition of the capital gain in a like-kind exchange, the debt on the replacement property must be equal to or greater than the debt on the relinquished property. Any reduction of debt would create taxable boot in the amount of the reduction. If the investor's goal for the exchange is to fully eliminate the tax on the sale, then the replacement DST properties must in aggregate have equal to or greater debt than the dollar amount of the debt paid off at the sale of the relinquished property. This debt requirement may eliminate many of the available DST properties from consideration. This is especially true if the investor is exchanging onto a single DST property. However, if the investor is acquiring multiple DST properties then the debt levels of the DSTs in the new portfolio may be blended to equal or exceed the debt level that was relinquished. In doing so, a prudent representative may propose using higher leveraged DSTs to blend with lower DSTs and effectively delivering much of the portfolio.

The issue of mortgage debt will be discussed in detail in chapter 17, but when selecting among DSTs, beyond the loan-to-value ratio needed for any 1031 purposes, the interest rate of the loan, loan term, loan covenants (prepayment penalties, etc.) and the level of amortization of principal are important to evaluate. While there tends to be consistency across the mortgage industry and it is difficult for one DST or another to distinguish itself in this regard, there are occasional examples of an assumed loan where the interest rate and or terms of the loan provide a significant advantage to the property compared to what would be available at that time on the market for a newly initiated loan. In any event, leverage is often the driving factor in selecting a DST property either for tax requirements or for economic substance.

Asset Class

Once the matter of debt has been considered, the investor will usually next consider the asset class of the property or properties contained in that DST, that is the type of property. Real estate assets are commonly broken down into the following different categories: multifamily, multitenant retail, single tenant retail, hospitality (hotels), senior care, student housing, self-storage, multitenant office, single tenant office and medical office. Currently in the DST/1031 market we do not see any hospitality or multitenant office properties, but I will mention a few key points about the other asset classes below as an introduction.

In selecting one or more assets classes, it may be wise to invest according to what one already knows or one's prior investment knowledge. Many investors have managed residential properties for years or decades and have a keen awareness in what makes a successful multifamily investment. Other investors may have worked extensively in retail and have a good sense of a retail asset's key success factors. One past example is a client who was a bio-medical engineer and knew that the tenant of an industrial laboratory DST was an innovative and growing biotech company. Ultimately, the tenant extended its lease and enjoyed a credit upgrade. The DST property sold five years later for a significant profit.

In general, commercial real estate properties are grouped according to lease type, that is either long-term net leases, shorter-term net leases, or various types of short-term or residential leases. Long-term net leases have contracted rental rates for the duration of the hold period. This type of property will be more predictable in its distributions, and for investors who would rest easier knowing the exact amount they will receive each month, net leased offerings offer this element. With any net leased property, the key issue is the tenant, the length of the lease, likelihood of lease renewal, the terms of the lease and the residual value of the real estate should it be necessary to find a new tenant. For the most part, leases in these classes will be longer than either the financing or the projected hold period. Net leases can be for twenty years or even longer though sometimes they are shorter, and a new offering may contain a lease which was contracted several years prior and thus the remaining period on the lease will be less.

Net Lease

Net leased or NNN leased means that the tenant will cover the costs of insurance, taxes and maintenance of the property. NN leased usually means that one element, such as the roof, is not covered by the tenant but rather by the landlord (the DST). In general, while this issue is very important on the level of the lease, it usually does not directly affect the DST investor. This is because either way these costs are factored into the net cash flow. Some investors do prefer the simplicity and security of a NNN lease, but it would not be accurate to say that NNN leased leases are inherently better than NN leases or even nonnet leased properties. Also, the properties are all professionally managed and so whether the maintenance is low (net leased) or high (multifamily, senior care) the result will be factored into the net cash flow of the DST.

Of course, a net lease is only as strong as the underlying tenant and no DST containing net leased properties will have a guarantee against a possible bankruptcy of the tenant. Still, especially with credit tenants, the likelihood of distributions being made on schedule and according to projections is high. Another key point to keep in mind with contracted net leases is the matter of rent bumps. Rent bumps will increase the income of the property over time and usually this increased income will pass through to investors in the form of increased distributions. A net leased offering with strong rent bumps has the stability of a net leased offering with an element of rent increases similar to what is possible with short term leases (see below). Of course, in addition to increasing distributions, increased income will also increase the market value of the property and its eventual sale price. Net leases with no rent bumps may be backed up by some of the most secure tenants, but with no increase in income over the hold period, there is a real possibility of the property remaining static in value, even to the point of being unable to overcome the transaction expenses and front-end securities load of the offering, which could result in the investor receiving back less than their full principal investment at the time of the disposition of the property. In any DST investment, the matters of securities load, as well as acquisition and disposition expenses, are critical and investors should consider the effect of these expenses and fees on the front end of the investment as well as the back.

Short-Term Leases

Regarding short-term leases, multifamily, senior care, self-storage, hospitality and in a sense multitenant retail, all require lease renewals during the hold period and provide the possibility of upwardly adjusting rents, though it is important to keep in mind that in a down market rents can also decrease during the hold. Of these groups, hospitality will have the shortest leases, daily, self-storage is typically month to month, apartments, senior care and student housing will all be yearly, while multitenant retail will have the longest leases.

Here is the basic trade off with long-term net leased properties as well as the basic risk. While net leased assets, barring the issue of bankruptcy, will have firm income projections including possible rent escalators, there is little to no possibility of exceeding these income projections. Adjustable rent properties, in contrast, can increase their rents over the hold period to whatever level the national and local market will support, but with the risk that rents can also decrease according to market demand.

The key points to consider with adjustable-rent properties are occupancy levels and rental rates which together will determine the gross income of a property, and after expenses, net operating income. A property which is attractive to renters, in a good location, and in a dynamic market will attract new tenants and very likely be able to raise rents over the hold. This will positively affect cash flow and the eventual sale price. Of course, with these same assets classes, lower demand and declining rents can have the opposite effect. This is a risk with any offering based upon variable rents and short-term leases.

Among the adjustable-rent asset classes, residence-based offerings have the benefit of being easier to finance. When financing for commercial properties tightens, residence-based properties of all types will typically be treated more favorably. While the DST investor has no direct involvement in the financing of a property, this benefit does pass through to the asset class.

Multitenant Retail

An asset class which in some sense straddles the long-term net leased properties and the residence based short-term lease properties is multitenant net leased retail properties. Leases in this asset classes tend to be from three to five years and may be to either credit or non-credit tenants. Key factors to look at when analyzing a multitenant short-term net lease property are of course location and also traffic counts. Recent syndicators of such properties have also placed a high emphasis on grocery anchored retail centers, even if the grocery store itself is not a part of the property for sale. The grocery store will tend to drive traffic to the location, it is less vulnerable to Internet competition, and the surrounding stores will often tend to be more Internet resistant such as hair/nail salons, food and beverage locations, etc. Linking back to the issues of location and traffic counts, sponsors of grocery anchored multitenant retail locations based upon short-term net leases remain optimistic about the attractive cash flow and appreciation potential of these properties.

When analyzing a single asset retail property with a large corporate tenant, take a look at the sales per square foot. This will be a good indication as to whether the corporate office will keep the store if they ever need to downsize and close underperforming stores. While many retailers may be private companies and this information may not be public, the sales per square foot for a particular store may always be found in the appraisal report for the property. Through a little research this number may be compared with other stores in the chain, the national average, or local competitors. If the sales per square foot is above average or in the top 25 to 30 percent then the store is certainly healthy and will be kept operating even if the economy slows, the retailer faces challenges, or it is acquired by a competitor. Please note that the appraisal is always a rich source of information on any property.

Multifamily

Multifamily properties can draw on a broad demographic for renters and this asset class is considered a basic commodity which will always be in demand. Important statistics for the multifamily investor to track are demographics, and home ownership and rental rates. For example, recent statistics showing an increasing population in the prime rental age group (twenty-five to thirty-five) as well as an increased tendency of this age group to rent as opposed to purchasing a home have boded well for multifamily investment. Of course, local market statistics such as population growth, average income, job and income growth, average age, etc. are also critical in choosing the right multifamily property. There are also matters of location and amenities to take into account. Overall over the long-term this asset class has achieved greater overall total returns than net leased based real estate assets albeit with more volatility. Currently this asset class is attracting a significant portion of the total capital coming into the syndicated 1031 space.

Another factor to consider with multifamily is whether there is planned new local construction. A quick satellite Google Map search can reveal any vacant lots or ongoing construction in the area if not already disclosed in the PPM. A newer more modern property can draw renters away from a previously stabilized property. Property management may then have a sales war with the new competition and have to offer more concessions such as discounted rent or free rent months to renters which may keep physical vacancy high but lower economic vacancy. However, new local construction in not always negative. The price of the competitor's new construction may be so high that they will have to offer the new apartments at higher rents than older properties in the area. If the demographics for the population support the additional supply of new units then the result may be a rent boost for our older property.

Student Housing

Student housing properties also benefit from the potential to increase rents and typically will have higher purchase cap rates (a higher cap rate translates to greater income per invested dollar) than class A or even class B multifamily properties, and they also can benefit from having a captive customer base with limited competition. When considering a student housing property, it is very important to consider the trending enrollment rate of the associated university as well as its reputation, size, and division. It is also important to understand the availability of on and off campus housing relative to the number of students projected to require housing. The best situation of course is where there is a large number of students requiring housing and relatively limited supply. Perhaps the most important criteria of a student housing property is location. For students who like to be able to reach campus within minutes of waking, a property which is a short walk or even adjacent to campus has a significant advantage while a property which is some distance from campus may suffer even if it checks off the other boxes. Student housing properties also tend to see higher occupancy rates and it is not uncommon to see occupancy at 100 percent. There is also the fact that most student housing leases tend to be one academic year meaning that if the property is fully leased up going into the fall academic year, it will very likely remain fully occupied into the following summer.

Senior Care

Senior care or assisted living properties will often have the highest acquisition cap rates of any residence-based asset class and with the burgeoning number of retirement age people in the country, this asset class is supported by strong demographic trends. Rents also tend to be significantly higher than at apartments, thus the potential rent increases and profit margins are correspondingly higher. However, risks are also considered correspondingly higher. Typical senior care properties will draw on a much smaller geographic area, often just a few square miles, and as properties often house significantly less than 100 residents, occupancy rates can be seriously affected by just a few vacancies. Also, it tends to take more time to find new tenants with the result that average occupancy rates across the asset class as a whole tend to be lower than those of the other residence-based offerings. Still, especially if the investor is able to diversify their real estate portfolio or exchange, the senior care asset class is quite attractive.

Self-Storage

Finally, we want to mention self-storage, an asset class which has had an excellent track record over at least the last two to three decades. Self-storage has a number of unique characteristics which provide economic advantages to the properties. As far as demand for storage space the colloquial saying is that when the economy is good, people buy more stuff and need a place to store it. When the economy is down people tend to downsize and need a place to store their stuff. There are also certain dynamics operating in the self-storage space which tend to benefit the investors. Unlike apartments or retail, modest incremental rent increases can total in the range of five dollars per month for the renter and most agree that they will likely not cancel their rental over such a small amount of money. But a 5 percent rent increase across the self-storage property has the same net effect on the net operating income of the property as a similar increase in another property. Also, with contracts usually from month to month, top tier operators of self-storage properties will take the opportunity to frequently increase rents by small amounts. If the tenant does vacate the unit, turnover is quite easy often only consisting of sweeping out the unit and marketing it to a new tenant. Similarly, the maintenance of a self-storage property overall is much easier and less expensive than that of an apartment. Usually the most expensive items will be an occasional resurfacing of the parking lot and maintenance of the office. All of these factors combine in this asset class to produce good cash flowing properties with an element of recession resistance, good income increase potential, low capital improvement demands, and potential appreciation upon sale due to increased income over the hold.

Property Management

Segueing from the self-storage asset class, syndicated real estate investors should also consider the matter of property management and possibly the operating company. In those asset classes where property management is of greater importance or where there is the aspect of an operating company, this will typically imply greater profit potential but also greater operating risk. In a NNN leased property the issue of property management is minimal, and any operations are on the side of the tenant, the profits of whom will not pass through to the investor. But in the case of apartments, student housing, self-storage and especially senior care, the issue of property management and operations are paramount. Property management directly affects occupancy and rental rates, and in the case of an operating company as in a senior care facility, the quality of the operating company will likewise directly affect the bottom line of the real estate.

Value-Add Potential

Another aspect to consider which applies to several asset classes is value add potential. Value add potential can be in the form of renovations to the property, capital improvements, or more effective operations. The DST structure does not permit capital improvements though they are permitted in limited partnership or LLC structures. But DSTs can engage in noncapital renovations and upgrades if the funds to do so are reserved at the time of the initial syndication or raised from the income of the property. A value add component can add significant potential for increasing cash flow over the hold period as well as appreciation potential but also implies additional risk. Beyond renovations, management and operations can be targeted by sponsors as areas of potential value add profit. Without changing the property at all sponsors may judge that they can significantly increase occupancy and rental rates, or decrease expenses, simply by improved management or marketing. Class B apartments are common targets for value add renovations while self-storage properties are often targeted by sponsors as under managed and ripe for short-term net operating increases without needing to add much capital to the property.

CAP Rates

The value of commercial properties is most commonly expressed by a capitalization rate or "cap rate" which is the ratio of the income to the sale price of the property. A property which produces five dollars of annual income and which sells at a 5 percent cap rate will sell for one hundred dollars. In this sense the income of the property determines the sale price of the property. Keep in mind that cap rates go up and down over time and different asset classes or conditions of properties sell at different cap rates. For example, currently class A multifamily properties are selling at cap rates just above 5 percent, sometimes even below 5 percent. This is considered quite low historically, meaning that the properties are very expensive. This low cap rate is based upon the assumption across the industry that the income of these properties will increase significantly and quickly thus justifying the high purchase price and providing appreciation. A senior care property in contrast, especially if it is not new construction, can sell for an 8 percent cap rate. This means that for one hundred dollars invested the senior care property will provide eight dollars of income while the multifamily property will only provide five dollars. But as we discussed to some extent above, these differing cap rates are often due to different levels of risk in a property or different perceptions of appreciation potential. Beyond the projected net cash flow of a property over the hold, investors should also consider the underlying capitalization rate of the property in question.

In any case, it is a pretty firm principle that in order for a property to sell for a profit, whether net leased or residential, rental income needs to rise. This is assuming that cap rates remain the same. If cap rates fall, this is in the favor of the seller at the time of sale and such movement can cause a property with flat income to be sold at a profit. On the other hand, if cap rates rise, this will go against the seller and can cause a property to be sold at a loss even if there is some increase in income but especially if income is flat. To be conservative, we should ask if a property can still project a positive outcome even if cap rates rise. To achieve this result residence-based offerings target increased income by increasing rents and by attaining or maintaining high occupancy levels. Net leased properties increase income by having built in rental increases in the leases, or by releasing the property at a higher rate.

Load and Fees

While it varies from DST to DST, most offerings will have between 88–91 percent of the total raise (equity and debt combined) available to invest directly in the property. This also will include any reserves which would be set aside for the operation of the property. The 9–12 percent which is allocated to various front-end fees, expenses and commissions is what we refer to as front end load or the securities load. It includes a number of items including selling commissions, due diligence costs and marketing costs, etc. As a side note, this level of front end load is pretty standard for most illiquid alternative investments such as private REITs, private debt, private equity or oil and gas investments. It is not particular to DSTs nor is the level of load unusual for the industry. In any case for the investor to receive back their full principal investment, this front-end load plus any closing costs front and back will need to be recouped by the appreciation of the property, or by the build-up of equity in the property by means of loan amortization. If there is neither appreciation in value nor any pay down of loan principal, the investor will not receive back their full principal investment at the time of sale. This is a complex point, but sophisticated investors and their brokers will need to pay attention to the matter of load, at least to determine that the load of any given offering is not excessive, or if it is above average if there is a reasonable explanation or increased profit potential to justify the extra expense.

Location

Usually a DST investor will consider options in a number of different states. This will bring up the issue of the state income tax rate in the state where the property is located. As DST investors are considered direct owners of the real estate, they are required to file for and pay state taxes in that state. Typically, any taxes paid in the state where the DST is located are deductible from the taxes of which the DST investor is a resident. But if the investor lives in a state with no income tax, they may want to consider giving priority to states which themselves have no income tax. These points are only mentioned in principle and as with all matters relating to taxes, both 1031 related and those related to income taxes, syndicated real estate investors should confer with their tax counsel to get concrete advice pertinent to their specific situation.

Diversification Strategy and Investment Philosophy

In conclusion there are a large number of different factors to consider when selecting a DST property for investment or exchange, from the age of the property, the characteristics of the real estate itself, the occupancy rate, the rental rate, the local market, the national market, the leases, the tenants, the financing, the management, etc. All of these factors need to be considered and balanced when selecting an appropriate DST as either a stand-alone property or as part of a diversified portfolio. These factors also need to be evaluated based on the investor's investment objective, whether that may be income, growth or a combination of income and growth. Due to these complexities it is especially important for the investor to choose their broker and sponsors wisely.

With lower investment requirements, an investor may want to diversity over multiple asset classes and geographic locations. One investment philosophy that has served many clients well is to diversify over income and growth-oriented DST asset classes. For example, half the portfolio may be invested in multifamily DSTs with rents escalating each year. By growing the net operating income (NOI) there is more upward pressure on the value of the property even if CAP rates (NOI/property asset value) remain stagnant. The other half of the portfolio may be invested in long-term national credit NNN retail properties. These supply constant and reliable cash flow but little upside potential. Another diversification strategy may be to diversity over a larger number of asset classes.

More will be discussed on diversifications strategies in chapter 18, but a strategy or investment philosophy employed in the selection of DST properties should correlate with the investor's prior experience, investment objectives, and risk tolerance. Building a well-diversified personal portfolio of investment-grade real estate is a key advantage of DST investing and should be the overarching goal of any DST property selection.

Chapter 12

The Closing Process

The closing of a syndicated real estate investment is simple and quick. Our focus is on the closing process for a DST investment, but most of the crucial points are pertinent to limited partnership, LLC or REIT closings as well. Especially when compared to traditional real estate closings, but also to syndicated TIC closings, a DST closing involves a mere fraction of the time and paperwork. Also, as in almost all cases the property will have been acquired by the DST prior to the closing of the individual investor, there is no closing risk as such. Therefore, the DST closing is not only quicker and easier, it is also far less risky for 1031 exchangers who have limitations related to the properties they may have identified and 1031 closing deadlines.

Four elements are required for a DST close: completion of all investment documents, broker-dealer review and approval, equity funding through the qualified intermediary, and the filing of certain documents required by the qualified intermediary

Making Equity Reservations

One important step in the DST investment process which takes place prior to closing is not commonly understood. This is the matter of making an equity reservation. Each DST will have a limited amount of equity available, and depending upon several factors, the timeframe to raise this equity might be quite short, even as short as a few days. Due to this situation, the common practice in the industry is for brokers to make equity reserves on behalf of their clients in a specific offering for a specific amount in order to hold their position, giving them time to close their relinquished property, complete paperwork, and send funds. Equity reserves are nonbinding to both parties and are based upon good faith agreement. Some sponsors will ask for paperwork to be completed in order to hold a reserve, but this is more of a gesture than a commitment. The practice across the industry is to not hold an investor to the reserve if they choose to pull back for any reason. No deposits are ever required. It is like preparing to sail together. The sponsor wants everyone happy as they load the boat, and therefore will not force a reservation if the client changes their mind.

In practice, the matter of reservations will depend very much on the sponsor, the broker, and the client. Different sponsors have different rules for granting reserves. Some require paperwork while most do not. Some will grant a reserve for thirty days while others may only grant seven days. Some sponsors will only grant reserves to those clients who have already sold their relinquished property, while others will grant reserves to those who have yet to sell. This also depends upon the desirability of any given offering and the speed at which the equity is selling out.

The reputation of the broker is also key in this regard. A broker who has a high rate of follow-through on their reserves will be given more regard than one who follows through at a lower rate. In particular, making reserves in two different offerings for the same equity is frowned upon in the industry, and would be a reason for the reputation of that broker to suffer.

The intent of the client is also key. A client who can give firm good-faith intent will be accommodated more than a client who gives "more likely than not" intent. Of course, if the client does not have good faith intent, it is best to be up front, and a reserve can still be made in agreement with the sponsor. Sometimes a "soft" reserve will be granted for a certain period of time, with the understanding that the client will either upgrade to firm intent or withdraw his reserve. Overall, a combination of a broker with a strong track record who knows how to work with the sponsors in the area of reserves, and a client who is ready to give firm good faith intent, will give a client better options and will often result in obtaining a reserve that would not be extended to others. Making reserves is an important part of the DST investment process, and an experienced broker with good relationships in the industry will benefit the client.

Completing Investment Documents

Returning to the matter of closing, in order to close a DST acquisition, the first step is to complete all the investment documents. These will include some form of a purchase questionnaire and a purchase agreement, as well as other possible documents (any applicable entity documents such as a trust agreement, partnership agreement or LLC agreement) and any new client or existing client documents required by the broker-dealer. The purchaser questionnaire is basically an information form, so the sponsor can register the investment properly, prepare tax reporting documents, and send distribution payments, as well as confirm the accredited status of the investor or entity. The purchase agreement is self-explanatory, and functions as the purchase contract.

On the side of the broker-dealer, the typical requirements will be a new account form, a financial statement signed by the investor, and an investment disclosure form. Other than basic contact information, these documents are used to confirm accredited status, and also to make sure that the DST investment is appropriate in terms of concentration risk, investment experience, hold period expectations, and financial objectives. As most 1031 investors will be compelled by the looming tax liability, and as they will in any case be coming out of an illiquid real estate-based investment, the suitability of a DST investment is rarely an issue.

Broker-dealers are required by law to conduct a Patriot Act check on every new client to confirm that they do not appear on any money laundering, wanted or terrorist watch lists. The broker-dealer is also required by FINRA to have a strict privacy of information policy, and information and documentation will never be shared with a third party.

Upon execution of these documents by the investor, they will be submitted to the broker-dealer for review and approval of the investment and provided to the sponsor. Some broker registered representatives let the investors grapple themselves with the documents sent by the sponsor together with the PPM. Better representatives, such as Cornerstone, will provide support during the execution of paperwork, making sure everything is clear, that all documents are properly signed, and then that the proper documents are distributed to the proper parties.

Some parties in the industry have begun to use digital signatures such as DocuSign, but because everyone is not yet on board, most transactions still require physical signatures. Still, the full transition in the industry to digital signatures would further simplify and speed up the investment process and is anticipated in the near future. In addition, as no real estate title is conveyed in the closing but an assignment of the interest there is no time consuming and expensive notary requirements.

The investor can complete all the documents for their DST acquisition in advance, but practically speaking, they cannot close on the acquisition of their replacement property until they have closed on the sale of their relinquished property. The equity proceeds from the sale of their relinquished property must pass through the account of their qualified intermediary, and from there be sent to the escrow account of the DST, in order for the closing to take place. In cases where the investor has completed all the paperwork and received broker-dealer approval in advance, the closing of the DST acquisition can take place in as few as one to two days from the close of their relinquished property. While this is not a particularly pressing matter, some investors prefer to keep their equity earning a return, and thus appreciate the quick exchange of funds into their DST replacement property.

Broker-Dealer Approval of the Investment

While the purchase agreement is the key legal document of the acquisition, the sponsor of a syndicated real estate investment, DST or other, cannot close on the investment prior to receipt of broker-dealer approval with the signature of a principal of the broker-dealer. Regarding the matter of approval, strictly speaking the sponsor also needs to approve of the investment. On very rare occasions the sponsor will be aware of a reputational or legal issue on the side of the investor and will decline the investment, but this is very infrequent. In contrast, the TIC investments of a decade ago were much more difficult. As the investor would have deeded title to the property, they also had to be individually vetted and approved by the lender, often requiring them to submit tax returns or have their credit checked. Due to the nonrecourse structure of the DST investment and the fact that the DST investor does not receive deeded title to the property, these lender or sponsor requirements are no longer relevant.

Core broker-dealer considerations in approving a DST investment trade are the client investor accreditation and suitability. Accreditation is certified not only with an initialed statement by the investor attesting to accreditation but also by an investor provided statement of net worth. The suitability of the DST investment for the investor is addressed in relation to stated DST hold periods and when the investor needs funds from the investment, other short-term liquidity needs, and the investor's stated risk tolerance. The sponsor will also evaluate concentration risk based on the investor's overall investment portfolio, net worth, and liquid assets. However, as the investor utilizing a like-kind exchange is exchanging investment real estate for DST investment real estate these concerns are mitigated, especially as many investors are exchanging from a single investment property into several more diversified DST properties.

Working with the Qualified Intermediary

Upon completion of all the documents, the closing department of the sponsor will work with the qualified intermediary (QI) of the exchanger to complete a few final documents, including an estimated closing statement. As described in more detail in chapter 7, the use of a QI is a strict requirement of any valid 1031 exchange to avoid the investor having constructive receipt of the funds. By this point in the process, the QI will have set up a special account to receive the proceeds of the sale of the relinquished property, and they will be ready to act on the investor's behalf to complete and fund the exchange. The sponsor will confirm with the QI that the requisite funds are available in the exchange account and that the investment documents are properly executed. The QI will also often require approval from the investor for the outgoing wire in the amount required. Most investors will have a QI in place for their exchange, but the broker-dealer can refer reputable qualified intermediaries with national reach to any exchanger who has need.

The Actual Close

When broker-dealer approval has been issued, the requisite funds have been wired to the escrow account of the DST, and all documents have been properly executed and distributed, the closing agent of the sponsor then closes the acquisition of the 1031 exchanger/investor. Most larger DST sponsors conduct daily closings; smaller sponsors close at least weekly. In effect, each DST has their own closing, usually conducted within a day of the receipt of their funds by the sponsor.

The closing process also introduces the investor to the DST sponsor. Initial communication directly from the sponsor to the investor begin during the process, including the welcome letter or package. After closing, the investor may correspond directly to the sponsor for information, forms or other questions. Of course, the broker representative should also be copied on all correspondence and be available to assist at any time during the hold period.

The Timeframe from Reservation to Close

While there are various documents and parties involved in the closing process, it is usual for a DST investor to complete paperwork, fund and close their DST acquisition within five to seven business days from the time that they finalized their decision of which DST to invest in and in what amount. For an investor who has already sold their relinquished property and who has funds available with their qualified intermediary, Cornerstone has on occasion completed paperwork, obtained broker-dealer approval, completed qualified intermediary documents, wired the funds, and completed the DST closing in the course of a single day.

What the Investor Can Expect after the Close

At the time of closing, the sponsor will provide a final closing statement to the investor showing the equity investment, debt allocation, total acquisition value, and percentage of ownership interest in the DST. This document will then be used by the 1031 exchanger and their QI to validate the various aspects of their exchange, equity invested, acquired debt, total acquisition value, and date of close. Because the DST investor does not acquire deeded title to the property, none of the issues related to title apply. The closing statement is the definitive document of the acquisition for investment and 1031 exchange purposes. Some sponsors will provide a certificate of beneficial interest in the DST, but this is not strictly required.

After close, the sponsor will provide a welcome packet to the investors, usually including copies of all pertinent investment and closing documents, and a confirmation of when the first distribution will be sent, as well as the schedule and arrangement of distributions going forward. The return of a DST begins to accrue from the day of closing, with distributions usually beginning the following month. Going forward from the closing, the sponsor will communicate directly with the investors, including periodic property updates, details on distributions, and yearly reports used for tax filings.

Note Regarding the DST Structure

Strictly speaking, the close of a DST acquisition is not the same as a fee simple real estate acquisition, because the fee simple interest in the property has already been acquired by the DST. The interests in the DST are then made available to investors via the DST closings; so, this closing is actually an assignment of interest in the DST from the depositor to the DST investor, the holder of the beneficial interest in the trust. This is also why there is no issue of title at the time of the DST closing, and also why there is no need for the numerous notarizations common in traditional real estate closings. Nonetheless, this closing process works for 1031 exchange purposes, specifically the 45-day identification and 180-day closing requirements. Thousands of 1031 DST acquisitions have been completed and reported since the issue of Revenue Ruling 2004-86.

In most cases, the DST investment will close well in advance of the expiration of the required 45-day identification period. In this case, the close and the closing statement is a de facto identification, and the investor need not separately identify the DSTs on a qualified intermediary form. However, some investors will complete the ID forms and submit them to the QI in advance of the forty-fifth day out of an abundance of caution. Of course, the closing in nearly every case is well in advance of the 180-day close date. On rare occasions, the 180-day close date may be relevant if the sponsor had not already closed on the property and something happens to delay that closing, such as delays in obtaining debt financing, but this is, again, extremely unusual.

The Close of Non-1031 Investments

Most investors, especially those who have closed on single ownership real estate in the past, are very pleasantly surprised by the efficiency and simplicity of the DST closing process. Especially with the assistance of an experienced and diligent broker representative, the required documentation can be reviewed and signed within a few hours' time, and the investment can be closed within days of making the investment decision. Returning to our earlier analogy, all the contented and like-minded investors have now been welcomed into the boat (the DST investment), introduced through the closing process to the captain (the sponsor), with optimistic expectations for a happy and prosperous five- to seven-year voyage (hold period).

Chapter 13

The Hold Period and What to Expect

If one is entering the hold period of a DST investment, then they have already purchased a DST. For many investors who are making their first investment into fractional ownership of an institutional-quality property, this is an exciting moment! Congratulations, you are now an owner of a DST!

DST properties are, generally speaking, fully stabilized and cash flowing properties that are available for investors to purchase as part of their exchange. Once the investor submits their payment either directly or through a qualified intermediary, the sponsor will issue a closing statement unique to that individual investment, a welcome package confirming the assignment and providing beneficial ownership interest certificates, and thus beings the hold period. Now that the transaction is complete, the hold period begins.

What Is the Hold Period?

So what is the hold period, and what should an investor expect during the hold period? The answer to this is simply that the hold period is the period of time from the date of the acquisition of the DST interest until the date the DST goes full-cycle and executes its exit. Most often, the exit will be in the form of selling the property to another buyer, thus creating a liquidity event for the DST investors. The length of the hold period will vary depending upon several factors such as the type of asset held in the DST, the location of the asset, the market demand in the local submarket, and the economy as a whole.

Duration of the Hold Period

In commercial real estate, it is common practice for properties to obtain ten-year loans as part of their financing, and this same time frame is often used for financing on properties held in a DST as well. As the DST may not refinance its debt one the offering is completed, it stands to reason that the DST will intend to execute its exit prior to the loan becoming mature. But how long should a DST property be held? Is there a specific time that an investor should anticipate?

Because DSTs are in essence a real estate investment, DST sponsors desire to hold onto the properties long enough to maximize their appreciation potential while still taking it full cycle prior to the maturity of its loan. This is often why offering materials for DSTs will listed a projected hold period of seven to ten years, as this allow the property time to grow in value while at the same time providing the DST with a window of time with which it can prepare the property for sale, obtain the best price, and execute the sale prior to the end of the ten-year period. In many cases, years seven to eight might be a reasonable estimate as to when a DST sponsor would aim to take the DST full-cycle. Waiting this length of time allows the property not only to achieve as much appreciation as possible, but to also ensure that the front-end load as part of the DST transaction can be overcome through the increase in property value.

Does this mean that all DSTs will sell their property at years seven to eight? The answer to this question is simply that the DST would look to sell at the time when it can obtain the best price. As such, if the DST were to receive an offer on the property presented investors with the best possible exit, then the DST may consider accepting the offer and take the property full-cycle even if investors are only three years into the hold period. Conversely, if the local market was not conducive to obtaining the best exit at the seven- or eight-year mark, then the DST might prolong the hold period until year nine if it was deemed to be in the best interest of the investors.

Hold Periods for All Cash DSTs

Those DSTs that do not include the use of any leverage, and thus, do not have any loans which will become due at any designated point in time, have the benefit of greater flexibility as to when to execute their exit strategy. Not having a loan allows these all-cash DSTs the freedom to hold the property for as long as is desired without the concern of a ticking clock forcing a decision to sell. While all-cash DSTs often are not able to provide as high of total returns to investors that leveraged DSTs can, not having to worry about a loan mature date does provide specific peace of mind to investor with lower risk tolerance.

Passive Hold

So what else should an investor expect during the hold period? Remember, that DSTs are a passive investment structure, thus, investors do not have to worry about performing any management services for the property. They do not need to be involved in negotiating the lease terms with the tenants, or attention to various maintenance needs. In brief, owners of a DST are able to repurpose the time they had spent previously on real estate management tasks onto other matters that may be of greater interest or import to them. Not having to actively manage these properties allows DST investors time to spend more time with family, learn to paint, travel to those wonderful destinations they always told themselves they would get to one day, or just stay home and relax. How they opt to spend this time is as varied as investors themselves, but the one thing they do have in common is that they do not need to spend any time actively managing their DST property.

Monthly Distributions

DSTs generally pay investors their distributions on a monthly basis. Most investors will elect at closing to receive their monthly distributions by way of electronic deposit directly into their bank account (i.e., direct deposit). This eliminates the need to deposit the funds and allows for even greater efficiency and passivity. However, the investor may also arrange for a physical check to be mailed to a home or office address. Distributions match the flow of cash thought the master lease structure. These payments initiate with the tenants and pass through to the master tenant and the trust manager and ultimately to the investors. Accordingly, most distributions will be made to the investors between the 5th to the fifteenth of the month following the month the income is earned.

Many sponsors will send an email to alert the investor that the distribution has been made and to check their statements. In addition, some sponsors will use the monthly distribution as an opportunity to share any news or communicate any pertinent financial or other information regarding the property to the investors for the period.

Initial distributions made following the close on the DST investment will typically be prorated for the prior month based on when the investment closed. Most sponsors use the date the investments funds were received to further benefit the investor if the closing was officially recorded on a date subsequent to finding. In some cases, especially if the investor's DST investment was closed close to the end of the month, the initial distribution may be made in the first half of the second month following the month of closing and would be a larger distribution as it would include the distribution for the prorated month of closing and the full month following the closing.

Unless, the investor elects out, a copy of the distribution email and any other correspondence will also be copied to the investor's registered representative.

Quarterly Reports

DSTs provide quarterly reports regarding the financial status of the property and any issues that may affect its performance. Quarterly reports include a summary of the performance of the property year-to-date (YTD), comparing the projected and actual expenses and income levels, status of the reserves, current occupancy, current distribution rate, and a listing of any upcoming short-term projects affecting the property such as clubhouse renovations, unit upgrades, pool resurfacing, marketing campaigns, etc. These regular reports ensure investors have visibility over the performance of their investment and a short-term forward-looking overview of the next three to six months of operations.

Year-End Tax Reporting

At the end of the year, DSTs provide investors with the tax information they need to properly file their taxes. These distributions, quarterly reports, and annual tax documents are the most consistent forms of communication that DST investors will receive during the hold period. The sponsor will strive to deliver the annual tax documents to the investors by February 15 to provide ample time to the investor to prepare their individual tax returns. In some rare cases, the report may be delayed into March or even April due to circumstances usually beyond the sponsor's control.

These documents include:

- *A Form 1098 for interest and principal paid on the assumed debt for the tax year.*
- *A pro forma income statement reporting the investor's proportionate share of the net income. These numbers are reported on the investor's Schedule E, similar to how a single ownership rental property would be reported.*
- *An allocation of cost between land and depreciable property. Please note each investor will have a different carry over basis*

and tax basis in the DST investment. However, based on the allocation of cost to the depreciable assets the investor's tax preparer should be able to calculate the applicable depreciation.

Based on these above three items of information, the investors or their respective tax preparer will be able to report their proportionate share of the income from the DST, deduct their proportionate share of the interest paid on the mortgage, and deduct their unique amount of depreciation to arrive at a net taxable income. These revenue and deduction items are reported on Schedule E of the investor's individual tax return with the net taxable income amount being brought forward to the investor's individual Form 1040. Please note that the reported net income minus the principle paid on the mortgage should equal the total cash that was distributed to the investor for the given year.

Other Communications

Beyond these anticipatory reports, DSTs will provide to investors any updates regarding the status of their property if any event occurs that could have caused a negative impact on the property, such as hurricane, tornado, flooding, blizzard, etc. DSTs will notify investors regarding the status of the property in the wake of these types of events as special notices, to ensure full visibility over the damage that was encountered (if any), and what steps are being taken to address and correct the damage.

It is not uncommon for DST sponsors to organize periodic conference calls with the DSTinvestments to provide for a detailed discussion regarding the property. These conference calls provide investors with the opportunity to ask specific questions to the sponsor that may be of concern to them, especially if there had been any recent issues that may have had a negative impact on the property.

Most of the larger sponsors have the resources to provide their own investor services department who are available to answer questions over the telephone and provide any documentation if requested.

At the time a DST investment closes, the sponsors will provide the investors with a welcome kit that will include the contact information for the investor services representative in their office, if someone in particular has been designated to perform that function.

Broker-Dealer Communications

Each year, the broker-dealer that approved the DST investment will send a letter to each investor to inquire about any changes to their address, contact information, or general account profile. Additionally, any significant life changes that may affect one's financial status and/or investment profile such as a change in occupants, change in earnings, divorce, children, or retirement should also be updated at that time if one's registered representative is not already of these changes. Having this information ensures that products and services are being provided to an investor that are suitable for their situation.

Consummation of the Hold Period

As the property reaches the end of its hold period, the DST will inform the investors of any potential offers that it may accept that would trigger a liquidity event. This notice would serve to inform the investors of the actual sale price of the property, as well as alert them that they may want to plan for their follow-on DST investment as part of their 1031 exchange as this particular DST goes full-cycle. This subject will be fully developed in the next chapter, The Final Disposition.

Conclusion

Having conducted their due diligence on both the sponsor and the DST offering prior to making a purchase, investors can enjoy the passive nature of their DST investment throughout the hold period by repurposing their time into other avenues of their life, knowing that the professional property and asset managers running their DST property are working hard on their behalf. DST investors are like passengers on a sailing ship, with the sponsor as the captain and the trustee and their staff as the crew. Investors should be confident that as the DST ship sails that they are in the experienced and capable hands of the captain and crew. We expect calm waters and smooth sailing, but in the event a storm pops up on the horizon, the captain (sponsor) will know how to navigate the ship and will communicate with the passengers until the ship is brought successfully to a safe-harbor and the final disposition of the DST property.

Chapter 14

The Final Disposition

Procedurally, the final disposition (the sale of the asset[s] of the syndicated real estate investment, including the distribution of equity proceeds to the investor) is even simpler than the closing process. Because the DST investment is fully passive, and the investor does not have deeded title to the property, the investors do not participate at any stage, either in the decision of when to sell the asset, nor in the closing process itself. The DST investor will receive notification from the sponsor that the property will be sold. Then, at the time of the sale, their portion of the equity proceeds will be sent either to their designated qualified intermediary or, if they will not be doing a follow-on 1031 exchange, directly to an account of their choice. At least one to two months in advance of the close and based upon the projected sale price and relatively predictable closing costs, the sponsor should provide the investor with a fairly good estimate of the investor's pro rata share of the equity proceeds, as well as their pro rata share of the loan balance at the time of close, allowing the investor to properly plan their follow-on 1031 exchange or other steps.

When Will the Sponsor Sell the Property?

Under normal circumstances, after a hold period of a certain number of years, the sponsor will decide that it is an opportune time to sell the assets of the DST and market the property for sale. Either the sponsor's internal real estate professionals or their external commercial real estate brokers will continuously be monitoring local and regional CAP rate movement for the asset class throughout the hold period. Consequently, the sponsor should be on top of the local market and aggressively poised to sell the property at the opportune time to maximize investor returns. It is also common for sponsors to receive unsolicited offers for a property held in a DST. The sponsor may include updates on such activities in their monthly or quarterly reporting, but usually it is the signing of a sale contract that results in a comprehensive update regarding the pending sale of the asset and the projected outcome for the investors. The process of selling an asset held by a DST is the same as any other. There will be certain contracted timeframes for the buyer to conduct due diligence and close, as well as requirements for deposits, etc. As with any real estate closing, causes for delay are numerous, and closings tend to occur later than initially projected. In any case, the sponsor should keep all the investors informed as the process proceeds, so that the actual closing does not catch anyone off guard. It will be a judgment call, but in principle the sponsor will seek to sell the property for the highest possible price and resulting in the greatest total return to investors.

How Mortgage Financing Limits the Hold Period

Due to the limitations on the DST structure stipulated in Revenue Ruling 2004-86, a DST is not permitted to refinance during the hold. For any properties acquired using mortgage financing, this means that the term of the financing functions as a practical backstop to the hold period of the property, and therefore of the DST itself. Furthermore, as most DSTs will use commercial debt with a ten-year term and resulting balloon payment, ten years will be a practical deadline for the hold period of most DSTs. In addition, since no sponsor/seller would want to be forced to sell due to an approaching maturity and balloon payment, eight to nine years should be considered the longest realistic hold period for the large majority of financed DSTs. (Note, in the case of distress or other situations which would require the DST to spring into an LLC, this back-end time limitation can be obviated. See chapter 3 for further discussion of the "springing" LLC.) On the other hand, if a property is held debt-free, there would be no such limitation; if the financing has a term longer than 10 years, the limitation would be longer accordingly. There are also occasional DSTs which use financing with a term less than ten years; this also might be the case if a mortgage was assumed by the DST at the time of acquisition. In these cases, the back-end time limitation will be less.

Defeasance Costs

Another loan-related factor which will weigh significantly upon the decision to sell is the matter of defeasance fees. Without going into their detailed characteristics and variations in loan contracts, in general, defeasance fees must be paid by the borrower (the DST) if the property is sold and the loan paid off prior to maturity. The amount of these fees depends upon a variety of factors, including current interest rates, and some loan contracts include defeasance fees for the first number of years of the loan term (e.g., the first five or seven out of ten). In any case, as these defeasance costs can be substantial, if there will be defeasance costs in the context of a certain sale scenario, it is very possible that the sponsor would delay the sale of the asset due to the fact that the cost of defeasance would substantially or entirely dilute the appreciation proceeds of the asset. This is also something to take into consideration when selecting a DST property.

Lease Term

The contracted lease term of the occupying tenant will also exert some forces on the hold period duration. The sponsor will not want to run off too much time from a long-term lease as the main value of a property may be the present value of the future lease payments. Accordingly, the sponsor may only hold a single tenant NNN lease retail DST for say five years of a twenty-year lease. Alternatively, if a tenant commits to renewing a lease the sponsor may want to take advantage of the created value by selling the property into the lease renewal.

Exchanging Out of a DST into a New Replacement Property

For the DST investor who intends to carry out a 1031 exchange out of the DST and into a new replacement property, the sale of the property and conclusion/close of their DST investment will be essentially the same as the close of any relinquished property. They will need to arrange for the services of a qualified intermediary, and the details of their 1031 account will need to be provided to the sponsor, so that the equity proceeds of the investor are sent accordingly, and the exchanger does not have constructive receipt of the funds. The sponsors are aware of this matter and will reach out to all the investors in advance, asking them for direction in this regard.

It is not required for investors to carry out a follow-on exchange. They can choose to receive the proceeds, pay the tax and exit the 1031 cycle if they would like. It is also important to note that 1031 exchange at the time of the sale of the DST is also an option for those investors who came in as direct cash investors, just as for those who invested via 1031 exchange at the front end. Because the DST investor is considered a direct owner of the real estate through the trust vehicle, whatever appreciation has built up over the hold period, plus the issue of depreciation recapture, will result in certain capital gains tax liability, which can be deferred by conducting a 1031 exchange. Whether or not a 1031 exchange is the right choice depends on the particular situation of the investor, the amount of appreciation or depreciation that will be realized at the time of the sale, the debt at the time of the sale, and on the analysis and advice of the investor's tax advisor.

A DST interest is considered "like kind" property for 1031 exchange purposes. Therefore, there is no requirement for the exchanger to exchange into another DST, though that will often be the practical and preferred choice of investors who have switched from active ownership of real estate assets to the passive ownership of DST interests. Rather, the exchanger coming out of a DST has all the viable 1031 options available to them. They can roll over into a new DST; they can exchange into any other like-kind property; or they can pay the tax and cash out. Including cashing out only a part of the sale proceeds and exchanging the remainder.

Sponsors will seek to win repeat business from investors by providing them with an attractive competitive return. In many cases, sponsors will prepare a follow-up DST for investment by the investors exiting their recently completed offering. For those investors who have a favorable impression of the sponsor, the asset class and the financial results, this is an attractive option, but as all funds will still need to go to the qualified intermediary, there will never be any requirement or pressure for the investor to take this option.

The Closing Statement of Sale of the DST Interest

Upon the completion of the sale of the property, each investor will receive a closing statement indicating the total sale price, closing costs, the satisfaction of any outstanding mortgage, the total equity proceeds, and their pro rata equity proceeds and pro rata debt. As closing costs are typically deductible from a 1031 exchange, the key numbers for the 1031 exchanger will be their equity proceeds, their portion of the debt satisfied at the time of close, and of course the date of close, from which time the forty-five-day identification and 180-day close timelines begin to toll. As with the sale of any 1031 relinquished property, the amount of the equity proceeds and debt, and their ratio, will weigh significantly on the investor's choices concerning any replacement properties. It is also very important to note that, for DSTs, 100 percent of the equity proceeds of the sale will be distributed to the investors after closing costs and a certain contracted disposition fee, because no profit split structure is permitted under the Revenue Ruling. The disposition fee does provide a certain return to the sponsor, which is actually welcomed by most, as it creates at least some alignment of financial interest between the sponsor and the investors. Strong due diligence review will nonetheless look out for inappropriately high offering disposition fees. For a further discussion of the disposition fee, please see chapter 4.

Cornerstone will work with the investor beginning several months in advance of the estimated closing date for the sale of the DST to identify suitable replacement DST properties, evaluate debt levels, make appropriate reservations, and coordinate QI services. In so doing, the closing and exchange transaction can be well planned, stress free, and any cash flow interruption will be minimized.

We hope this section has provided a roadmap to the DST offering and provided some context and perspective to an otherwise unfamiliar and uncharted industry. More importantly, we trust we have provide some insights into choosing trusted business partners including broker-dealers, registered representatives, and sponsors. We also hope the information conveyed in this section has bolstered investor confidence and empowered the private real estate investor to utilize the effectiveness of Section 1031 exchange tax deferral to build a well-diversified personal portfolio of institutional-grade real estate.

Analyzing the DST Offering

Chapter 15

Due Diligence

Due diligence: the analytical process of the facts and circumstances associated with an investment, intended to provide an investor with a full disclosure of facts and risks in order to arrive at an investment decision.

> Cornerstone and its broker-dealer are committed to performing thorough due diligence on each prospective DST offering before it is presented for investor consideration.

Performing the necessary due diligence on any investment is both recommended and necessary. However, due to the timing restrictions involved with a 1031 exchange, investors are often rushed, thereby making it difficult to gather enough information to make a suitable replacement property decision. Furthermore, most real estate is sold by the seller under the contract law principle of buyer beware or "caveat emptor" that controls the sale of real property after the date of closing and puts the responsibility of discovery and investigation on the buyer.

In direct contrast to real estate law, securities laws require the DST issuer, legal counsel, and broker dealer all to conduct reasonable investigations and disclose all material facts and observations to the buyer in the form of a full disclosure prospectus or private placement memorandum (PPM). The full disclosure PPM and the underlying due diligence not only provide the investor with assurance of the facts on which to base a DST investment decision, but also provide a vehicle for the investor to conduct his or her own due diligence on multiple DST offerings within the forty-five-day identification time constraint of Section 1031. Because a DST is sold subject to the 1933 Securities Act, it has all the tax advantages of real estate, yet with the governance, regulation, and oversight provided under securities law.

Four Levels of Due Diligence in a DST offering

Cornerstone and its broker-dealer are committed to performing thorough due diligence on each prospective DST offering before it is presented for investor consideration.

Syndicated DST investments offered through Cornerstone must pass through four layers of due diligence before being offered to its clients. The first three layers of due diligence are performed by the sponsor, the lender and the sponsor's legal counsel, while a fourth layer is performed by the broker-dealer.

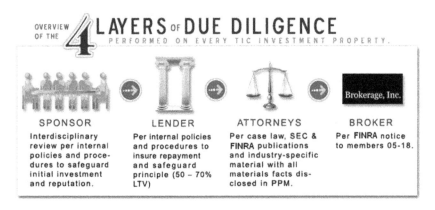

Level 1: Sponsor Due Diligence

The sponsor searches the national real estate market looking for stabilized investment-grade properties. They conduct a significant due diligence process for each potential property candidate. As the DST sponsor is considered the issuer of a private securities offering, under Section 12 of the 1933 Securities Act it could be held liable for any material misrepresentation or omission in connection with the offer or sale of the property contained within its prospectus or other communications. The sponsor must therefore be able to prove that it made reasonable investigation and has a reasonable basis to believe, and did believe at the time, that there were no material misrepresentations or omissions. This is the essence of due diligence: a reasonable investigation resulting in a reasonable ground to believe, and an actual state of mind in which the underwriter does believe, that its statements are correct.[31]

At the sponsor level, the acquisition team will vet the property by commissioning an appraisal, an environmental study, and a 10-year property condition assessment. The sponsor will also complete a full real estate and financial underwriting for the property. The sponsor will typically engage a third party due diligence firm such as Mick Law, FactRight, or Buttonwood to provide independent reports on the property and offering on behalf of the broker-dealers. If satisfied with the results of the due diligence, the sponsor acquires or contracts to purchase the property and the DST offering is initiated.

Level 2: Lender Due Diligence

Once the sponsor identifies a property for acquisition, as the majority of these syndicated DST real estate offerings are leveraged, the sponsor will arrange nonrecourse debt financing with a lender. The lender will then also conduct their own due diligence on the property prior to loan approval. In most cases the lender is providing the majority of the financing in the capital stack, and accordingly will conduct a vigorous due diligence review of the property and evaluate the ability to repay the loan principal and interest. This is particularly true after the Great Recession, with more stringent federally regulated underwriting standards.

As part of its due diligence process, the lender will confirm the property value using a third-party appraisal, ensure there are no environmental risk exposures by requiring an environmental report, determine the amount of reserves that are necessary to maintain the property in good condition using a conditions report, and analyze the net operating income the property is earning.

The foundational step in commercial real estate loan underwriting is verifying the appropriate net operating income (NOI). While the borrower will submit a rent roll and a NOI pro forma, the lender will almost always build their own pro forma for loan underwriting purposes, which may result in a different net operating income (NOI) calculation. Lender adjustments to NOI may comprise increasing the vacancy and credit risk factor to account for tenant rollover risk, the market environment, and deducting capital reserves from NOI.

Once the NOI is confirmed, the lender will input the NOI into its internal loan policy guidelines and other underwriting criteria. The two most commonly used loan underwriting criteria used are the Loan to Value Ratio (LTV) and the Debt Service Coverage Ratio (DSCR).

Loan to Value Ratio (LTV)

The loan to value ratio compares the total loan amount borrowed in relation to the value of the property.

$$LTV = \frac{Loan\ Amount}{Property\ Value}$$

For example, assuming a loan amount for a commercial real estate property was $600,000 and the appraisal came in with a value of $1,000,000, the LTV ratio would simply be $600,000/$1,000,000, or 60 percent. Various lenders typically have different LTV requirements which are determined by each lender's internal strategic growth goals and existing portfolio concentrations. LTV guidelines may also vary by asset class to reflect associated risk. For example, a multitenant office is often considered have greater risk than a fully leased apartment building, and accordingly the LTV on an office building may be lower. Of course, an important issue with the loan-to-value ratio is how the lender determines the value of the property.

A third-party appraisal firm is engaged to provide a full appraisal report on the property, but the lender may adjust the value per its own internal estimation.

Debt Service Coverage (DSCR)

The debt service coverage ratio is simply the ratio of NOI to the annual debt service requirement for the property. This is a key ratio to most lenders, as it safeguards that the property has the necessary cash flow to cover the loan payments. The DSCR formula can be calculated as follows:

$$DSCR = \frac{\text{Net Operating Income}}{\text{Annual Debt Service}}$$

The DSCR provides the lender a margin of safety. By requiring a 1.30x DSCR, for example, the lender is creating a built-in cushion in the property's cash flow above the annual debt service. At a 1.30x DSCR, the property's NOI could decline by 25 percent and still cover the loan payments. Similar to the LTV ratio, the DSCR is set by the bank's internal loan policy, and may vary by asset class, tenant credit worthiness, and other factors. Higher risk properties such as hotels will normally have higher DSCR requirements than more stable operating properties like apartments.

Maximum Loan Analysis

The main purpose for the maximum loan analysis is to determine the maximum acceptable loan amount based on the NOI, the DSCR, and the LTV requirements. In most cases, the lender will then take the lesser of the two loan amounts calculated based on the LTV computation and the DSCR calculation.

JOHN HARVEY CPA, MBT, TRAWNEGAN GALL, AND DAVID KANGAS

Level 3: Due Diligence in the Preparation of the Private Placement Memorandum

Once the debt side of the offering is negotiated, the sponsor will then structure the equity side of the acquisition through a private placement offering. Such private placement offerings necessitate the sponsor to retain a law firm to write a private placement memorandum (PPM) disclosing all risks and material facts related to the offering. Legal counsel, which is contracted to draft the PPM for the offering, will also conduct their own due diligence on the property and offering.

Several courts will permit a claim for malpractice against a lawyer only by those in privity with the lawyer, and the 1933 Act does not directly impose any obligation on counsel to ensure the accuracy of a prospectus.[32] Nonetheless, some courts have held that an attorney may be liable to a specific third party who the attorney is aware will be relying on the attorney's work, even in the absence of privity, and that a lawyer may be liable for a negligent misstatement. A primary example of an attorney being held liable for failing to discover and prevent fraud is FDIC v. Clark under a suit for legal malpractice. As stated above, sellers of securities are liable under Section 12 of the 1933 Act for violation of disclosure requirements. An issuer's (sponsor's) attorneys are often charged with being "sellers" by reason of their extensive involvement in document preparation and the offering process. The Supreme Court in Printer v. Dahl confirmed that Section 12 reference to "seller" extends beyond those who pass title. Accordingly, the attorney who prepares the private placement memorandum has a reasonable duty to discover and disclose any material misstatements or omissions made by the seller in connection with the offer or sale involving a prospectus or oral communication.

The legal counsel will also compose the tax opinion that is included in the PPM for each offering. The tax opinion specifically compares the specific DST to the IRS Revenue Ruling 2004-86 and should be able to issue a "should" or higher-level opinion that this particular DST does qualifies as replacement property for a 1031 exchange. On this point, to date we are not aware of a single DST which has been disqualified by the IRS as a replacement property.

Level 4: Broker-Dealer Due Diligence

Once the PPM has been prepared, the PPM together with all information used in the underwriting of the offering is presented to a FINRA member securities broker-dealer. Adding an additional layer of protection to the investor, the brokerage conducts their own due diligence study on the sponsor and the property before signing a selling agreement.

In March of 2005, FINRA issued Notice to Members 05-18. This notice reminded FINRA members that when offering fractional ownership interests that are securities to customers, members and their associated persons must comply with all applicable NASD rules, including those addressing suitability and due diligence. The notice classified the TIC (and similarly the DST) interest as a nonconventional interest and the applicability of NASD Notice to Members 03-71. Specifically, that FINRA members are responsible to

- conduct appropriate due diligence;
- perform reasonable-basis suitability analysis;
- perform customer specific suitability analysis for recommended transactions;
- ensure the promotional materials used by the members are fair, accurate, and balanced;
- implement appropriate internal controls; and
- provide appropriate training to registered persons involved in the sale of these products.

With respect to due diligence, the member should make reasonable investigations to ensure that the offering document does not contain false or misleading information. Such investigation should include background checks of sponsor's principals, review of agreements (e.g., property management, purchase and sale, lease, and loan agreements), property inspection, and understanding the degree of likelihood that projections will occur.

In addition, in April 2010, FINRA released Regulatory Notice 10-22, Obligation of Broker Dealers to Conduct Reasonable Investigations in Regulation D offerings. In the notice, FINRA provides guidance regarding a FINRA member's obligation to conduct a reasonable investigation of an issuer, the securities offered in connection with Regulation D, and the issuer's representations about it. This duty emanates from the broker-dealer's special relationship to the customer (investor), and that its recommendation rests on the conclusions from a reasonable investigation.

The industry practice is for the broker-dealer to begin the due diligence process by collecting all the applicable due diligence items on its Due Diligence Request form. For each offering submitted, the broker-dealer analysts independently review the offering materials provided and the third-party due diligence reports. These reviews focus on both the quantitative and qualitative aspects of both the sponsor and its specific DST offering.

The Broker-Dealer's Sponsor-Level Review

On an annual basis, the broker-dealer offering DSTs should perform the following sponsor-level examinations as part of their review:

1. *Examination of the sponsor's financial statements and financial position. In most cases audited financial statements are required and analyzed to determine the depth of financial resources and liquidity.*
2. *Examination of the sponsor's organizational capabilities, including depth of real estate expertise, customer service capacity, and operational manpower.*
3. *Review of the track record of the sponsor both for full cycle and currently operating properties with respect to estimated projections and actual performance.*

4. *Background check on the principals of the sponsor, including the search for the existence of any criminal records, bankruptcy, or judgments, as well as their track record in the field of syndicated real estate.*

The Broker-Dealer's Property-Level Review

As a DST sponsor brings various DST offerings to the market throughout the year, the broker-dealer will perform a due diligence review of each DST offering. The review may be separated into an examination of the actual property and the examination of the offering documents. Analysis of the properties themselves from a real estate perspective include but are not limited to

1. *property tours (site visits),*
2. *tenant interviews,*
3. *lease agreement review,*
4. *review of loan covenants and recourse carve-outs,*
5. *appraisal assessment,*
6. *environmental issues,*
7. *the adequacy of tenant improvement, loan and other reserves, and*
8. *an analysis of the national and local market using third-party real estate data firms.*

The property-level data is compared to the information provided within the offering documents for reasonability as compared to historical data and the overall market in which the property is located. The quantitative metrics compared include (but are not limited to) acquisition cap rate, occupancy, expense ratios, capital improvement plans, value add components of the business plan, anticipated investment hold period, and anticipated exit cap rate and absolute disposition price.

The fee structure charged by the sponsor is analyzed and compared to other sponsors, as well as third party vendors that perform similar services. The areas of compensation that focuses of interest are: acquisition fees and costs, asset management fees, property management fees, master lease profit margins and disposition fees.

The offering documents are analyzed for appropriate disclosure of the key terms of the legal and operative documents for the investment: the trust agreement, the master lease, asset/property management agreements, loan agreements, and tax opinion letter.

> Cornerstone's broker-dealer rejects approximately 30% of the offerings presented. The reasons for rejection are varied and can relate to the property itself, the sponsor, the financing, or the market.

The operative and legal documents are also reviewed for completeness, consistency, and reasonable structure to give the sponsor the ability to operate the property effectively and the investors a reasonable structure for investment.

Investment Committee Vote

After a potential offering has gone through the due diligence process, the due diligence analyst typically presents their findings, together with the third-party due diligence report, to an investment committee, where it is again reviewed for potential approval. Each member of this committee should have many years of commercial real estate experience and an aptitude for the 1031 exchange marketplace. Once an offering has gone through this examination by internal and external parties, and is found to be a sound offering, it may be approved by the investment committee and will then be presented for investor consideration.

Cornerstone's broker-dealer rejects approximately 30 percent of the offerings presented. The reasons for rejection are varied and can relate to the property itself, the sponsor, the financing, or the market. It is important to note that this final level of due diligence is after the sponsor, the lender and the legal counsel have all approved the offering, meaning that those offerings declined may be available to investors through other broker-dealers.

Investor Due Diligence

In our view, the investor would be hard pressed to find a real estate property that has gone through as much interdisciplinary due diligence as a syndicated DST property. However, in addition to the four layers of due diligence inherent in each DST offering, the investor should also conduct his or her own due diligence investigation. The prudent investor should carefully review the full set of offering materials, including the PPM, supplemental statements, and offering summary. The investor will have to sign several forms from both the sponsor and the broker-dealer that they have read the PPM and understand the risks of the investment.

In addition to the offering documents, the investor may find helpful information from an internet search on the demographics of a property location, business reports and press releases for major tenants, and industry trends and data. A surprising amount of information may also be obtained on the internet regarding tenant financial statements and credit ratings. Most sponsors will pay for travel and accommodations for the investor to visit the DST property, and will provide a tour. Cornerstone highly recommends a property tour for investments that are financially material to the investor.

Chapter 16

Analyzing the PPM Document

All DSTs are structured and offered as securities under the Securities Act of 1933 which requires the investor to be provided with a private placement memorandum (PPM). The PPM is created out of significant due diligence from the real estate company, the lender, and the securities industry. The PPM is designed to be a stand-alone document and should disclose everything the investor in a new offering will need to know in order to make an informed investment decision. This includes: the offering structure, SEC disclosures about the interests being purchased, property information, information on the trust manager and the master tenant, risks involved with the investment, financing information, use of proceeds, conflicts of interest, and investor suitability data. The PPM also includes the purchase questionnaire and purchase agreement, which is the actual sales contract for the offering. This is the document that the investor will sign and send in with their investment funds. The PPM is prepared by the insurer (the sponsor) of the offering.

Regulation D of the 1933 Securities Act became effective April 15, 1982 and is one of the key exemptions under SEC rules for sponsors that wish to raise money by selling equity. Reg D contains the kind of exemptions that allow entrepreneurs looking to raise equity for private or limited offerings to avoid time and expense associated with registering an offering with the SEC. By using a PPM pursuant to a Reg D offering, DST sponsors can meet the requirements of the Securities Act in a manageable and cost-effective fashion, while providing potential investors with the disclosures and protections required by the act.

At a minimum, a PPM should contain the following:

1. *Cover page and securities legends*
2. *Purchaser suitability requirements for investors*
3. *Summary of the offering*
4. *Risk factors*
5. *Estimated use of proceeds*
6. *Compensation and fees*
7. *Description of the market*
8. *Description of the project*
9. *Basic underwriting assumptions*
10. *Acquisition and contribution of the property*
11. *Financing terms*
12. *Description of the master lease*
13. *Master lease capitalization*
14. *Summary of the trust agreement*
15. *Summary of the property management agreement*
16. *Summary of the purchase agreement*
17. *Business plan*
18. *The trust manager and their affiliates*
19. *Conflicts of interest by management*
20. *Prior performance of sponsor and its affiliates*
21. *Federal income tax matters*
22. *Financial statements*
23. *Financial projections*
24. *Litigation*
25. *Tax opinion*

By design, the PPM is lengthy and detailed, and can be a daunting document for the average investor. Many investors may prefer to simply review an executive summary, or marketing material with glossy pictures and general statements about how well the investment will do. This is not a good idea. The PPM is the sponsor's opportunity to disclose all the risks and conflicts associated with their offering, as well as the various opportunities and potential rewards of the investment. A properly written PPM educates and protects the investor, discloses the risks and opportunities of the investment, and protects the sponsor from certain types of liability. It is also the investor's opportunity to objectively evaluate those risks and conflicts. If one breaks down the various sections, the PPM can be a very useful guide to compare one DST investment against another.

In the opening pages of the PPM there are some standard SEC disclosures that are common in all PPMs for direct participation programs. These disclosures are in bold type. Some investors may consider these risk disclosures unlikely for the type of investment offered. For example, a DST property may be an all-cash investment, with no debt, with a highly rated credit tenant with a long-term lease, and yet have the same SEC disclosures as an investment into an oil and gas well wildcat drilling offering. Investors should seriously consider all these risk disclosures and be aware that some risks are more likely, while others are less likely, such as the risk of illiquidity vs. the risk of a tornado.

Typically, a PPM will include copies of the trust agreement, master lease agreement, loan agreement, management agreement, and the subscription documents. These are the actual documents that will govern operation of the property and are therefore critical in the review of the investment. No prospective investor should invest or commit to invest in any offering where they have not first fully reviewed each of these documents. In addition, regardless of their desire to invest in the offering, no investor should ever invest in an offering if they are not willing and able to comply with the terms and conditions contained in these documents.

Other Helpful Sections

There are several sections of the PPM that an investor may find particularly helpful when reviewing an offering. These sections of the PPM may be compared side by side for several contemplated DST offerings.

Estimated Use of Proceeds

Per industry best practices, each DST offering PPM will contain an Estimated Use of Proceeds section. Also called a source and uses table, the Estimated Use of Proceeds section may be presented in table form and contain a column for offering equity proceeds and a column for loan proceeds, assuming debt is being used. All the applicable costs and fees for the property acquisition will be disclosed in the table and presented as a total dollar amount, as a percentage of offering proceeds, and as a percentage of total capitalization.

> Cornerstone recommends that the appraisal value be greater than the acquisition price for the sponsor, and that the amount going to the direct acquisition be no lower than 90% of the proceeds from total capitalization.

The Use of Proceeds table is divided into two sections. The first section discloses fees and expenses associated with organizing the offering, including selling and marketing. These include organization and offering expenses, sales commissions, management and broker-dealer fees, marketing and due diligence allowances, and reserves for working capital.

The second section of the Use of Proceeds table includes acquisition and other costs directly associated with acquiring the property. These items include the actual down payment for the property purchase, loan-related costs, other closing costs, and trust-controlled reserves. These are considered as the proceeds that will "go into the ground" to directly acquire the subject DST property. As a rule, Cornerstone recommends that the amount going to the direct acquisition be no lower than 90 percent of the proceeds from total capitalization. These percentages may be quickly and easily compared between DSTs by comparing the percentage of proceeds used for acquisition of the property vs. the percentage of equity used for offering and commission expenses, assuming comparable leverage.

In contrast with most standard single-ownership real estate fees, which are typically expressed as a percentage of the total price of the property, the DST PPM expresses fees and expenses as a percentage of invested equity proceeds. If approximately half of proceeds for the acquisition of the property come from a lender (i.e., 50 percent leverage), then the total offering and commission expenses should not be greater than approximately 10 percent of equity proceeds or approximately 5 percent of the total proceeds (equity and debt). To determine the true load, the equity and lender reserves should be backed out, as these reserves will ultimately go into the property to improve the property and hopefully drive up net operating income ("into the ground"); or if the reserves are not utilized, these reserves will ultimately be returned to the investors when the property is sold.

While 10 percent of equity proceeds may seem high, when translated to 5 percent as a percentage of total proceeds and compared to a standard single-ownership real estate purchase with typically a 3 percent to 6 percent real estate commission, closing costs, appraisals costs, and lender fees, then the DST fees and expenses seem competitive. It should also be noted that DST costs and expenses are underwritten into the total sales price and not paid by the investor directly. With a standard single-ownership real estate transaction, the investor would have to pay out of pocket for the appraisal and other costs, even if he did not ultimately decide to invest.

Appraisal

Typically, within the section of the PPM entitled "The Property" or the section entitled "The Project" will be a subsection under "Appraisal" or "Appraised Value." Here the investor can learn the date and the value that the property has been appraised for by a third-party, independent, qualified appraiser. The appraised value may then be compared to the acquisition price that the sponsor paid for the property and the total offering price that the DST investors are paying for the property. These numbers should be readily available in the Investment Summary in the appendix of the PPM.

As a rule, Cornerstone recommends that the appraisal value be greater than the acquisition price for the sponsor. An appraisal less than the sponsor acquisition price is a case for concern and should be mitigated by other factors to warrant a buy decision by the DST investor. An appraised value greater than the sponsor acquisition price and less than the net offering price will greatly help to burn off any load on the property from the various costs and fees associated with the offering. The net offering price is the total offering price less any equity and debt reserves. An appraisal greater than the net offering price is a very positive factor that would greatly support a buy decision by the DST investor absent other negative factors. Cornerstone prefers that sponsors earn their acquisition fee and other fees by buying the property well and then marking the property at or below market for the net offering price to the investors.

Please note that the property appraisal has a treasure of information on the subject property and is issued by an independent third-party licensed professional. The appraisal is a valuable source of information and should be reviewed as an integral part of any due diligence study.

Master Lease Structure

The PPM section entitled "Master Lease or Summary of the Master Lease" will have two key items of disclosure. The first is the master tenant capitalization, and the other is the master lease rent structure. As we discussed in chapter 3, the master tenant is a special purpose entity in the form of a limited liability company (LLC). Thus, a newly registered entity will be guaranteeing the lease payments under the master lease agreement. Most DST sponsors will capitalize the master tenants with a demand note in addition to the reserves that are put into place at the capitalization of the DST. Most demand notes are between $250,000 and $500,000 and would be payable by the sponsor to the master lessee in case tenant rents and reserves were insufficient to meet obligations for master tenant rent payments, tenant improvements, leasing commissions, and other expenses.

In past cases, the demand note capitalization has worked well and has been readily funded by the sponsor. However, if the sponsor has issued multiple demand notes for other sponsored DST offerings, and in the event of an economic or market downturn, the sponsor may be insolvent or unwilling to fund all its outstanding demand notes. This risk should also be highlighted in the Risk Factors section of the PPM. Accordingly, Cornerstone prefers to see a cash capitalization of the master lease in lieu of, or in addition to, a demand note capitalization.

> Cornerstone believes that any rent growth assumptions greater than 3% per annum may warrant further review.

The second key disclosure under the "Master Lease Structure" section of the PPM is the master lease rent structure. As discussed in chapter 3, the master lease may have three possible rent payment structures. The structure used by the sponsor for the DST master lease will be described in this section of the PPM, including the base rent, additional rent (bonus rent), and possible supplemental rent structures. With respect to the underwriting of the rental revenue underpinning the master lease rent payments, the investor should also review the assumptions for occupancy and rent growth. These assumptions may be found in the assumptions section of the PPM or on the financial projection statements in the PPM appendix. Cornerstone believes that any rent growth assumptions greater than 3 percent per annum may warrant further investigation. In addition, a fair and conservative vacancy rate should be assumed for multitenant properties. The investor should check that the sponsor is not using either aggressive rent growth assumptions or vacancy factors to engineer an unachievable cash flow projection.

Compensation and Fees

In addition to the acquisition costs and fees in the Estimated Use of Proceeds, the investor should also review disclosures in the Compensation and Fees section of the PPM. Here the investor may determine the amount of compensation paid to the sponsor and its affiliates during the operating period, such as the property management and asset management fee, and any liquidation period fees, such as the disposition fee. Cornerstone recommends that any management fee greater than 3 percent, and any disposition fee greater than 4 percent, warrant further investigation. A 3 percent property management fee based on monthly gross income from the property is within norms for the property management industry. The 4 percent disposition fee should be subject to a return of capital to the investors. This fee should also be shared with the procuring real estate broker for the sale of the property.

Risks

The investor should review the "Risk Factor" section of the PPM. Here all known risks are disclosed, including DST structure risks, real estate risks, master tenant risks, master lease risks, property risks, financing risks, operation of the property risks, offering risks, and tax risks.

The Trust Manager

The PPM will have a section on the trust manager and its background. The names of all the principals and officers of the sponsor will be disclosed, with a short resume for each person. Most importantly, any disclosable items, such as civil or criminal convictions and bad actor or fraud disclosures from FINRA, will be reported here, if any.

Prior Performance of Sponsor

Some of the most valuable information the PPM may disclose is information on the track record of the sponsor. In this section of the PPM, the investor may gain insight into how well the sponsor has performed with past DST and other syndicated real estate offerings. The information on past performance must be disclosed in the PPM per securities law as a material matter. The sponsors may disclose their past performance data in either paragraph or table form, or both. The table form is often most helpful, as it allows for an easy comparison between the PPM projected distributions (cash flow) and the actual cash distributions.

The information disclosed on the currently operating programs should present a full picture of the performance of the property and the sponsor. If the sponsor has experience with past offerings of multiple asset classes, then for comparison purposes it is best if the information is categorized by asset class or type, such as multifamily, retail, industrial, and so forth. The data on current programs should include the name of the program, the location of the property, asset class, equity raised, purchase price, years held, prior year(s) PPM projected distributions (as a percentage of equity raised), and prior year actual annualized distributions.

In addition to the performance data on current programs or properties, the performance data for properties that have gone full-cycle and have been sold should also be disclosed in this section of the PPM. Information on full-cycle properties should include the name of the program, the location of the property, asset class, date acquired, date sold, purchase price, and sales price. The property annual average rate of return and total return should also be disclosed, to present the returns including cash flow as well as appreciation.

The saying that no one is perfect may also be applied to DST sponsors. Any properties that have underperformed or produced adverse returns, such as a loss on invested capital, should be explained in detail. Often, the story of the sponsor's performance can best be seen in how well they handle unforeseen adverse situations.

Cash Flow Projections

Within a section of the PPM typically entitled Assumptions, the PPM reader should find a table disclosing all the assumptions and the detailed projection calculations for the DST cash flow over the intended hold period. These assumptions may be compared to the detailed financial statement for the property, reporting gross revenue, administrative, managerial, and operating expenses, and net operating income. These historical financial statements are usually included in the appendices of the PPM, for the past twelve months (the trailing twelve) of performance at a minimum. Some PPMs will contain financials for the past several years.

The Forecasted Statement of Cash Flows will begin at the top with the property's effective gross rent less expenses to provide the effective net operating income (NOI). The effective NOI is essentially the available cash that will cascade through the master lease payment structure as reported on this statement. Accordingly, the statement starts with the amount projected for base rent and debt service. Next, the statement discloses the amount over the additional rent breakpoint available for the asset management fee, the trust reserves, and to project the additional rent cash return. Finally, the statement will project the supplemental rent, and show the split of this amount between the master tenant (typically 10 percent) and the supplemental rent cash flow to the investors (typically 90 percent). Remember that the master tenant must have some income from the master lease activity to be a valid economic agreement. The total of the base rent, additional rent, and supplemental rent should equal the total projection of annual cash flow to the DST investors.

Different DST sponsors use different rent structures for their master lease. Therefore, the reports will differ per the master lease structure employed. However, the basic concept is the same. For example, the statement for a prolific and well-known DST sponsor will begin with projections for base rent, then go to supplemental rent, with no additional rent. The projected cash flow to the DST investor is the total of the projected base rent and supplemental rent. The remaining income is used to service the debt, reserves, and to pay the master tenant.

A Free Recourse to the Investor

The PPM may be requested for any DST offering free of charge and should be requested through the investor's registered representative. The sponsor will usually overnight a full PPM package, including the actual PPM document, executive summaries, sponsor backstory articles, and subscription forms, to the perspective investor at no additional expense and without commitment. Some sponsors can provide these documents electronically by email or internet hyperlink. Cornerstone recommends that a prospective investor order a PPM from a current DST offering well in advance of an exchange, in order to become familiar with the document and to set expectations as to what types of properties, cash flows ranges, and leverage levels to anticipate for the time when the investor is executing an exchange.

A well-designed PPM is a logical, concise, and informative document that embodies and conveys the findings of various levels of due diligence. The sponsors and attorneys that draft the PPM often have years of experience in composing PPMs over many real estate offerings and have perfected their PPM presentation. Accordingly, the DST PPM should be considered a valuable resource to the investor and an advantage of investing in real estate through a DST private placement offering. Multiple DST investments within and without an asset class may be efficiently and effectively compared and contrasted given the similar structure of DST PPMs. The PPM for a DST in which the investor has invested should be kept for reference throughout the hold period of the investment and beyond.

Chapter 17

Debt Structures

The use of leverage in real estate may provide strategic financial and tax advantages. Similar to acquiring stock using a margin account, the use of leverage allows the investor to effectively multiply his or her purchasing power to acquire real estate with a value of two to three times the investor's cash equity investment. The DST annual master lease payments are often presented as a percentage of equity invested, to provide the investor with a cash-on-cash return expectation. However, the investor is acquiring a fractional ownership in the entire property, including the equity and debt portion of the capital stack. Accordingly, leverage allows the investor to benefit from potential appreciation growth on the full value of the real estate. In an appreciating economic environment, this can multiply the overall internal rate of return (IRR) or annual average return as a percentage of equity invested.

On the other hand, leverage can be just as effectively a disadvantage in a down market. Leverage can serve to multiply any decrease in property value as a percentage of invested equity. Furthermore, in the event of reduced cash flow there is a danger of not having sufficient cash to service the monthly payments on the debt. Accordingly, as disclosed in every PPM, the use of leverage presents the possibility in real estate (including the DST investment) of the investor losing his or her entire investment—the worst case, nightmare scenario for any investor.

JOHN HARVEY CPA, MBT, TRAWNEGAN GALL, AND DAVID KANGAS

Learning from History

In the run-up to the Great Recession, real estate investors, including TIC sponsors, were using increasingly higher leverage. Investors and lenders assumed that continued CAP rate compression (increasing values) would ultimately reduce the loan-to-value percentages and provide for greater returns. Loan-to-value (LTV) percentages were often in the 70 percent to 80 percent range in many cases. When conservative annual rent increase projections of less than 3 percent ultimately turned out to be negative, and increased vacancies stressed many TIC properties (as well as typical single ownership property), these factors stressed the cash flow to the point that the managers could not make debt service. As the recession dragged on, reserves were eventually exhausted, and cash calls for additional capital were made to TIC investors. If funds from investor cash calls were insufficient to service the debt, the lender foreclosed on the property. Thus, many TIC properties that had utilized higher leverage were forced into foreclosure—as well as many non-TIC conventional ownership real estate properties.

It should be noted that the foreclosure risk was not only a factor of higher LTV and aggressive underwriting, but also a factor of asset class and its associated lease terms. Most affected by the debt crisis were hospitality assets. With the toxic combination of daily lease term and lower business travel demand due to unemployment in double digits, average daily occupancy plummeted, and more hospitality TIC investments were lost to foreclosure than any other asset class. With lease terms as short as three to five years, the next most adversely affected asset classes were multitenant retail and office properties, due to factors such as tenant bankruptcy and increased vacancy. Multifamily assets fared more favorably, depending on location and the amount of leverage. In most cases, multifamily with annual leases only suffered cash flow reduction due to stagnating or decreasing rental rates, while other multifamily performed well because of the high rate of single family home foreclosures and increased demand for rental units.

Investors in the asset class of single-tenant NNN retail with major credit tenants and long-term leases did not seem to feel the effects of the recession. These investors continued to enjoy monthly cash flow with no reduction, and in many cases with contractual rent escalations that came into effect during the recession years. While the tenant's balance sheet may have had a temporary decrease in value, being some of the best companies in America, they survived the recession and soon recovered as economic growth benefited from the stimulus of fiscal policies.

Structured for the Lender

Following the 2008 financial crisis, the DST structured to qualify for Section 1031 tax deferral also meets the requirements of prospective lenders, as it has structural provisions that permit the lender to securitize the loan on a secondary market (i.e., CMBS lenders and B piece buyers). The DST structural provisions that are particularly advantageous for the lender are

- single entity on title in the form to the trust (opposed to numerus individuals);
- a special-purpose entity;
- bankruptcy-remote;
- lower loan-to-value levels; and
- a very passive holder of real estate (the trustees will have minimum powers and the beneficiaries will have no powers with respect to the mortgaged property).

The Promissory Note

The loan is evidenced by a promissory note. The loan is secured by the properties, and the trust will be liable for repayment of the loan as owner of the properties. Upon the unlikely event of default under the loan with respect to any property, the lender will have the right to foreclose on all the properties. If this were to occur, the beneficial owners would be likely to lose their entire investment in the trust. The loan documents provide that under certain circumstances, the removal or resignation of the master tenant or transfer of the interests without the lender's prior written consent will constitute an event of default under the loan.

Loan Terms

Commercial mortgages are typically amortized over thirty years, but unlike a single-family mortgage, the principle is due and payable in a balloon payment after the tenth year. This is also true for DST debt. Interest rates are typically fixed and tend to be at a slight discount compared with similar loans to an individual investor, due to the credit worthiness of the sponsor trustee. With interest rates still at historic lows, any variable interest rate financing should be looked at with extreme caution and is virtually nonexistent in today's DST marketplace.

Interest-Only and Financial Engineering

DST debt amortization varies from offering to offering. On the more conservative side of the spectrum, some DSTs structure their debt with amortization beginning from day one, while other more aggressive DSTs may structure their debt as interest only for the entire ten-year term. In the middle are DSTs with debt that begins to amortize in year three, five, or even seven. If rents do not escalate or there are no other cost savings, the beginning of amortization may shift more net operating income to principal amortization and reduce cash flows.

The question of whether to fully amortize or use interest-only financing may be a more philosophical one. Some investors prefer to have more of the yield from a property in their pockets as cash flow. This is especially true if the debt is at a lower, more conservative loan to value ratio. In this case, the loan may be said to be preamortized, as while the debt level remains constant, it will still be at the same level as a higher leverage loan balance that amortized down to the same level by the end of the hold period. Other investors prefer to pay down the mortgage and realize the cash return once the property is sold with a lower debt level. In this case, even if the property value declines, there is still a possibility for the return of the amount of capital originally invested.

As with a stock purchased on a margin account, debt leverages the value of property that a dollar of equity can buy and provides an arbitrage to turbo-charge cash flow as a percentage of equity invested. Accordingly, the prudent investor should consider to what extent the sponsor is using leverage to financially engineer the desired cash flow. To compare apples to apples, an investor should compare total yield to total yield, with the yield being both the cash flow and the amortization on the loan. It should also be noted that debt amortization may create "phantom income" to the investor. Phantom income is the yield allocated to principal debt payments, so the investor does not receive the cash but must realize the income for tax purposes. Depreciation and other expenses may help to shelter a portion of phantom income, but the effect on after-tax cash return can be material.

Nonrecourse Financing

Generally, commercial loans are nonrecourse to the investors, and no personal guarantee is required of the investor. However, there are exceptions with traditional real estate due to the creditworthiness of the tenant or the investor and the amount of leverage. With DST properties, there is never the requirement for the investor to guarantee his or her portion of the debt. While loan is assigned to each specific investor according to his or her percentage interest in the trust, no personal guarantee is required; the lender's only recourse is against the DST property itself—effectively sheltering the investor's personal assets from exposure to the debt risk should the proceeds from a foreclosure sale not fully satisfy the loan principal.

An advantage to the DST is that the lender does not qualify the investors. This is because the individual is not on title and the DST trustee signs the carve-out provisions. This fact also allows for ease of transference in case of inheritance, divorce, or secondary market sales. This was not the case with the TIC, where all investors are subject to lender approval.

Recourse Carve-Outs

In nearly all nonrecourse commercial loans, the lender requires the investor(s) to sign carve-out provisions within the debt instrument. These carve-outs are to make the investor(s) liable both jointly and severally in case they perform any so-called "bad boy acts" such as fraud or other actions that directly damage the property or its financial capacity. This is also true for TIC investments; however, a significant advantage to the DST structure is that the trustee to the DST and not the DST member investors sign the carve-out provisions. This makes the DST loan an absolutely nonrecourse loan to the DST investor, with no possibility for the lender to access the investors' other assets.

> Zero cash flow, highly leveraged DSTs are used by Cornerstone within a portfolio of multiple DSTs to effectively blend the LTVs of multiple replacement 1031 DST properties to match the relinquished debt and avoid mortgage boot.

High Leverage Zero Cash Flow Offerings

For tax planning purposes, at any given time, there may be on the market a DST with very high leverage. These DSTs with as high as 84 percent loan-to-value are specially designed to assist DST investors who need to replace higher leverage from their relinquished properties in order to avoid mortgage boot on their 1031 exchange. These DST offerings are called "zeros," as the lender will sweep all the net cash flow in order to hyper-amortize the debt. While there is no monthly cash flow to the investors, these DSTs have typically produced between 12 percent and 14 percent annual yield due to the amortization. In most cases, these zeros are used by Cornerstone within a portfolio of multiple DSTs to effectively blend the LTVs of multiple replacement 1031 DST properties to match the relinquished debt and avoid mortgage boot.

The tenant on the zero-cash-flow, highly leveraged DST will of necessity be of higher credit worthiness to satisfy the lender's underwriting standards. Typical tenants are pharmacies such as Walgreens and CVS. The return on the zero DST is recognized once the property or properties are sold. These investments may be considered a type of high yield savings account that effectively help to de-lever part of the portfolio in the short-run by investing in DSTs with leverage below the relinquished debt level and the entire portfolio in the long-run due to hyper-amortization of the DSTs with higher debt. Cornerstone believes that deleverage is always a good thing!

Mezzanine Loans for Closing

Lastly, the sponsor may use mezzanine financing to close on a property in advance of the equity raise. These short-term loans are at higher interest rates and are paid off as equity is raised and closed into the DST. Sponsors who use mezzanine debt to close will have a higher carrying cost and less profit from the acquisition if it takes longer to raise the equity from DST investors. Most DSTs have a shelf life of approximately thirty to sixty days, so the interest costs are usually a reasonable expense for the sponsor. The sponsor and not the investors would realize the loss from longer-term mezzanine interest costs, and in the unlikely event that not all the equity is raised, the sponsor will in most cases retire the mezzanine debt with their own funds and be a coinvestor with the other DST investors.

The byproduct is advantageous to the DST investors, as the sponsor will have more skin in the game, and their interests more closely parallel the investors'.

Pre- and Post-Exchange Debt Financing

An exchange investor should note that incurring debt on a relinquished property prior to an exchange to pull cash out tax free may be deemed by the IRS as taxable boot based on the step transaction rule. While there is little case law, debt incurred after the exchange on the replacement property should not be considered taxable boot. Per Revenue Ruling 2004-86, a DST is a fixed income trust, is immutable, and cannot secure financing subsequent to the initial acquisition debt financing.

Debt in Moderation

The right amount of debt can maximize the return potential of a real estate investment. While 1031 exchange mortgage boot requirements may demand a certain level of debt to avoid taxation, care should be taken to ensure that the investor does not incur more debt than is prudent given the investor's overall financial situation and risk tolerance. When higher levels of debt are necessary, loan amortization should be utilized to reduce the leverage over time. Furthermore, it should be noted that, while the debt on a DST may be nonrecourse, if the investor eventually exchanges out of a DST into a single-ownership property, the replacement debt on that property may be recourse to the investor. As a rule of thumb, 50 percent loan-to-value is a prudent standard and is in line with most current DST loans-to-value. All things in moderation!

Chapter 18

Diversification Strategies

To date, modern portfolio theory, or MPT, has represented the investment industry's best attempt toward maximizing return and minimizing losses. MPT is a mathematical formulation of the concept of diversification in investing, with the aim of selecting a collection of investment assets that has collectively lower risk than any individual asset.

MPT assumes that investors are risk averse, meaning that given two portfolios that offer the same expected return, investors will prefer the less risky one. Thus, an investor will take on increased risk only if compensated by higher expected returns. Conversely, an investor who desires higher expected returns must accept more risk. The exact trade-off will be the same for all investors, but different investors will evaluate the trade-off differently based on individual risk aversion characteristics. The implication is that an investor will not invest in a portfolio if a second portfolio exists with a more favorable risk-expected return profile.

An investor can reduce portfolio risk simply by holding combinations of instruments that are not perfectly positively correlated. In other words, investors can reduce their exposure to individual asset risk by holding a diversified portfolio of assets. Diversification may allow for the same portfolio expected return with reduced risk.

While the principles of MPT are applicable to DST investments, it should be noted that DSTs are not efficiently priced, and therefore the modeling may break down. However, there are some correlations between risk and return for most DSTs. DSTs with higher risks do in many cases have a higher return, and those DSTs with lower risk in most cases will have a lower return. These may include the following:

- DSTs with higher leverage and higher foreclosure risk do typically have a higher return.
- All-cash deals have no foreclosure risk and typically lower returns.
- DST properties with lower credit rated tenants and higher risk of vacancy generally have higher returns.
- DST properties with higher credit rated tenants and lower risk of vacancy generally have lower returns.
- DST properties in more tertiary markets and higher risk of retenanting have higher returns due to higher CAP rates.
- DST properties in more infill locations and lower risk of retenanting have lower returns due to lower CAP rates.

DST Diversification Strategies

With a $100,000 minimum investment requirement for investors in a like-kind exchange and a $25,000 minimum investment for nonexchange investors, DSTs are an excellent investment vehicle to obtain diversification within a real estate portfolio. As presented and demonstrated in chapter 2, Section 1031 exchange investors have been able to diversify from a concentration risk in a single investment property into multiple DSTs with different asset classes, offering sponsors, and geographic locations. These investors have used various diversification strategies to reduce risk.

Asset Class Diversification

The four main asset classes are multifamily, retail, office, and industrial. Presented below is a graph of these four main asset classes and their average CAP rate over time. In addition to what has been called "the four food groups" of asset classes, there are other real estate asset classes that have a business component. These include hotels, senior care, and parking lot properties. It should be noted that the investor is only exchanging into the actual, tangible, immovable real estate, as the business component does not qualify for 1031 exchange. The business component is operated by an unrelated tenant or operating company lease. However, these assets typically do have a higher cash flow than the four classic asset classes.

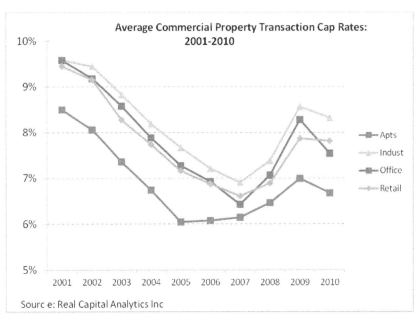

Source: Real Capital Analytics Inc

Asset class diversification is an essential strategy to reduce risk associated with industry exposure. With an exchange equity of $200,000 or greater, an investor may diversity into two or more asset classes with as little as $100,000 in each asset class. DST asset classes include multifamily, retail, office, industrial, hospitality, medical office, student housing, self-storage, senior care, and even oil and gas. In these uncertain times, a popular strategy has been for investors to diversify half an exchange portfolio into single asset retail with credit tenants and long-term leases, and the other half of the portfolio into multifamily apartment complexes. This strategy allows for flat but stable cash flow in case of recession, due to long-term lease contracts from major corporations, yet also provides for cash flow escalation from annual rent increases customary with residential units. The relatively flat valuation of retail is countered by the application potential of residential due to NOI growth.

A trend in the industry has been to combine multiple assets into a single DST. We have seen two or three noncontiguous class A 350-unit multifamily complexes placed into a single DST for as many as 1,000 rental units in a single DST. On the retail side, one sponsor is packaging as many as 20 pharmacy stores in a single DST, and another sponsor is packaging as many as twenty retail assets with various institutional grade credit tenants in a single DST. Accordingly, with as little as $100,000 equity investment, the investor could diversify into as many as twenty geographic locations and credit tenants. With a $200,000 investment, the investor could diversify over forty geographic locations and credit tenants. Hypothetically, for a $200,000 investment, an investor could diversify into twenty single-tenant retail stores and one thousand class A residential units, thereby diversifying from a single tenant who may be struggling to make rent to 1,020 renters including some of the best companies in America.

Sponsor Diversification

There are many DST sponsors active in the DST industry as outlined in chapter 8. These sponsors differ in size, specializations, and experience. Many investors favor the larger, more institutionalized sponsors, while others prefer a more personalized and more agile sponsor. Cornerstone highly recommends diversifying over multiple sponsors to protect against litigation or other systemic threats to the financial stability of a sponsor. Sponsor diversification typically goes hand-in-hand with both geographic and asset class diversification, as different sponsors will have DSTs of different asset classes and locations at the time the investor is executing an exchange or direct investment.

Geographic Diversification

Diversification over different geographic locations can reduce risk exposure to local economies and markets. Economic and real estate markets can vary from state to state and region to region. For example, Texas, with its energy industry, fared better than most other states during the recession. Also, some states, like California and New York, experienced significant real estate price bubbles and significant property devaluation during the recession, while other less populated states experienced more stable and gradual real estate value escalations with less volatility. Geographic diversification can also reduce risk exposure to local disasters and acts of nature such as hurricanes and earthquakes. Still, some investors prefer to diversify into nonincome tax states such as Texas, Florida, Nevada, Alaska, South Dakota, Washington, Wyoming, New Hampshire, and Tennessee.

Build a Personal Portfolio

The possibilities for diversification with DSTs are only limited by the investor's financial objectives and imagination. Multiple DSTs from one or more exchanges can be combined into a well-diversified personal portfolio of institutional grade properties spanning multiple sponsors, locations, and asset types. Whether you are looking for cash flow free from concentration risk to fund retirement or building up a personal real estate portfolio of institutional properties over your career to supplement professional income, a well-diversified DST portfolio may be the solution. Below is an industry graphic representing the diversity of equity investment into DST properties in 2020.

2020 DST Asset Equity Placement

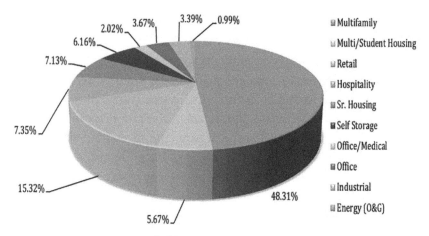

Data provided by Mountain Dell Consulting

Multifamily Properties

The most popular type of investment property for small investors tends to be multifamily apartment properties. We all have some familiarity with housing because everybody has to live somewhere. Many have lived in an apartment at some point in their life, therefore being familiar with residential-income properties. Real estate investors may often get their start by converting a current residence into a rental, rather than selling, when purchasing a new residence. They thereby gain experience with the ownership of residential-income property. Such an investor may, by trading up, end up with multiple small residential-income properties; eventually, such an owner might consolidate several smaller properties into a multiunit apartment building. These types of properties, over time, have generated strong appreciation and relatively little downside.

Apartment properties also tend to be very attractive to the financial sector. Because they generally show lower rates of default relative to other types of property, they tend to attract generous lending programs. Such financing can dramatically increase an investor's purchasing power, as well as significantly increase the cash flow when the property is refinanced.

Apartment properties do, however, have potential downside. First of all, they are management-intensive. Any owner of residential units has probably received a call in the night about an electrical or plumbing issue, or a tenant locked out of their unit. Residential income properties tend to be rented to individuals with fewer financial resources, many living paycheck to paycheck. Evicting a tenant can be time consuming and expensive in a jurisdiction with strong tenant-rights laws or regulations. More desirable tenants with a stronger financial background may leave the property as soon as they are able to purchase a residence. Nationally, apartment rental markets were heavily impacted by renters purchasing a new home during the recent period of historically low interest rates.

Apartment properties may provide less cash flow than other property types. Apartments can trade at capitalization rates (cap rates) typically one to two hundred basis points below other forms of real estate, due to a high degree of investor acceptance (and therefore demand) combined with increasingly restrictive development requirements and strong historic appreciation.

Retail NNN-Leased Properties

NNN-leased properties, in contrast to apartment properties, tend to be leased on a long-term basis to highly creditworthy tenants, who will then be fully responsible for management and operating expenses. In a true NNN-leased property, the tenant will be responsible for utilities, maintenance, management, insurance, property taxes, etc. In a bondable lease, the tenant is also responsible for the structural aspects, including damage or destruction of the property itself. In leases that are not NNN, the landlord is responsible for some or all the property operating expenses.

NNN-leased properties are intended to be a passive asset. For the tenant with an 'investment grade' credit rating, the lender evaluates the lease more than the underlying real estate to establish debt limits and interest rates. This may result in significantly greater loan proceeds and lower interest rates compared to similar properties leased to a noninvestment-grade tenant. This can increase the purchasing power and/or cash flow available to the investment-grade investor. NNN-leased properties can therefore provide the owner with a long-term, passive investment with steady, predicable cash flow.

NNN-leased properties, like apartments, can also have their downside. The lease tends to be flat (no increases) for the entire term, the typical tradeoff for a long-term lease to a credit-worthy tenant, or at most, minimal rent increases over the term. The investor will thus not enjoy an increase in cash flow over the hold period and will not receive inflation protection through increasing rents. NNN-leased properties are, in this aspect, quite similar to bonds, as if it were a bond with ownership of the underlying real estate.

A related potential downside is that the pricing for NNN-leased properties also tends to act like a bond. Cap rates for NNN-leased investments tend to go up with a rise in interest rates, thereby reducing prices. Conversely, cap rates also tend to go down with interest rates, increasing prices. NNN-leased properties show a much more direct correlation to interest rates compared to other property types from an income perspective because of their similarity to bonds.

Office Properties

Over the past decade, the office building as a DST asset class has included the downtown high-rise skyscraper, medical office buildings, and single-tenant headquarters for large corporations. Leases are typically five to seven years, which is significantly shorter than retail but allows for more potential rent escalations as well as greater vacancy risk. The vacancy risk was particularly acute during the Great Recession, which caused rents and occupancy levels to plummet in the office sector. Conservative due diligence would look for mission-critical assets for larger multinational and publicly traded companies, as well as significant reserves for tenant improvements and debt service.

Senior Care and Healthcare Properties

With the baby boomers reaching their retirement years, the senior care asset class has increased in popularity with DST investors to the extent that some sponsors are specializing in this single asset class. Although historic returns do not predict future performance, many of our clients who invested in senior care DSTs and TICs over the past decade have done extremely well, with double digit cash flows and total annualized returns in the double digits on properties that have gone full cycle. Within senior care are facilities that offer services that range from Alzheimer's care to assisted living. While DST properties are not efficiently priced for risk and return, the properties that have a business component such as senior care or hospitality tend to offer higher cash flow. Please note that the 1031 exchange investor is not acquiring the business but the real property that is in turn leased to the business operator. It should also be noted that the complexities of a senior care business have challenged some of these operators, and a few of the TIC senior care properties have failed with investors losing a significant portion if not all their investment. Conservative due diligence would require operators that have a long and successful operating history, as well as facilities that depend less on government subsidy from Medicare and Medicaid.

Industrial Properties

Industrial complexes and warehouses are less glamorous but can be cash cows if the fundamentals are right. Included in this class are self-storage and parking lots.

Hospitality Properties

Hotels are often considered the most glamorous, and past DST offerings have included national operators such as Marriott and Hilton. With lease terms of not years but a single day, rents per unit can be increased almost instantaneously due to increase RevPAR (revenue per available room), and cash flows are typically higher than other asset classes to compensate for the downside vacancy risk which can be immediate and substantial. During the Great Recession, hospitality assets were especially hard hit, with unemployment above 10 percent and business travel virtually nonexistent. In the past, these assets were highly leveraged, and over the industry many had zero cash flow for an extended period; several TIC properties were lost to foreclosure. However, those that survived were the first to recover, and we have seen record returns for hotel TICs that have come full cycle and sold in recent years. Due diligence should research the demand generators in the area of the hotel, including major corporations, airports, and universities.

DST Diversification Plan

Cornerstone has a software tool that will provide a full DST diversification plan for the investor. The plan will use the investor's 1031 exchange equity and debt amounts to present any number of current DST offerings into a single portfolio. The tool will provide cash flow and yield (with amortization) projections over an eight-year hold period. The tool will blend the LTVs of the selected DSTs to determine the overall leverage and calculate cash boot, mortgage boot, and additional tax basis (if any). Contact a Cornerstone registered representative to explore the possibilities for DST diversification that are available for your exchange.

> Cornerstone has a tool that will provide a full DST diversification plan for the investor.

Chapter 19

Depreciation and Tax Matters

In addition to the incredible benefit of deferring capital gain tax and depreciation recapture by utilizing a Section 1031 exchange, real estate, including DST properties, provides for the shelter of rental income from federal and state taxes up to the annual tax depreciation deduction. This is because depreciation is essentially not a cash expense but an accounting concept and tax deduction. The property may be and hopefully will be actually appreciating. However, under the matching principle of GAAP accounting and as permitted under the Internal Revenue Code, the cost basis of the property may be allocated and deducted on an annual basis over a recovery period to net against the rental income it is producing each year. This allows income and costs to be matched in the reporting year and allows for a true reporting on annual net income or taxable income. The 2017 Tax Cuts and Jobs Act retained and did not change the recovery periods for commercial real estate. Under IRC section 168, depreciation for tax purposes continues to allow for a straight-line allocation (also known as MACRS) of the cost of the real property and improvements over a recovery period of twenty-seven-and-a-half-years for residential and thirty-nine years for nonresidential commercial properties.

Both the recovery period and the depreciation method are the same.

If either the recovery period or the depreciation method for the replacement property is the same as for the relinquished property, then the period or the method that is the same is used to depreciate the replacement property (Treas. Reg. § 1.168(i)-6(c)(3)(iii)). Thus, the replacement MACRS property is depreciated over the remaining recovery period, and by using the same straight-line depreciation method, of the relinquished MACRS property. In practice, this is nearly always the case when residential property is exchange for other residential property using a twenty-seven-and-a-half-year recovery period, and when nonresidential commercial property is exchanged for other nonresidential commercial property using a thirty-nine-year recovery period.

Recovery period or depreciation method of the properties is not the same.

Longer recovery period. If the replacement property's recovery period is longer than that of the relinquished property, depreciation for the exchanged basis beginning in the year of replacement is determined as though the replacement property had originally been placed in service by the acquiring taxpayer in the same taxable year the relinquished property was placed in service, but using the longer recovery period. Thus, the depreciable exchanged basis is depreciated over the remaining recovery period of the replacement MACRS property. This is the case when residential property is exchange for nonresidential commercial property where the formerly used twenty-seven-and-a-half-year recovery period is replaced with a thirty-nine-year recovery period. However, the new thirty-nine-year recovery period begins from the same date on which the original residential property was placed into service.

Shorter recovery period. If the replacement property's recovery period is shorter than that of the relinquished property, depreciation of the replacement property is based on the longer period of the relinquished property. Thus, the depreciable exchanged basis is depreciated over the remaining recovery period of the relinquished MACRS property. This is the case when nonresidential commercial property is exchange for residential property where the formerly used thirty-nine-year recovery period is continued to be used (not the twenty-seven-and-a-half-year recovery period).

Please note that depreciation should not be taken for the period of time that the exchange is with the qualified intermediary (assuming the replacement property is acquired after the relinquished property is sold). A convention such as a midmonth or mid-year convention may be used for the date that the replacement property is placed into service.

<u>Change in method.</u> In the event that the depreciation method of the replacement property is less accelerated than that of the relinquished property (such as with the use of the 200 percent or 150 percent declining balance methods), depreciation for the exchanged basis is determined as though the replacement property had originally been placed in service by the acquiring taxpayer at the same time the relinquished property was placed in service, but using the less accelerated method. On the other hand, if the replacement property's method is more accelerated than that of the relinquished property at the time of disposition, depreciation for the replacement property is determined using the same method as the relinquished property, that is, the less accelerated method.

Depreciable and nondepreciable (land) property

If land or other nondepreciable property is acquired in a like-kind exchange for, or as a result of an involuntary conversion (section 1033) of, depreciable property, the land or other nondepreciable property is not depreciated. If both depreciable property (MACRS) and nondepreciable property are acquired in a like-kind exchange for, or as part of an involuntary conversion of, MACRS property, the basis allocated to the nondepreciable property is not depreciated and the basis allocated to the replacement MACRS property is depreciated.

If MACRS property is acquired, or if both MACRS and nondepreciable property are acquired, in a like-kind exchange for, or as part of an involuntary conversion of, land or other nondepreciable property, the basis in the replacement MACRS property that is attributable to the relinquished nondepreciable property is treated as though the replacement MACRS property is placed in service by the acquiring taxpayer in the year of replacement. Thus, the depreciation allowances for the replacement MACRS property are determined by using the applicable recovery period, depreciation method, and convention prescribed under section 168 (as described above) for the replacement MACRS property at the time of replacement.

Depreciation Recapture

Capital gain tax rates are currently at historical lows, but tax rules require investors to recapture at a higher tax rate the portion of the gain on the sale that relates to allowable depreciation over the period the asset was held. The current tax rate for depreciation recapture is 25 percent. The higher tax rate approximates the taxpayer's tax rate for the ordinary income against which he or she claimed the depreciation deduction over the past years. The mandatory flat 25 percent tax rate for depreciation recapture simplifies compliance as the taxpayer does not have to research all the numerous and varied top marginal tax rates that applied to his or her ordinary income over the hold period. Furthermore, the tax rules require the recapture for both allowed and allowable depreciation. So even if the taxpayer did not claim the depreciation deduction in past years or only claimed a lesser portion the amount of depreciation that the tax law allowed, he or she must recapture the fully allowable depreciation at the 25 percent tax rate.

To add insult to injury, the depreciation recapture must first be applied to any part of the recognized taxable gain. In other words, if a taxpayer takes any cash out of an exchange or assumes less debt on the replacement property or recognizes any other type of taxable boot from a Section 1031 exchange, then that boot will be taxed at the 25 percent rate until all the allowable depreciation has been fully recaptured. Only after the allowable depreciation is fully recaptured will the lower long-term capital gain rates apply to the remainder of the gain. In many cases, this effectively means that all the cash taken out of an exchange will be taxed at 25 percent (not to mention the possible application of the Affordable Care Act tax at 3.8 percent and possible state and local taxes).

Fortunately, the tax code considers depreciation recapture as essentially a capital gain that is just taxed at an ordinary income level tax rate. Accordingly, depreciation recapture recognition may be fully deferred by employing a Section 1031 exchange. Needless to say, depreciation recapture is a significant factor in motivating an investor to participate in a like-kind exchange.

Property Placed in Service Between 1981 and 1986

A further complication is that the portion of the gain that is unrecaptured § 1250 gain depends, as shown below, on when the property was placed in service. For real estate placed in service after 1980 but before 1987, the treatment of gain on sale depends on whether the real estate is residential or nonresidential.

Residential Real Estate

If you depreciated residential pre-1987 realty using straight-line depreciation, the tax results if you sell it will be the same as for a sale of post-1987 property, as described above. But if (as was possible) you, at any time, used a declining balance method to depreciate the real estate, the gain on sale would be taxed as follows:

- Gain, to the extent of the depreciation claimed that exceeds what would have been allowable under straight-line depreciation, will be recaptured as ordinary income, and thus taxed at rates as high as 35 percent in 2003 and later years (ordinary income rates); the amount of excess depreciation subject to recapture may be less for certain low-income housing.

- Gain, to the extent of the depreciation that isn't recaptured as ordinary income, will be taxed at a rate of 25 percent.
- The balance of the gain will be taxed at a rate of 15 percent.

Nonresidential Real Estate

As is the case for residential pre-1987 realty, if you depreciated non-residential pre-1987 realty using just straight-line depreciation, the tax results if you sell it will be the same as for a sale of post-1986 property, as described above. But if, as was possible, you, at any time, used a declining-balance method to depreciate the realty, the gain on sale would be taxed as follows:

- Gain, to the extent of the full amount of depreciation allowable to the time of sale, would be recaptured as ordinary income, and thus taxed at ordinary income rates;
- The balance of the gain would be taxed at a rate of 15 percent.

Pre-1981 Property

The following rules apply if you sell real estate placed in service before 1981:

- The excess of depreciation claimed over straight-line depreciation is recaptured as ordinary income, and thus taxed at ordinary income rates. (The amount of excess depreciation subject to recapture may be less for certain residential real estate or for real estate acquired before 1970.)
- Gain, to the extent of the balance of depreciation allowable, is unrecaptured § 1250 gain, taxed at a rate of 25 percent.
- The balance of the gain, if any, would be taxed at a rate of 15 percent.

If you have further questions about the above rules, or would like to compute the potential tax that you face, be sure to contact your tax advisor.

Tax Season Issues

According to Regulation §1.1245-2(b), a taxpayer is generally required to report all gains or losses on the disposition of capital assets, including the transactions giving rise to capital gains or losses, in a separate computation on the tax return (Reg. §1.1202-1[a]). However, there is no statutory authority that requires the reporting of a full tax-deferred exchange. In any event, it may be wise planning to attach a schedule to report a problematic exchange to start the statute of limitations running on the issue.

> Conservative advisors such as Cornerstone will usually recommend that their client report the exchange even where no tax is generated, in order to start the clock running on the statute of limitations.

Schedule D and Form 4797

An exchange of like-kind property can be reported on Schedule D or on Form 4797, whichever applies. The instructions to Schedule D (Form 1040) state that all exchanges must be reported. The instructions apply to even fully tax-deferred exchanges. Thus, while again there is no statutory authority for this instruction, it does present a dilemma. On the one hand, those who are more aggressive in their tax compliance will probably continue to report as little as possible, based upon the reasoning that if your exchange is nontaxable, the IRS would not impose a penalty at a later date. On the other hand, conservative advisors such as Cornerstone will usually recommend that their client report the exchange even where no tax is generated, in order to start the clock running on the statute of limitations. If the taxpayer does choose to report the exchange, it should be done as simply as possible. A short "memo box" recapitulation on a single sheet of paper would be ideal. This recapitulation could then be attached to Schedule D or Form 4797.

Form 8824

If a taxpayer has a like-kind exchange, Form 8824 Like-Kind Exchanges must be filed in addition to Schedule D or Form 4797. Form 8824 requests specific information about the exchange including

- description of the properties;
- date of disposition of taxpayer's property;
- dates of identification and acquisition of the replacement property;
- certain related party information. The balance of the form concerns computations of realized gain or loss, recognized gain, basis of property received, and deferred gain.

Chapter 20

Investment Risk Factors

As with any investment, there are risks inherent in the investment. This is true if you are investing in direct ownership real estate, stocks, bonds, mutual funds, or alternative real estate investments such as a DST property. To provide our readers with a fair and balanced presentation, we have devoted this entire chapter to presenting these DST risks. Remember that a DST risk is not a DST disadvantage. The disadvantages including illiquidity, lack of control, and the inability to raise capital, have been discussed in earlier chapters on the DST and its structure.

While assessing risks, two additional points should be noted. Firstly, many of the risks disclosed in the PPM document are standard disclosures for a direct participation program (DPP). For example, a DST with an all-cash, no debt, triple net Walgreens store as the only asset will have some of the very same disclosures as a PPM for an oil and gas wildcat drilling offering. The two offerings could not be more divergent as far as investment risk, but both would share many of the same DPP disclosures.

Secondly, the reader should be aware that the sponsor's counsel will disclose every conceivable risk, no matter how remote. It is often thought that the PPM is designed to make the investor drop the book and run the other direction. However, we believe that an investor equipped with these insights will be able to discern each risk disclosure on its own and in view of the total offering.

In the sections below, we present the standard risk disclosures for a PPM for a multifamily property DST. The risks are typically sectioned by risks related to the trust structure, operating risks, risks related to the master lease, real estate risks, financing risks, risks related to private offerings, and tax risks. Please note that in various places we use "XXX" in place of dollar amounts as these numbers vary from offering to offering.

Risks Related to the Trust Structure and Operating Risks

Beneficial owners possess limited control and rights. The trust will be operated and managed solely by the trustee and the manager. Purchasers, as beneficial owners, will have no right to participate in any aspect of the operation or management of the trust. The trustee and the manager will not consult with the beneficial owners when making any decisions with respect to the trust and the property, including whether to sell the property or effectuate a transfer distribution. The beneficial owners waive any right to file a petition in bankruptcy on behalf of the trust or to consent to any filing of an involuntary bankruptcy proceeding involving the trust. The manager will collect the rents due from the master tenant under the master lease and make distributions therefrom in accordance with the terms of the trust agreement. The manager will seek to sell the property in accordance with the provisions of the trust agreement, which provides that the manager has sole discretion to determine when it is appropriate to sell the property. The trustee may remove the manager only for cause (fraud or gross negligence causing material damage to, or diminution in value of, the property), but only if the lender consents (to the extent there is an outstanding loan) and only if 65 percent or more of the interests consent in writing to such removal.

Beneficial owners do not have legal title. The beneficial owners will not have legal title to the property. The beneficial owners will not have any right to seek an in-kind distribution of the property or divide or partition the property. The beneficial owners do not have the right to sell or cause the sale of the property.

The trustee and the manager have limited duties to beneficial owners. The trustee of the trust and the manager will not owe any duties to the beneficial owners other than those duties set forth in the trust agreement. In performing its duties under the trust agreement, the trustee will only be liable to the beneficial owners for its own willful misconduct, bad faith, fraud or gross negligence. Similarly, the manager will only be liable to the beneficial owners for its own fraud or gross negligence.

The trustee and the manager have limited powers, and the trust may therefore face increased termination risk. In order to comply with the tax law regarding investment trusts and Section 1031 Exchanges, the trust agreement expressly prohibits the trustee and the manager from taking a number of actions, including the following: (a) selling, transferring or exchanging the property except as required or permitted under the trust agreement; (b) reinvesting any monies of the trust, except to make permitted modifications or repairs to the property or in short-term liquid assets; (c) renegotiating the terms of the loan or entering into new financing, except in the case of the bankruptcy or insolvency of the master tenant or another tenant; (d) renegotiating the master lease or entering into new leases, except in the case of the master tenant's bankruptcy or insolvency; (e) making modifications to the property (other than minor nonstructural modifications) unless required by law; (f) accepting any capital from a beneficial owner (other than capital from a purchaser that will be used to fund the supplemental trust reserve or repurchase the depositor's class 2 beneficial interests and thereby reduce the depositor's ownership interest in the trust); or (g) taking any other action that would, in the opinion of tax counsel to the trust, cause the trust to be treated as a business entity for federal income tax purposes.

As a result, the trust may be required to effectuate a transfer distribution in order to take the actions necessary to preserve and protect the property. See "Summary of the Trust Agreement." While the property will remain subject to the loan after such conversion or transfer, the beneficial owners will no longer be considered to own, for federal income tax purposes, a direct ownership interest in the property.

Management and indemnification. The manager will have administrative authority with respect to the trust. The trust agreement will provide for indemnification by the beneficial owners of the trustee against liabilities not attributable to the trustee's own willful misconduct, bad faith, fraud or gross negligence, and of the manager against liabilities not attributable to the manager's own fraud or gross negligence. Such indemnity and limitation of liability may limit rights that beneficial owners would otherwise have to seek redress against the trustee and the manager. Beneficial owners will have personal, recourse liability for payment of any indemnity owed to the trustee or the manager.

Rev. Rul. 2004-86. The utilization of a DST (like the trust) to acquire and hold property for purposes of a Section 1031 Exchange is based primarily on Rev. Rul. 2004-86, which sets forth terms under which a trust will be treated as an "entity" that is taxable as a "trust" rather than taxable as a partnership. It is possible that the IRS could modify or revoke Rev. Rul. 2004-86 or, in the alternative, determine that the trust does not comply with the requirements of that ruling. A determination that the trust is not taxable as a trust (within the meaning of Treas. Reg. § 301.7701-4) could have a significant adverse impact on the beneficial owners.

Sale. The manager shall sell the trust estate upon its determination (in its sole discretion) that the sale of the trust estate is appropriate; provided, however, that absent unusual circumstances, it is currently anticipated that the trust will hold the trust estate for at least two years. This sale will occur without regard to the tax position, preferences or desires of any of the beneficial owners, and the beneficial owners will have no right to approve (or disapprove) of the sale of the property. The beneficial owners will not have the right to sell the property. A beneficial owner may or may not be able to defer the recognition of gain for federal, state or local income tax purposes when a sale occurs.

Transfer to newly formed Delaware Limited Liability Company. If the manager determines that it is necessary to effectuate a transfer distribution, the trust will transfer the property to the Springing LLC, a newly formed Delaware limited liability company. The Springing LLC will be treated as a partnership for federal income tax purposes, and the beneficial owners will become members in the

Springing LLC. Unlike interests in the trust, membership interests in the Springing LLC will not be treated as interests in real property for federal income tax purposes (including for purposes of Code Section 1031). Thus, if the trust transfers the property to the Springing LLC in a transfer distribution, it is unlikely that any of the beneficial owners will thereafter be able to defer the recognition of gain on a subsequent disposition of their membership interests in the Springing LLC or the property under Code Section 1031.

The transfer of the property to the Springing LLC will occur under the circumstances set forth in the trust agreement without regard to the costs incurred as a result of such transfer. It is possible that such transfer will result in the imposition of (i) state and/or local transfer, sales or use taxes; or (ii) federal income tax (although no federal income tax would be imposed under current law).

In the event of an adverse effect on the income of the trust, the trust is not permitted to obtain additional funds through additional borrowings or additional capital, and therefore could be required to effectuate a transfer distribution so as to seek to raise capital through the springing LLC. If, after a transfer distribution, additional funds are not available from any source, the Springing LLC may be forced to dispose of all or a portion of the property on terms that may not be favorable to the beneficial owners. Further, apart from potential adverse economic consequences of a transfer distribution, a transfer distribution may have adverse tax consequences for the beneficial owners. See "Federal Income Tax Consequences."

The trust agreement restricts beneficial owners' rights to information. The trust agreement eliminates certain rights to information the beneficial owners would have otherwise had under the Delaware Statutory Trust Act (the "DST Act"). While the sponsor believes this is reasonable, necessary and prudent to protect the interests of legitimate purchasers in the trust from "greenmail" or other attacks by parties such as so called 'vulture investors' that are potentially harmful to the investment program, this would nevertheless mean that a purchaser will have less access to information from the trust than a purchaser would be entitled to under the DST Act, including contact information for other beneficial owners.

Real Estate Risks

Accuracy of anticipated results of operations. The anticipated results of operations for the trust as set forth in this Memorandum, including the pro forma financial projections attached as Appendix I: Financial Forecast, are based upon current estimates of income and expenses relating to the operation of the property, should be considered speculative and are qualified in their entirety by the assumptions, information, limitations and risks disclosed in this Memorandum. If the assumptions on which these estimates are based do not prove correct, the beneficial owners who own interests in the trust will have difficulty in achieving their anticipated results. The anticipated results of operations assume occupancy levels and certain net rental rates. There can be no assurance that the property can achieve stabilization or maintain the occupancy level or rate increases anticipated. Some of the other underlying assumptions inevitably may not materialize and unanticipated events and circumstances may occur. Therefore, the actual results achieved during the life of the ownership of the property may vary from those anticipated, and the variation may be material. As a result, the rate of return to the trust and the beneficial owners may be lower than that projected. Any return to the beneficial owners on their investment will depend on the ability of the master tenant, the property manager and the property submanager to operate the property profitably and ultimately sell the property at a profit, which, in turn, will depend upon economic factors and conditions beyond their control.

Risks of real estate ownership. The investment by beneficial owners will be subject to the risks generally incident to the ownership of real property, including changes in national and local economic conditions, changes in the investment climate for real estate investments, changes in the demand for or supply of competing properties, changes in local market conditions and neighborhood characteristics, the availability and cost of mortgage funds, the obligation to meet fixed and maturing obligations (if any), unanticipated holding costs, the availability and cost of necessary utilities and services, changes in real estate tax rates and other operating expenses, changes in governmental rules and fiscal policies, changes in zoning and other land use regulations, environmental controls, acts of God (which may result in uninsured losses), and other factors beyond the control of the trust. Any negative change in the general economic conditions in the United States could adversely affect the financial condition and operating results of the trust.

The trust also will be subject to those risks inherent in the ownership of income-producing real property, such as occupancy, operating expenses and rental schedules, which in turn may be adversely affected by general and local economic conditions, the supply of and demand for properties of the type selected for investment, the financial condition of tenants and sellers of properties, zoning laws, federal and local rent controls and real property tax rates. Certain expenditures associated with real estate equity investments are fixed (principally mortgage payments, if any, real estate taxes, and maintenance costs) and are not necessarily decreased by events adversely affecting the income from such investments. The ability of the trust to meet its obligations will depend on factors such as these and no assurance of profitable operations can be given.

The property is subject to risks relating to its local real estate market. Weakness or declines in the local economy and real estate market could cause vacancy rates at the property to increase and could adversely affect the trust's ability to sell the property under favorable terms. The factors which could affect economic conditions in the market generally include business layoffs, industry slowdowns, relocations of businesses, changing demographics, infrastructure quality and any oversupply of or reduced demand for real estate. Declines in the condition of the market could diminish your investment in and value of the property.

Risks of investing in multifamily rental properties; competition. The rental of multifamily residential space is a highly competitive business. Ownership of the property could be adversely affected by competitive properties in the real estate market, which could affect the operations of the property and the ultimate value of the property. Success in owning the property, therefore, will depend in part upon the ability of the master tenant, the property manager and the property submanager (i) to retain current tenants at favorable rental rates; (ii) to attract other quality tenants upon the termination of existing leases if the existing tenants fail to renew or as otherwise needed; and (iii) to provide an attractive and convenient living environment for the tenants.

Although the property will be leased to the master tenant throughout the term of the trust, the master tenant is a newly formed entity with limited financial resources. The financial performance of the property therefore will be dependent to a significant degree on the ability of the master tenant, the property manager and the property submanager to retain current tenants, to attract new tenants and, as planned, to increase rental rates, all of which may in turn depend on factors both within and beyond the control of the manager, the trust, the master tenant, the property manager and the property submanager. These factors include changing demographic trends and traffic patterns, the availability and rental rates of competing residential space, and general and local economic conditions. The loss of a tenant or the inability to maintain favorable rental rates with respect to the property would adversely affect the value of the property and/ or the ability of the master tenant to pay rent, which could result in the lender declaring the loan in default and foreclosing on the property. This could result in the purchasers losing their entire investment in the property. The occurrence of a casualty resulting in damage to the property could also decrease or interrupt the payment of tenant rentals, which could adversely affect the master tenant's performance under the master lease. The end user tenant leases generally allow the end-user tenants to terminate their leases if the leased premises are partially or completely damaged or destroyed by fire or other casualty. Such leases will also permit the end-user tenants to partially or completely abate rental payments during the time needed to rebuild or restore such damaged premises. The leases or local law may permit tenants to assign their leases or sublet the premises they occupy, but such assignment or subletting generally will not relieve the tenant of its primary obligations under the lease.

Dependence upon the property manager. The financial performance of the property will depend upon ability of the property manager and property submanager to attract and retain tenants who will meet their rental obligations on a timely basis, care for their living space and preserve or enhance the reputation of the property. The financial performance of the property and the related ability of the property manager and the property submanager to meet the financial projections contained herein will depend upon many factors, a significant one being the tenants' timely payment of rent under their leases and care for their living spaces. If a large number of tenants become unable to make rental payments when due, decide not to renew their leases or decide to terminate their leases, this could result in a significant reduction in rental revenues, which could adversely affect the ability of the master tenant to make payments under the master lease, including payment of principal and interest on the loan, which could adversely affect the value of the property and/or result in the lender declaring the loan in default and foreclosing on the property. This could result in the purchasers losing their entire investment in the property. In addition, the failure by a large number of tenants to properly care for their units or common areas or to preserve or enhance the reputation of the property could lead to increased repair and maintenance costs or otherwise adversely affect the value of the property. Failure on the part of a tenant to comply with the terms of his or her lease may give the master tenant the right to terminate the lease, repossess the applicable premises and enforce payment obligations under the lease. However, the cost and effort involved in pursuing these remedies and collecting damages from a defaulting tenant could be greater than the value of the lease. There can be no assurance that the master tenant will be able to successfully pursue and collect from defaulting tenants or relet the premises to new tenants without incurring substantial costs, if at all. If other tenants are found, the property manager or property submanager may not be able to enter into new leases on favorable terms. The financial projections assume a minimum occupancy rate and certain net rental rates for the property to enable the master tenant to comply with its obligations under the master lease, but there can be no assurance that the property will maintain the minimum occupancy rate or that the minimum net rental rates will be achieved. The loan documents provide that the lender must approve any change of the master tenant or property manager, which may make it difficult and/or costly to make a desired change in the management of the property.

Competition from apartment communities in the surrounding geographic area. A number of apartment communities of similar size and amenities are located in the property's immediate apartment submarket. There are a number of Class A apartment communities in the surrounding region that may be more attractive to renters. Competing apartment communities may reduce demand for the property, increase vacancy rates, decrease rental rates and impact the value of the property itself. There may also be additional real property available in the general vicinity of the property that could support additional multifamily properties. An analysis of Axiometics data as of Q2 2017 on all existing, planned, and under construction apartment communities in the property's submarket vicinity reveals seven Class A apartment communities comprising approximately X,XXX units currently in lease up and an additional three communities comprising approximately X,XXX units under construction. Further, there is one additional project comprising XXX units in the planning stages. If newer housing is built, it may siphon demand away from the property, as newer housing tends to be more attractive to prospective tenants. It is possible that tenants from the property will move to existing or new apartment communities in the surrounding area, which could adversely affect the financial performance of the property. Competition from nearby apartment communities could make it more difficult to attract new tenants and ultimately sell the property on a profitable basis. The property could also experience competition for real property investments from individuals, corporations and other entities engaged in real estate investment activities. Other properties and real estate investments may be more attractive than the property. There is no assurance that the property manager or the property submanager will be able to attract residents to the property given these facts.

Leases for the property generally have short terms, and the property manager or property submanager may be unable to renew leases or re-let units as leases expire. Most of the existing leases for the units at the property have lease terms of twelve months. Consequently, the property's performance may in large measure depend upon the effectiveness of the property manager's and property submanager's marketing efforts to attract replacement tenants and to maintain the occupancy rate for the property, which may require significant time and money. If tenants decide not to renew their leases upon expiration or decide to terminate their leases, the property manager and property submanager may not be able to relet their units. Even if the tenants do renew or their units are relet, the terms of renewal or re-leasing may be less favorable than current lease terms. If the property manager and property submanager cannot promptly renew the leases or relet the units, or if the rental rates upon renewal or re-leasing are significantly lower than expected rates, then the property's financial operations and condition will be adversely affected and this, in turn, may adversely affect the property's cash flow, the ability of the master tenant to pay all rents due under the master lease and the ability of the trust to service its debt and pay distributions to the beneficial owners.

Changes in laws could adversely affect the property. Various Federal, state and local regulations, such as fire and safety requirements, environmental regulations, the Americans with Disabilities Act of 1990 (the "ADA"), nondiscrimination and equal housing laws, land use restrictions and taxes affect the property. If the property does not comply with these requirements, the trust may incur governmental fines or private damage awards. New, or amendments to existing, laws, rules, regulations or ordinances could require significant unanticipated expenditures or impose restrictions on the operation, redevelopment or sale of the property. Such laws, rules, regulations or ordinances may adversely affect the ability of the trust to operate or sell the property.

Risks Relating to the Master Tenant and the Master Lease

Limited capital of the master tenant. The financial stability of the master tenant may affect the financial performance of the property. The master tenant's capitalization is supported solely by the demand note from the sponsor. The sponsor is under no obligation to contribute capital to the master tenant. If the master tenant requires funds in excess of property net operating income to pay the rent (subject to a limited right of deferral) or satisfy its other obligations under the master lease, it will need to call upon the sponsor to contribute the amount of its demand note. However, no assurance can be given that the amount of the demand note will be sufficient to enable the master tenant to pay the rent or to fund its obligations under the master lease, or that the sponsor will be able to fund the demand note if called upon by the master tenant to do so. If the master tenant is unable to pay the rent or satisfy its obligations under the master lease, the master tenant would be in default under the master lease. A master tenant default also constitutes an event of default under the loan agreement (as defined below), which could result in suspension or termination of distributions to beneficial owners and/or a foreclosure of the property by the lender. In addition, the costs and time involved in enforcing the trust's rights under the master lease may be significant. If the trust terminated the master lease, it may not be able to lease the property on terms similar to the master lease. If the trust were unable to enter into a new master lease for the property, the returns to purchasers would likely be materially adversely affected. In addition, if the trust were unable to enter into a new master lease, it would likely become necessary for the trust to effectuate a transfer distribution, in order to engage in leasing activities, which would likely give rise to adverse tax consequences to purchasers. Absent insolvency or a bankruptcy by the master tenant, the trustee may not be empowered to execute such a replacement master lease. Furthermore, if the master tenant is unable to pay the rent or satisfy its obligations under the master lease, the trust may be unable to pay the debt service on the loan and the lender could foreclose on the property. In such event, the purchasers could lose their entire investment in the property and suffer adverse tax consequences.

The sponsor's affiliate may be unable to fulfill its obligations under the demand note. The sponsor has made the demand note in favor of the master tenant in order to capitalize the master tenant. However, there can be no assurance that the sponsor will be able to satisfy its obligations pursuant to such demand note. The net worth or current assets of the sponsor may be insufficient to support its obligations under its demand note at the time of being called. If the sponsor is required to perform on outstanding or future demand notes, guaranties or other debt obligations or otherwise experiences an adverse financial event, it is possible that XXX may not have sufficient funds or resources to perform its obligations under its demand note and may be unable to fulfill its obligations to the master tenant. In the event of the insolvency or bankruptcy of the sponsor, the master tenant would be required to compete with any other creditor claims that may be asserted against the same assets of those entities and any secured creditor claims would be superior to those of the master tenant under the demand note, which is unsecured. The assets of the sponsor and its affiliates are subject to the various risks of real estate ownership, syndication and management, including, but not limited, to market value fluctuations and uncertainty of profitability of business operations. The ultimate value of these existing assets will depend upon their ability to successfully implement their respective business plans, which in turn depends upon competition and other market factors. If the sponsor is unable to pay its demand note when called upon, the master tenant may have insufficient funds to pay the rent or property expenses, including without limitation the base rent upon which the trust relies in order to be able to pay the debt service on the loan. Any failure of the master tenant to pay the rent would materially and adversely affect returns to the purchasers, may cause the trust to terminate the master lease, and may cause a default under the loan resulting in foreclosure and a complete loss of the property and the entire investment of the purchasers.

Performance of the master tenant under the master lease. The ability of the trust to meet its obligations is dependent upon the performance of the master tenant and its payment of rent and other payments required under the master lease.

The master tenant has a limited right to defer rental payments under the master lease. Under the master lease, if the property's operating cash flow is insufficient to pay all the associated expenses of the property (not including the Asset Management Fee), the full base rent, then in such event, the master tenant has a limited right to defer and accrue a portion of the additional rent and supplemental rent payments due under the master lease (but not any portion of the base rent required to make debt service payments due under the loan documents). Because the master tenant may accrue a portion of the additional rent and supplemental rent, it will not be required to call the demand note from XXX in order to make up such a shortfall. In such an instance, purchasers may receive less or more varied distributions than they would have if the master tenant were required to call the demand note to fund any such rent shortfall. Furthermore, if future cash flow from the property or disposition proceeds are insufficient to pay the accrued rent and XXX is unable to fund the demand note when called, then the trust may never receive the full amount of any such accrued rent, which could materially and adversely affect the returns to the purchasers.

Additionally, if the master tenant elects to defer payment of a portion of the rent, although the issue is not completely settled under existing law, under Section 467 of the Code, beneficial owners may be required to report and pay tax on rent in accordance with the rent schedule attached to the master lease, even though the master tenant may have elected to defer the payment of a portion of such rent. As a result, beneficial owners may be required to recognize rental income even though rent is not being fully paid, and therefore beneficial owners may have to use funds from other sources to pay tax on such income.

Risks Relating to an Investment in the Property

Valuation. The Appraisal reflects a market value "As Is" for the property of $53,000,000 as of August 18, 2017. The net purchase price of $XX,XXX,XXX for the property is lower than the $56,898,729 aggregate purchase price of the interests, which includes $XX,XXX,XXX in equity for the interests, assuming the maximum offering amount is sold, and $XX,XXX,XXX for the loan. Thus, the trust will be subject to immediate dilution and the beneficial owners may recover less than their invested capital upon any eventual sale of the property. There can be no assurance that the value of the property will appreciate, or appreciate at a rate sufficient to provide a positive return on investment.

Property Not a Diversified Investment. By the terms of the trust agreement (as well as the terms of the loan documents), the trust generally is not permitted to acquire real property other than the property or any other assets or make any other investments. Because an investment in interests represents an investment in one property, it is not a fully diversified investment. Accordingly, the poor performance of the property would likely materially and adversely affect your investment in an interest.

Physical Condition of the Property; No Representations to Purchasers. The trust will not make any warranties or representations to the purchasers regarding the condition of the property. The sponsor has received a property condition assessment report dated as of June XX, 20XX (the PCA), prepared by XXX Consulting LLC. The PCA concluded that the property was in "generally good condition." The PCA identified a small number of immediate needs for repairs in the amount of $X,XXX for testing and inspection of the site main backflow preventer and the individual sprinkler riser backflow preventers located in the riser closets. The PCA also recommended recurring capital reserves for likely repairs and replacements necessary during the next ten years. The estimated total of the immediate and future capital needs is $XXX,XXX.

Following completion of the sale of the maximum offering amount, the trust would have approximately $XXX,XXX in the supplemental trust reserve, plus $XXX,XXX from the lender Replacement Reserve, plus a projected $XXX,XXX contributed from property operations over a ten-year period (to total $X,XXX,XXX), versus $XXX,XXX estimated capital repair items estimated by the PCA. There can be no assurance of the accuracy of the PCA with regard to future capital expenditure requirements of the property, or that the sponsor has budgeted adequately in the Financial Forecast for all such repairs, replacements, and other expenditures that are or become necessary. If the immediate repairs reserve and supplemental trust reserve are insufficient (including due to the possibility that reimbursements and other compensation items due the sponsor or its affiliates may be or have been drawn from resources credited, held or controlled by the trust, including the supplemental trust reserve), the trust's rent could be used by the trust to reserve for or pay such expenses (instead of being used to pay distributions to purchasers), or those expenses and costs could possibly be so significant as to require additional capital to be infused which could not be done except through a transfer distribution, which would likely have material and adverse tax consequences for purchasers.

The preparers of the PCA issued reliance letters entitling the trust, among others, to rely on the PCA and to enforce any claims against the preparers of the PCA if they failed to identify any particular property deficiency. However, such letter would not necessarily entitle a purchaser to rely on the PCA or enforce legal claims against parties that prepared the PCA or its underlying information. In addition, there can be no assurance that the preparers would be held liable for any losses in connection with deficiencies in the property that were not identified in the PCA. Furthermore, there can be no assurance that financial wherewithal of such preparers would be sufficient to cover any loss that may arise, should they be held liable.

Environmental problems are possible and can be costly. Federal, state and local laws and regulations relating to the protection of the environment may require a current or previous owner or operator of real estate to investigate and clean up hazardous or toxic substances or petroleum product releases at or affecting the property. The owner or operator may have to pay a governmental entity or third parties for property damage and for investigation and clean-up costs incurred by such parties in connection with any such contamination. These laws typically impose clean-up responsibility and liability without regard to whether the owner or operator knew of or caused the presence of the contaminants. Even if more than one person may have been responsible for the contamination, each person covered by the environmental laws may be held responsible for all the clean-up costs incurred. In addition, third parties may sue the owner or operator of a site for damages and costs resulting from environmental contamination emanating from that site.

The property has been evaluated for environmental hazards on behalf of the lender pursuant to a noninvasive Phase I Environmental Site Assessment Report, dated June XX, 20XX, prepared by XXX Consulting, based on a site visit conducted in June XX, 20XX. The Phase I Report, which consisted of a walk-through observation of the accessible areas and interviews with facility personnel and local agency representatives, interviews with relevant personnel, limited observations of surrounding properties, and a records review including regulatory databases and historical use information revealed no evidence of recognized environmental conditions in connection with the site and no further investigation was recommended.

A Phase 1 environmental assessment report generally will not involve any invasive testing, but instead is limited to a physical walk through or inspection of the property and a review of the related governmental records. Accordingly, the sponsor cannot provide any assurance to potential purchasers that actual environmental problems with the property will be exposed by the Phase 1 Report. In light of the material risks and potential liability associated with the discovery of an environmental hazard at the property, the purchasers of the interests should be certain that they understand, and can accept, the risks associated with any known and unknown hazardous substances affecting the property. In addition, it is possible that an environmental claim may be raised in such a manner that liability could penetrate any limited liability protections otherwise available to shield the owners of an entity from liability, thereby allowing such claims to be enforceable against the purchasers. Finally, it is possible that the existence of any environmental issues with the property may make it more difficult, and perhaps impossible, to obtain financing for the property.

Construction of improvements. Under applicable tax rules, if the trust were to cause the construction of more than minor, nonstructural improvements, this activity could require a transfer distribution, which may have adverse tax consequences for the beneficial owners.

Risk of mold contamination. Mold contamination has been linked to a number of health problems, which could result in litigation by tenants seeking various remedies, including damages and the ability to terminate their leases. Recently there have been an increasing number of lawsuits against property owners and managers alleging personal injury and property damage caused by the presence of toxic molds. Some of these lawsuits have resulted in substantial monetary judgments or settlements. Insurance carriers generally exclude mold-related claims from standard policies and price mold endorsements at prohibitively high rates. The assessment of the property in connection with the Phase I Report included an evaluation of any apparent mold growth (AMG). No AMG was observed within the dwelling units or common areas accessed. The site representative was not aware of AMG issues at the site and no tenant complaints were reported. As such, no further evaluation is recommended. No assurance can be given either that an undetected mold condition does not presently exist at the property or that a mold condition will not arise in the future. A mold condition would create the risk of substantial damages, legal fees and possible loss of tenants.

The supplemental trust reserve may be inadequate. The master tenant, subject to the express terms of the loan documents and the master lease, may draw upon the supplemental trust reserve for landlord costs and other property costs and expenses. To the extent that property expenses increase, or unanticipated expenses arise, and the available reserves are insufficient to meet such expenses, the trust may be forced to use some or all the rent payment received from the master tenant to pay such obligations of the trust, or to effect a transfer distribution in order to raise the necessary capital through the Springing LLC for such purposes, because the trust itself is prohibited from raising additional capital. Further, to the extent that the aggregate of the organization and offering expenses, loan-related costs and other closing costs exceed the amounts projected, then any such shortfall will be funded first from savings in other categories and may be funded next from any other available reserves of the trust, including from the supplemental trust reserve. In addition, construction of more than minor, nonstructural improvements out of reserves established by the trust may require the trust to effectuate a transfer distribution, which may have adverse tax consequences for the beneficial owners.

Energy shortages and allocations. There may be shortages or increased costs of fuel, natural gas or electric power, or allocations thereof, by suppliers or governmental regulatory bodies in the area where the property is located. We are unable to predict the extent, if any, to which such shortages, increased prices, or allocations will occur or the degree to which such events might influence the ability of the property to meet stated goals. If such shortages occurred or such costs increased, however, they could materially and adversely affect the income derived by the trust from the property, the value of the property and the value of the interests.

Risks Related to Financing of the Property

Risks of leverage. The trust owns the property subject to the loan. This use of leverage may increase the return on invested capital. However, it also presents an additional element of risk in the event that the cash receipts from the operation of the property are insufficient to meet the principal and interest payments on such indebtedness. In order to comply with tax requirements for Section 1031 Exchanges, the trust is not permitted to obtain new financing and beneficial owners are not permitted to make additional capital contributions to the trust. Thus, if the cash flow from the property is insufficient to allow the master tenant to make the required payments under the master lease, including payments required to service the loan, the lender may foreclose on the property and the beneficial owners' equity in the property may be reduced or lost entirely. A transfer distribution may make it possible to delay or avoid a foreclosure (because the Springing LLC is not restricted from refinancing the property or raising new capital) but may, itself, cause adverse tax consequences for the beneficial owners. See "Federal Income Tax Consequences." Moreover, the cost of any refinancing of the property after a transfer distribution, in the form of interest charges and financing fees imposed by lenders or affiliates of the sponsor, might significantly reduce the profits or increase losses resulting from operation of the property.

Although the trustee can remove the manager in certain limited circumstances, the lender will likely require that there be an adequately capitalized successor manager. This requirement may limit the ability of a trustee to remove the manager, since the exercise of such right would give rise to a default under the loan absent the lender's consent. The trust cannot incur any additional borrowings or refinance the property.

Scheduled debt payments could adversely affect the property's financial condition. In the future, the property's cash flow could be insufficient to meet required payments under the loan documents or to pay cash flow to the trust at expected levels. As a result of any shortfall, the manager may be forced to postpone capital expenditures necessary for the maintenance of the property, suspend distributions to beneficial owners, or may require a sale or transfer distribution. There can be no assurance that the manager will be able to sell the property upon acceptable terms, if at all, or that after a transfer distribution the Springing LLC would be able to raise additional or sufficient capital to avert a loan default and possible foreclosure of the property by the lender.

Events of default. The loan is "nonrecourse," meaning that the lender may only seek recovery from the liquidation of its collateral (principally, the property) for any amounts that remain due under the loan after a default. However, the loan documents contain certain events that would allow the lender to proceed against the trust to repay amounts due on the loan, in addition to foreclosing on the property and the other collateral for the loan. Thus, if such events occur, "springing" liability to the trust may result, including an amount equal, in certain instances, to the full amount of the loan. The events under the loan documents for which the trust may have liability beyond the value of the lender's collateral include, but are not limited to the following:

- failure to pay rents or security deposits owed to lender upon an event of default under the loan documents;
- failure to maintain insurance policies required by the loan documents;
- failure to apply insurance proceeds as required by the loan documents;
- failure to comply with the provisions of the loan documents relating to the delivery of books and records, statements, schedules and reports;
- failure to apply rents to the ordinary and necessary expenses of owning or operating the property;
- waste or abandonment of the property;
- grossly negligent or reckless unintentional material misrepresentation or omission by the trust, the master tenant or the sponsor in connection with on-going financial or other reporting required by the loan documents, or any request for action or consent by the lender;
- failure of the master lease to be subordinate to the lien of the mortgage (defined below) or failure of the master lease to be terminated if so elected by the lender in accordance with the loan documents;
- failure to effect a transfer distribution;
- failure of the trust or the master tenant to comply with the single-asset entity requirements of the loan documents;
- occurrence of a transfer not permitted by the loan documents;
- occurrence of certain bankruptcy events;
- fraud, written material misrepresentation or material omission; and

- the trust's indemnification obligations under the loan documents.

Lender's approval rights. The lender has numerous rights under the loan documents, including the right to approve certain changes in ownership and management. Prospective purchasers are encouraged to review a complete set of the loan documents prior to subscribing for the interests.

Restrictions on transfer and encumbrance. The terms of the loan prohibit the transfer or further encumbrance of the property or any interest in the property except with the lender's prior written consent, which consent may be withheld, or otherwise permitted under the loan documents. The loan documents provide that upon violation of these restrictions on transfer or encumbrance, the lender may declare the entire amount of the loan, including principal, interest, prepayment premiums and other charges, to be immediately due and payable. If the lender declares the loan to be immediately due and payable, the trust will have the obligation to immediately repay the loan in full. If the trust is unable to obtain replacement financing or otherwise fails to immediately repay the loan in full, the lender may invoke its remedies under the loan documents, including proceeding with a foreclosure sale that is likely to result in the beneficial owners losing their entire investment in the property. Further, since the trust is prohibited from borrowing additional funds or from accepting additional capital contributions, the trust would in such a situation be required to effectuate a transfer distribution into the Springing LLC.

Ability to repay the loan. The ability of the trust to repay the loan will depend in part upon the sale or other disposition of the property prior to, at the latest, the maturity date of the loan. There can be no assurance that any such sale can be accomplished at a time or on such terms and conditions as will permit the trust to repay the outstanding principal amount of the loan. Financial market conditions in the future may affect the availability and cost of real estate loans, making real estate financing difficult or costly to obtain for potential buyers of the property.

In the event that the trust is unable to sell the property prior to the maturity date of the loan, the trust may be required to effectuate a transfer distribution in order to allow the Springing LLC to seek to refinance the loan. However, market conditions and the interest rate environment at that time could cause the cash flow from the property to fluctuate and could impact capitalization rates, both of which could negatively impact the value of the property and limit the Springing LLC sale or refinancing options. The Springing LLC may not be able to obtain refinancing on terms as favorable as the loan. If additional funds are not available from a sale, refinancing or additional capital contributions to the resulting Springing LLC, the Springing LLC may be subject to the risk of losing the property through foreclosure. Any such transfer distribution or foreclosure may have adverse tax consequences for the beneficial owners. See "Federal Income Tax Consequences."

Availability of financing and market conditions. Market fluctuations in real estate financing may affect the availability and cost of funds needed in the future for the property. Moreover, credit availability has been restricted in the past and may become restricted again in the future. Restrictions upon the availability of real estate financing or high interest rates for real estate loans could adversely affect the property and the ability of the trust to sell the property at a profit or at any price.

Risks Relating to the Operation of the Property

Insurance and uninsured losses. The master tenant has obtained general liability and business interruption insurance for the property. If a loss occurs that is partially or completely uninsured, the beneficial owners may lose all or a part of their investment. The trust may be liable for any uninsured or underinsured personal injury, death or property damage claims. Liability in such cases may be unlimited. While insurance may help reduce the risk of loss, it increases costs and thus lowers the potential return to the beneficial owners.

Regulatory matters. The value of the property may be adversely affected by legislative, regulatory, administrative, and enforcement actions at the local, state and national levels in the area, among others, of environmental controls. In addition to possible increasingly restrictive zoning regulations and related land use controls, such restrictions may relate to air and water quality standards, noise pollution and indirect environmental impacts such as increased motor vehicle activity.

Reliance on management. Under the trust agreement, the manager has the right to make administrative decisions on behalf of the trust. Also, the manager has the sole discretion to determine when to sell the property and on what terms. The manager has other extensive powers and authority, some of which are limited by the express terms of the trust agreement. In the event of a transfer distribution, however, the manager or its affiliate, as the manager of the Springing LLC, would be granted expanded powers and the right to receive additional compensation. Accordingly, no purchaser should purchase interests unless such purchaser recognizes that the trust is limited in its ability to manage the property and such purchaser is willing to entrust such limited management of the property and the power to sell the property to the trustee and the manager, and after a transfer distribution the purchaser is willing to entrust all aspects of the management of the Springing LLC to the manager as its manager. See "The Manager" and "Summary of the Trust Agreement—Termination of the Trust to Protect the property; transfer distribution." Furthermore, under the trust agreement, the trustee has the power and authority to remove the manager for cause (fraud or gross negligence causing material damage to, or diminution in value of, the property), but only if the lender consents (to the extent there is an outstanding loan) and only if 65 percent or more of the interests consent in writing to such removal.

Conflicts. The manager and its affiliates are subject to conflicts of interest between their activities, roles and duties for other entities and the activities, roles and duties they have assumed on behalf of the trust. Conflicts exist in allocating management time, services and functions between their current and future activities and the trust.

None of the arrangements or agreements described, including those relating to the purchase price of the property or compensation, is the result of arm's-length negotiations. See "Conflicts of Interest."

No substantial assets of the sponsor, manager, or master tenant. The sponsor, manager and master tenant are newly formed entities and do not have any substantial assets. Thus, there is no assurance that the sponsor, manager or the master tenant will have the financial resources to satisfy their obligations under the trust, the master lease or the property management agreement. Neither the sponsor, the manager nor the master tenant is obligated to invest or provide additional capital on behalf of the trust, the beneficial owners or the property. The sponsor has agreed to initially capitalize the master tenant with the demand note in the amount of $XXX,XXX. This Memorandum does not contain financial statements for the sponsor, the manager or the master tenant.

Compensation and fees. The sponsor and certain of its affiliates will receive certain compensation from the trust for services rendered regardless of whether any sums are distributed to the beneficial owners.

Offering Risks

No market for interests. The transfer of interests will be subject to certain limitations. Moreover, it is not anticipated that any public market for interests will develop, and the transfer of interests may result in adverse tax consequences for the transferor. Consequently, purchasers of interests may not be able to liquidate their investments in the event of emergency or for any other reason. Moreover, purchasers are specifically notified that interests are not likely to be readily accepted as collateral for outside financing. Any purchase of interests, therefore, should be considered only as a long-term investment.

Purchase price of interests. The purchase price of the interests is based on the purchase price of the property, and includes organization and offering expenses, sales commissions, marketing/due diligence expense allowances, managing broker-dealer fee, loan-related costs, other closing costs, sponsor's acquisition fee, and the supplemental trust reserve. If the trust is unable to sell the property at a price which would net (after repayment of the loan and other applicable expenses) at least the aggregate of the purchase price paid for the interests, the purchasers would suffer a loss on their investment.

Risk that purchaser will not acquire interest. After identifying the property, a prospective purchaser may not be accepted, or may be rejected as an investor for any reason or for no reason at all and such purchaser may therefore lose the benefit of a Section 1031 Exchange. It is suggested and anticipated that purchasers will attempt to mitigate these risks by identifying multiple properties in connection with their Section 1031 Exchange.

Impact of leverage on Section 1031 Exchange. The property is subject to financing in the form of the loan. Code Section 1031 generally requires taxpayers to offset debt on their relinquished property with equal or greater debt on their replacement property (or additional cash from another source). purchasers who are exchanging relinquished property with a larger amount of debt than the proportionate amount of the loan they are deemed to have assumed for tax purposes in connection with the acquisition of an interest may recognize taxable gain (although additional cash from another source may offset the reduction in debt). Each purchaser will have its own unique debt and other Section 1031 Exchange issues. Therefore, each purchaser must seek the advice of its own independent tax advisor as to qualification for tax deferral under Code Section 1031 and the Treasury Regulations promulgated thereunder, including the debt replacement rules.

Ownership of remaining interests. Except for the retained interest to be held by the depositor, any remaining interests held by the sponsor or its affiliates (including the depositor) at the end of the twenty-four-month period beginning on the date of the initial closing must be sold to unrelated third parties or contributed to the trust for the benefit of the beneficial owners, as determined by the depositor. Such unrelated persons could be employees or have other relationships with the sponsor and its affiliates. Such persons could have conflicting interests with those of the beneficial owners and in the event of a transfer distribution could hold interests sufficient to provide control over actions taken by the Springing LLC.

Timing of sale of the property. Beneficial owners should not expect a sale within any specified period of time. Although the trust agreement allows the manager to sell the property at any time that, in the manager's discretion, a sale is appropriate, it is currently anticipated that the trust will hold the property for at least two years. The decision to sell the property will be made at the sole discretion of the manager, and the beneficial owners will not have any right to participate in the decision to sell the property.

Operation as a Limited Liability Company after a transfer distribution. If a transfer distribution occurs and the property is transferred to the Springing LLC, the manager of the Springing LLC will have exclusive discretion in the management and control of the business and affairs of the Springing LLC. A copy of the limited liability agreement of the Springing LLC is attached to the trust agreement as an exhibit. The members of the Springing LLC will not have the right to take part in the management or control of the business or affairs of the Springing LLC. The members are permitted to vote only in a limited number of circumstances and can remove the manager of the Springing LLC only for cause. The manager has the right to sell the property at any time that, in the manager's discretion, a sale is appropriate. Such sale could occur at a time that would be adverse to the interests of any given member either from a financial or tax standpoint. The manager of the Springing LLC, as a holder of membership interests in the Springing LLC, if any, may have conflicts of interest with respect to the Springing LLC and the members. The manager of the Springing LLC is entitled to certain limitations of liability and to indemnity by the Springing LLC against liabilities not attributable to its fraud or gross negligence. Such indemnity and limitation of liability may limit rights that members would otherwise have to seek redress against the manager of the Springing LLC. See "Summary of Certain Provisions of "Springing LLC" Limited Liability Company Operating Agreement."

An affiliate of the manager is expected to serve as the manager of the Springing LLC and will be a newly formed entity with limited financial resources. It will have no obligation to invest in or otherwise provide capital to the Springing LLC. Thus, the Springing LLC may not be able to satisfy its financial obligations, which could negatively impact the beneficial owners who, upon the occurrence of a transfer distribution, would become members of the Springing LLC. A member may become liable to the Springing LLC and to its creditors for and to the extent of any distribution made to such member if, after giving effect to such distribution, the remaining assets of the Springing LLC are not sufficient to pay its outstanding liabilities (other than liabilities to the members on account of their membership interests in the Springing LLC). It is not expected that there will be any market for membership interests in the Springing LLC. Thus, members may not be able to liquidate their investments in the event of an emergency or for any other reason.

No Minimum offering contingency. There is no minimum amount of offering proceeds that must be raised, or minimum number of purchasers required in connection with this offering. Accordingly, if the sponsor is unable to sell all the interests, the depositor will retain class 2 beneficial interests. The ownership of beneficial interests in the trust by the depositor, an affiliate of the sponsor, involves certain risks that potential purchasers should consider, including, but not limited to, the fact that there may be conflicts of interest between the objectives of the purchasers and that of the sponsor, or, if the offering is not fully subscribed, that a significant amount of the trust's beneficial interests will not have been acquired by disinterested purchasers after an assessment of the merits of the offering.

Tax Risks

General. There are substantial risks associated with the federal income tax aspects of a purchase of an interest, especially if the purchase is part of an exchange designed to qualify as a Section 1031 Exchange. The following paragraphs summarize some of these tax risks to a purchaser with respect to the purchase of an interest. A further discussion of the tax aspects (including other tax risks) of a purchase of an interest is set forth under "Federal Income Tax Consequences." Because the tax aspects of this offering are complex and certain of the tax consequences may differ depending on individual tax circumstances, each prospective purchaser is strongly encouraged to and should consult with and rely on its own tax advisor about this offering's tax aspects in light of such purchaser's individual situation. No representation or warranty of any kind is made with respect to the IRS' acceptance of the treatment of any item of income, deduction, gain, loss, credit or any other item by a purchaser and there can be no assurance that the IRS will not challenge any such treatment.

Acquisition of the interests may not qualify as a Section 1031 Exchange. An interest may not qualify under Code Section 1031 for tax-deferred exchange treatment, and even if it does a portion of the proceeds from a purchaser's sale of his or her property to be relinquished (the "relinquished property") could constitute taxable "boot" (as defined below). Whether any particular acquisition of an interest will qualify as a tax-deferred exchange under Code Section 1031 depends on the specific facts involved, including, without limitation, the nature and use of the relinquished property and the method of its disposition, the use of a qualified intermediary and a qualified exchange escrow and the lapse of time between the sale of the relinquished property and the identification and acquisition of the replacement property (the "replacement property" or "replacement properties"). Neither the sponsor nor its affiliates, counsel or agents are examining or analyzing any prospective purchaser's circumstances to determine whether such purchaser's acquisition of replacement property qualifies as a Section 1031 Exchange. Moreover, no opinion or assurance is being provided to the effect that any individual prospective purchaser's transaction will qualify under Code Section 1031. Such examinations or analyses are the sole responsibility of each prospective purchaser, who must consult with his or her own legal, tax, accounting and financial advisors before purchasing an interest. If the factors surrounding a prospective purchaser's disposition of the relinquished property and his or her acquisition of the interests do not meet the requirements of Code Section 1031, the disposition of the relinquished property will be taxed as a sale and the IRS will assess interest and possibly penalties for failure to timely pay such taxes. Also, merely designating an interest in connection with a purchaser's Section 1031 Exchange does not assure the purchaser that there will be interests available to purchase when the purchaser executes the Purchase Agreement and actually causes his, her, or its qualified intermediary to transfer funds to complete the purchase of the interests.

Form of ownership. On August 20, 2004, the IRS issued Revenue Ruling 2004-86, 2004-33 I.R.B. 191, which held that, assuming the other requirements of Code Section 1031 are satisfied, a taxpayer's exchange of real property for an interest in the DST described in the ruling satisfies the requirements of Code Section 1031. The IRS based its holding on the following conclusions: (1) the DST is treated as an entity separate from its owners (and not as a coownership or agency arrangement); (2) the DST is an "investment" trust and not a "business entity" for federal income tax purposes; (3) the DST is a "grantor trust" for federal income tax purposes, with the holders of interests in the DST treated as the grantors of the DST; and (4) the holders of interests in the DST are treated as directly owning interests in real property held by the DST. There are no authorities that directly address the tax treatment of the trust other than Rev. Rul. 2004-86. It is possible that the IRS could revoke Rev. Rul. 2004-86 or, in the alternative, determine that the trust does not comply with the requirements of that ruling or the underlying authorities. A determination that the trust is not taxable as a trust (within the meaning of Treasury Regulation Section 301.1.7701-4) likely would have a significant adverse impact on the beneficial owners. Because the holding of Revenue Ruling 2004-86 is based on certain factual assumptions regarding the DST, not all of which apply to the trust, and because there are provisions in the trust agreement which are not mentioned in the limited facts laid out in the ruling, there can be no guarantee that the interests will satisfy the requirements of Code Section 1031.

Classification for purposes of Code Section 1031; No Ruling. We believe the offering described in this Memorandum is structured in a manner that the interests should be treated for federal income tax purposes as direct ownership interests in real estate and not as interests in a partnership. If the interests were to be treated by the IRS or a court as interests in a partnership, then no purchaser would be able to use its acquisition of interests as part of a Section 1031 Exchange to defer gain under Code Section 1031. The IRS may challenge the tax treatment related to the interests as described in this Memorandum.

We have obtained an opinion from tax counsel in connection with the offering that (i) the trust should be treated as an investment trust described in Treasury Regulation Section 301.7701-4(c) that is classified as a "trust" under Treasury Regulation Section 301.7701-4(a); (ii) the beneficial owners should be treated as "grantors" of the trust; (iii) as "grantors," the beneficial owners should be treated as owning an undivided fractional interest in the property for federal income tax purposes; (iv) the interests should not be treated as "securities" under Code Section 1031; (v) the interests should not be treated as certificates of trust or beneficial interests for purposes of Code Section 1031; (vi) the master lease should be treated as a true lease and not a financing for federal income tax purposes; (vii) the master lease should be treated as a true lease and not a deemed partnership for federal income tax purposes; (viii) the discussions of the federal income tax consequences contained in this Memorandum are correct in all material respects; and (ix) certain judicially created doctrines should not apply to change the foregoing conclusions. The issues which are the subject of such opinion have not been definitely resolved by statutory, administrative or case law. This opinion is based on the facts and circumstances set forth in the opinion and is not a guarantee of the current status of the law, and, as such, it should not be treated as a guarantee that the IRS or a court would concur with the conclusion in the opinion. If any of such facts or circumstances were to change, the tax consequences to purchasers described in the opinion and in this Memorandum could change. See "Federal Income Tax Consequences."

Identification. Treasury Regulation Section 1.1031(k)-1(c)(4) permits taxpayers to identify alternative and multiple replacement properties under Code Section 1031. All properties acquired within

45 days of the sale of the relinquished property are deemed to have been properly identified. In addition, taxpayers are permitted to identify three properties without regard to the fair market value of the properties (the "three property rule") or multiple properties with a total fair market value not in excess of 200 percent of the value of the relinquished property (the "200 percent rule"). In the event that the IRS successfully challenges the valuation of a replacement property under the 200 percent rule, and as a result the replacement properties identified by the taxpayer exceed 200 percent of the value of the taxpayer's relinquished property, the taxpayer's identification may be treated as invalid, which may invalidate the taxpayer's like-kind exchange under Code Section 1031. A taxpayer also may identify any number of properties if it acquires at least 95 percent of the identified properties (the "95 percent rule"). The identification rules of Code Section 1031 are strictly construed, and a purchaser's exchange will not qualify for deferral of gain under Code Section 1031 if too many properties are identified or if the deadlines for identification are not met. Prospective purchasers will have to rely on the 200 percent rule or 95 percent rule with respect to the offering and should seek the advice of their tax advisors prior to subscribing for the interests or making an identification. For purposes of both the 200 percent rule and the 95 percent rule, "fair market value" means the fair market value of the property without regard to any liabilities secured by the property. Thus, a taxpayer identifying under the 200 percent rule for an unencumbered relinquished property having a value of $20 million could only identify replacement property(ies) having an aggregate gross fair market value (without regard to any liabilities which may encumber such property(ies)) of $40 million, in which case the identification of a single replacement property having a $30 million equity value but which is secured by a $20 million liability (and, thus, having a $50 million gross value) would violate the 200 percent rule. The identification rules of Code Section 1031 are strictly construed, and a purchaser's exchange will not qualify for deferral of gain under Code Section 1031 if too many properties or properties having too much value (including by reason of not excluding the effect of the loan for "fair market value" purposes) are identified, if the properties

are not correctly identified, or if the deadlines for identification are not met. Prospective purchasers will have to rely on the 200 percent rule or 95 percent rule with respect to the offering and should seek the advice of their tax advisors prior to subscribing for the interests or making an identification.

Possible adverse tax treatment for closing costs and reserves. Funds from a Section 1031 exchange may not be used for certain costs associated with the property. Each purchaser of an interest will be obligated to pay its pro rata share of closing costs, financing expenses, reserves and other costs of the offering. A portion of the proceeds of the offering will be used to pay each purchaser's pro rata share of such costs. In addition, a portion of the proceeds of the offering may be treated as having been used to purchase an interest in reserves established by the sponsor rather than for real estate. Under certain conditions, these costs, as well as reserves relating to the property, may not constitute property that is like-kind to real estate for purposes of Code Section 1031. In particular, a portion of the offering proceeds will be used to fund the supplemental trust reserve. You may elect to pay these costs with personal funds separate from your Section 1031 Exchange funds. You may elect to pay these costs with personal funds separate from your Section 1031 Exchange funds. Because the tax treatment of certain expenses of the offering, closing costs, financing costs or reserves is unclear and may vary depending upon the circumstances, no advice or opinion of tax counsel will be given regarding the tax treatment of such costs and the treatment of proceeds attributable to the reserves, which may be taxable to those purchasers who purchase their interests as part of a Section 1031 Exchange. Therefore, each prospective purchaser should seek the advice of a qualified tax advisor as to the proper treatment of such items.

The use of certain exchange proceeds may result in taxable "boot." Any personal property that may be part of the property, amounts used to establish reserves and impositions or other items that are not attributable to the purchase of real estate will not be treated as an interest in real estate and may be treated as "boot." It is possible that such amounts, if sufficient additional funds are borrowed by the purchasers in excess of the indebtedness of a purchaser's prior investment, will not be treated as boot. It is also possible that reserves will be treated as cash boot. In addition, the IRS could take the position that the increase in the purchase price of the property paid by the purchasers would not be considered as an interest in real estate and may be treated as "boot." In addition, to the extent that the portion of the debt acquired with the purchase of an interest in the property is less than the purchaser's debt on the relinquished property, such difference will constitute "boot" and may be taxable depending on the purchaser's basis in the relinquished property. In the event any item is determined to be "boot," the taxpayer will have current income for any such "boot" up to the amount of gain on the exchange of the real property. No opinion is being provided by the trust, the manager, the sponsor or their affiliates or counsel with respect to the amount of "boot" in the transaction. Prospective purchasers must consult their own independent tax advisor regarding these items.

Potential significant tax costs if interests were deemed to be interests in a partnership. If purchasers are treated for federal income tax purposes as having purchased interests in a partnership, the purchasers who purchased their interests as part of a Section 1031 Exchange would not qualify for deferral of gain under Code Section 1031, and each purchaser who had relied on deferral of such purchaser's gain from a disposition of other interests in real property would immediately recognize such gain and be subject to federal income tax thereon. Additionally, since such determination would of necessity come after such purchaser had purchased his interest, such purchaser may have no cash from the disposition of its original interest in real property with which to pay the tax. Given the illiquid and long-term nature of an investment in the interests, there would be no practical means of generating cash from an investment in the interests to pay the tax. In such circumstances, a purchaser will have to use funds from other sources to satisfy this tax liability.

Deferral of tax under state law. Some states adopt Code Section 1031 in whole, other states adopt it in part and still other states impose their own requirements to qualify for deferral of gain under state law. In addition, while many states follow federal tax law by treating the owner of an interest in a fixed investment trust as owning an interest in the assets held by the trust, other state laws may differ and could result in the imposition of income or other taxes on such entities. Therefore, each purchaser must consult his own tax advisor as to the qualification of a transaction for deferral of gain under state law. See "Federal Income Tax Consequences."

Transfer distribution to the Springing LLC. If a transfer distribution occurs, the property will be transferred from the trust to the Springing LLC and the membership interests in the Springing LLC will be proportionally distributed by the beneficial owners. It is anticipated that the manager or its affiliate will serve as the manager of the Springing LLC. The Springing LLC will be treated as a partnership for federal income tax purposes. A transfer distribution may occur under the circumstances set forth in the trust agreement without regard to the tax consequences that arise as a result of the transaction. Under current law, such a transfer should not be subject to federal income tax pursuant to Code Section 721. The transfer could be subject, however, to state or local income, transfer or other taxes. In addition, there can be no assurances that such transfer will not be taxable under the federal income or other tax laws in effect at the time the transfer occurs. Because a transfer distribution could occur in several situations, it is not possible to determine all the tax consequences to the beneficial owners in the event of a transfer distribution. Prospective purchasers should consult their own tax advisors regarding the tax consequences of a transfer distribution and the effect of the property being held by the Springing LLC rather than the trust.

Deferral of tax upon Sale of Springing LLC membership interests. Unlike interests in the trust, membership interests in the Springing LLC will not be treated as direct ownership interests in real property for federal income tax purposes (including for purposes of a Section 1031 Exchange). Thus, if the trust transfers the property to the Springing LLC in a transfer distribution, it is unlikely that any of the beneficial owners who receive membership interests in the Springing LLC will thereafter be able to defer the recognition of gain under Code Section 1031 upon a subsequent disposition of the property or their membership interests in the Springing LLC.

Delayed closing or inability to close. Prospective purchasers who are completing a Section 1031 Exchange should be aware that closing on their replacement property must occur before "the earlier of (i) the day which is 180 days after the date on which the taxpayer transferred the property relinquished in the exchange, or (ii) the due date (determined with regard to extension) for the transferor's return for the taxable year in which the transfer of the relinquished property occurs." See Code Section 1031(a)(3)(B). No extensions will be granted, or other relief afforded by the IRS to taxpayers who do not satisfy this requirement. Therefore, a delayed closing on the acquisition of an interest could adversely affect the qualification of an exchange under Code Section 1031. Prospective purchasers are strongly encouraged to "identify" the maximum number of alternative Replacement Properties and not to identify only the property in this offering.

Compliance with Revenue Ruling 2004-86. Tax counsel believes that the powers and authority granted to the trustee, manager, beneficial owners, and the trust in the trust agreement fall within the limited scope of the powers and authority that may be exercised by a trustee of an "investment trust." The trust agreement authorizes the trust to own the property, receive distributions from the property, and make distributions thereof, enter into any agreements with qualified intermediaries for purposes of a beneficial owner's acquisition of an interest pursuant to Code Section 1031, and notify the relevant parties of any defaults under the transaction documents. Additionally, the trust agreement expressly denies the manager any power or authority to take actions that would cause the trust to cease to constitute an investment trust within the meaning of Treasury Regulation Section 301.7701-4(c). Furthermore, the trust agreement expressly prohibits the trustee, manager, beneficial owners and the trust from exercising any of the enumerated powers that are prohibited under Revenue Ruling 2004-86.

The trust has been structured with a view to the trust addressed in Rev. Rul. 2004-86. However, distinctions exist between the trust agreement and other related arrangements and the trust and other related arrangements described in Revenue Ruling 2004-86. Tax

Counsel believes these distinctions are not material. If, however, the IRS or a court were to disagree with the opinion of tax counsel, the interests may be treated for federal income tax purposes as interests in a partnership and not as interests in real estate, and purchasers would not be able to use their acquisition of interests as part of a Section 1031 Exchange to defer gain under Code Section 1031. For a complete discussion of the trust in comparison to the arrangement described in Revenue Ruling 200486, purchaser may request the opinion of tax counsel.

Status as a true lease for federal income tax purposes. Transactions structured as leases may be recharacterized for federal income tax purposes to reflect their economic substance. For example, in appropriate circumstances a purported lease of property may be recharacterized as a sale of the property providing for deferred payments. Such a recharacterization in this context would have significant (and adverse) tax consequences. For example, if the master lease were to be recharacterized as a sale of the property, then a purchaser would be unable to treat the acquired interest as qualified "replacement property" in a Section 1031 Exchange in that the interest would constitute an interest in real property that the purchaser would not hold for investment. That is, the purchaser would be treated as having immediately sold the acquired interest in the property to the master tenant with the master tenant being treated as purchasing the property (and all the interests therein) from the purchasers in exchange for an installment note for federal income tax purposes. As a result, purchasers attempting to participate in Section 1031 Exchanges would not be treated as having received qualified replacement property when they acquired their interest because the purchaser would be treated as having made a loan to the master tenant. As the owner of the property for federal income tax purposes, the master tenant would be entitled to claim any depreciation deductions. To the extent that payments of "rent" were recharacterized as payments of interest and principal, the payment of principal would not be treated as the receipt of taxable income by the purchasers and would not be deductible by the master tenant, as applicable. All of these consequences could have a significant impact on the tax consequences of an investment in an interest.

Rev. Proc. 2001-28 sets forth advance ruling guidelines for "true lease" status. We have not sought, and do not expect to request, a ruling from the IRS under Revenue Procedure 2001-28. These ruling guidelines provide certain criteria that the IRS will require to be satisfied in order to issue a private letter ruling that a lease is a "true lease" for federal income tax purposes. In the event of an examination by the IRS, the IRS and, ultimately, the courts of applicable jurisdiction, would consider these ruling guidelines, together with existing cases and rulings, for purposes of determining whether a lease qualifies as a true lease for federal income tax purposes. However, tax counsel does not believe that strict compliance with Rev. Proc. 2001-28 is required to conclude that the master lease should be characterized as a true lease for federal income tax purposes. Rather, tax counsel believes that satisfying most of the material ruling guidelines should be sufficient for purposes of determining the characterization of the master lease for federal income tax purposes. We will receive an opinion of tax counsel that tax counsel believes the master lease satisfies most of the pertinent material conditions set forth in Rev. Proc. 2001-28 and that the master lease should be treated as a true lease rather than as a financing for federal income tax purposes. Similarly, if the master tenant were treated as a mere agent of the trust rather than as a lessee, the power of the master tenant to make improvements to the property and to re-lease the property could be attributed to the trust, and the trust could be deemed to have powers prohibited under Rev. Rule 2004-86. We have considered the issue and, after having consulted with tax counsel, have concluded that that master tenant should not be treated as an agent of the trust. However, there is no assurance that the IRS would agree with these positions.

Tax penalties. The opinion was written to support the promotion or marketing of this transaction, and each purchaser should seek advice based on the purchaser's particular circumstances from an independent tax advisor.

Limitations on losses and credits from passive activities. Losses from passive trade or business activities generally may not be used to offset "portfolio income," such as interest, dividends and royalties, or salary or other active business income. Deductions from such passive activities generally may only be used to offset passive income. Interest deductions attributable to passive activities are treated as passive activity losses, and not as investment interest. Thus, such interest deductions are subject to limitation under the passive activity loss rule and not under the investment interest limitation rule. Credits from passive activities generally are limited to the tax attributable to the income from passive activities. Passive activities include trade or business activities in which the taxpayer does not materially participate and any rental activity. The purchaser's income and loss from the trust will constitute income and loss from passive activities. A taxpayer may deduct passive losses from rental real estate activities against other income if: (i) more than half of the personal services performed by the taxpayer in trades or businesses are performed in a real estate trade or business in which the taxpayer materially participates, and (ii) the taxpayer performs more than 750 hours of service during the tax year in real property trades or businesses in which the taxpayer materially participates. See "Federal Income Tax Consequences—Other Tax Consequences—Limitations on Losses and Credits from Passive Activities."

Foreclosure/Cancellation of Debt Income. In the event of a foreclosure of a mortgage or deed of trust on the property, a purchaser would realize gain, if any, in an amount equal to the excess of the purchaser's share of the outstanding mortgage over its adjusted tax basis in the property, even though the purchaser might realize an economic loss upon such a foreclosure. In addition, the purchaser could be required to pay income taxes with respect to such gain even though the purchaser may receive no cash distributions as a result of such foreclosure.

If property debt were to be cancelled without an accompanying foreclosure of the property, then a purchaser could have to recognize cancellation of debt income (subject to the applicability of one or more of the cancellation of debt exclusions, in which event such exclusion(s) might constitute only a "deferral" of such income effectuated by the purchaser's reduction of tax attributes – including tax basis), which would be taxed as ordinary income, for federal income tax purposes. Also, the purchaser would not be able to offset any such cancellation of debt income with any loss recognized by a purchaser that would constitute a capital loss for federal income tax purposes (including any loss recognized by a purchaser from the sale of his interest in the likely event that the interest could not be considered Section 1231 Real Property).

Limitation on losses under the at-risk rules. A purchaser that is an individual or closely held corporation will be unable to deduct losses from the trust, if any, to the extent such losses exceed the amount such purchaser is "at risk." Losses not allowed under the at-risk provisions may be carried forward to subsequent taxable years and used when the amount at risk increases. The rules regarding the applicability of the at-risk rules to a particular purchaser are complex and vary with the facts and circumstances particular to each purchaser. Prospective purchasers should consult their tax advisors with respect to the tax consequences to them of the rules described herein.

No decision rights regarding sale requirements for the property. The purchasers will not have any vote or decision-making authority with respect to the sale of the property. If the manager determines, in its sole discretion, that the sale of the property is reasonable, then the trust may sell the property. This sale will occur without regard to the tax position, preferences or desires of any of the purchasers, and the purchasers will have no right to approve (or disapprove) of the sale of the property. A purchaser may or may not be able to defer the recognition of gain for federal, state or local income tax purposes when this sale occurs.

Tax liability in excess of cash distributions. It is possible that a purchaser's tax liability resulting from its interest will exceed its share of cash distributions from the trust. This may occur because cash flow from the property may be used to fund nondeductible operating or capital expenses of the property. Thus, there may be years in which a purchaser's tax liability exceeds its share of cash distributions from the trust. The same tax consequences may result from a sale or transfer of an interest, whether voluntary or involuntary, that gives rise to ordinary income or capital gain. If any of these circumstances occur, a purchaser would have to use funds from other sources to satisfy its tax liability. See "Federal Income Tax Consequences—Other Tax Consequences."

Risk of audit. An audit of the tax returns of a beneficial owner by the IRS or any other taxing authority could result in a challenge to, and disallowance of, some of the deductions claimed on such returns. An audit also could challenge the qualification of a Section 1031 Exchange. No assurance or warranty of any kind can be made with respect to the deductibility of any items, or of the qualification of a Section 1031 Exchange, in the event of either an audit or any litigation resulting from an audit. An audit of a purchaser's tax returns could arise as a result of an examination by the IRS or any state or local taxing authority or any other taxing authority of tax returns filed by the sponsor or its affiliates, or a beneficial owner or any information returns filed by the trust.

Purchasers' tax liquidity. It is possible that a purchaser's taxable income resulting from their interest will exceed any distribution of cash attributable thereto. This may occur because cash flow from the property may be used to fund nondeductible operating or capital expenses of the property, including reserves and payments of principal on the loan. Thus, there may be years in which a purchaser's tax liability exceeds his, her or its share of cash from the property. In addition, a sale or exchange of the property at an economic loss without a Section 1031 Exchange could result in ordinary income, depreciation recapture or capital gain to a purchaser without any accompanying net cash proceeds from the sale or disposition of the property to pay income taxes on such items. This is a particular risk for certain purchasers, such as persons acquiring an interest in a Section 1031 Exchange, whose income tax basis in an interest may be substantially lower than his, her or its cash investment in the property. If this were to occur, an Investor would have to use funds from other sources to satisfy his, her or its tax liability.

Changes in federal income tax law. The discussion of tax aspects contained in this memorandum is based on law presently in effect and certain proposed Treasury Regulations. Nonetheless, prospective purchasers should be aware that new administrative, legislative or judicial action could significantly change the tax aspects of an investment in an interest. Any such change may or may not be retroactive with respect to transactions entered into or contemplated before the effective date of such change and could have a material adverse effect on an investment in an interest.

Reportable transaction disclosure and list maintenance. A taxpayer's ability to claim privilege on any communication with a federally authorized tax preparer involving a tax shelter is limited. In addition, taxpayers and material advisors must comply with disclosure and list maintenance requirements for reportable transactions. Reportable transactions include transactions that generate losses under Code Section 165 and may include certain large like-kind exchanges entered into by corporations. The sponsor and tax counsel have concluded that the sale of an interest should not constitute a reportable transaction. Accordingly, the trust and tax counsel do not intend to make any filings pursuant to these disclosure or list maintenance requirements. There can be no assurances that the IRS will agree with this determination by the trust and tax counsel. Significant penalties could apply if a party fails to comply with these rules, and such rules are ultimately determined to be applicable.

State and local taxes. In addition to federal income tax consequences, a prospective purchaser should consider the state and local tax consequences of an investment in an interest. Prospective purchasers must consult with their own tax advisors concerning the applicability and impact of any state and local tax laws. Purchasers may be required to file state tax returns in some or all the states where the property are located in connection with the ownership of an interest.

Accuracy-related penalties and interest. In the event of an audit that disallows a purchaser's deductions or disqualifies a purchaser's Section 1031 Exchange, purchasers should be aware that the IRS could assess significant penalties and interest on tax deficiencies. The Code provides for penalties relating to the accuracy of tax returns equal to 20 percent of the portion of the tax underpayment to which the penalty applies. The penalty applies to any portion of any understatement that is attributable to (i) negligence or disregard of rules or regulations, (ii) any substantial understatement of income tax, or

(iii) any substantial valuation misstatement. A substantial valuation misstatement occurs if the value of any property or the adjusted basis of such property is 150 percent or more of the amount determined to be the proper valuation or adjusted basis. This penalty generally doubles if the property's valuation or the adjusted basis is overstated by 200 percent or more. In addition to these provisions, there is a 20 percent accuracy-related penalty is imposed on (i) listed or (ii) reportable transactions having a significant tax avoidance purpose. This penalty is increased to 30 percent if the transaction is not properly disclosed on the taxpayer's federal income tax return. Failure to disclose such a transaction can also prevent the applicable statute of limitations from running in certain circumstances and can subject the taxpayer to additional disclosure penalties ranging from $10,000 to $200,000, depending on the facts of the transaction. Any interest attributable to unpaid taxes associated with a nondisclosed reportable transaction may not be deductible for federal income tax purposes. See "Federal

Income Tax Consequences—Other Taxes

Alternative minimum tax. The alternative minimum tax applies to designated items of tax preference. The limitations on the deduction of passive losses also apply for purposes of computing alternative minimum taxable income. Prospective purchasers should consult with their own tax advisors concerning the applicability of the alternative minimum tax.

Medicare tax. Income and gain from passive activities may be subject to the Medicare Tax. Certain purchasers who are US individuals are subject to the Medicare tax, an additional 3.8 percent tax on their "net investment income" and certain estates and trusts are subject to an additional 3.8 percent tax on their undistributed "net investment income." Among other items, "net investment income" generally includes passive investment income, such as rent and net gain from the disposition of investment property, less certain deductions. Prospective purchasers should consult their tax advisors with respect to the tax consequences to them of the rules described above.

In conclusion, the purchase of an interest involves a number of risks. Do not acquire an interest if you cannot afford to lose your entire investment. Carefully consider the risks described in the PPM for each contemplated DST investment, as well as the other information in the PPM before deciding to purchase an interest. Consult with your legal, tax and financial advisors about an investment in an interest. The risks described above are not the only risks that may affect an investment in an interest. Additional risks and uncertainties that not presently known or have not been identified may also materially and adversely affect the value of a DST interest, the property or the performance of an investment.

Chapter 21

Why Not a TIC?

Tenancy-in-common (TIC) offerings have been almost entirely replaced by DST offerings since the Great Recession. This is largely due to the DST advantages presented in the foregoing chapters, not least of which are the ability of the trustee to make critical decisions without unanimity, and the requirement of lenders to have a single entity on title. However, there are a few TIC offerings on the market each year, particularly for all-cash debt-free properties. Accordingly, a discussion on the structure, advantages, and disadvantages of a TIC interest may be helpful to close the discussion of fractional ownership investments for 1031 exchange.

Tenancy-in-Common (TIC)

Similar to a DST, a TIC is a co-ownership structure under which multiple investors pool their funds to own one entire property. Each investor owns an undivided fractional interest in an entire property, and participates in a proportionate share of the net income, tax shelters, and growth. However, unlike a DST offering, each TIC owner receives a separate property deed and title insurance for their percentage interest in the property and has all the same rights and privileges as a single (fee simple) owner. Like a DST, the purchase of a TIC interest is treated as a direct interest in real estate, qualifying as like-kind real estate for Section 1031 exchange.

Common Law

The term *tenant* is understood to describe a person who rents or leases a piece of property. In the context of common law concurrent estates (such as a TIC), however, a tenant is a co-owner of real property; this is used as a way to hold concurrent or simultaneous title ownership of real property. Far from a new concept, tenancy in common had its legal footing in English common law that developed from the rights of freemen established by the signing of the Magna Carta by King John in 1215. The reader may be familiar with other common law concurrent titles, such as joint tenancy, joint tenancy with the right of survivorship, cotenancy and tenancy by the entirety. At common law, tenancies in common were not originally favored, due to the fact that at the death of one tenant, the entire property was divided into several shares among the tenants according to their percent of ownership, whereas the English Lords desired to retain large tracts of land within a family.[33]

Revenue Procedure 2002-22

This important ruling, known as Revenue Procedure 2002-22, was issued by the IRS in March of 2002, and includes fifteen factors to determine if a co-ownership arrangement such as a tenants-in-common format, is likely to be treated as a partnership for income tax purposes and therefore not qualify to enjoy the § 1031 exchange provisions. For your information, a full version of the Revenue Ruling in included in Appendix B. The specifics of the ruling are summarized below.

Prior to Revenue Procedure 2002-22, TIC sponsors had to request a private letter ruling to be certain that their investors' exchange position would be honored by the IRS. As these private letter rulings began to pile up, IRS officials determined that it would be a good idea to formally issue a ruling, that while not a safe harbor, would set forth the conditions under which the co-owners of real estate will not be considered partners relative to § 1031.

To the delight of promoters of TIC syndications structured for investors wanting to complete § 1031 exchanges, Revenue Procedure 2002-22 gave tacit approval to this ownership format as long as the terms of the TIC arrangement do not conflict with any of the fifteen factors spelled out in the ruling. In so doing, some observers believe that the IRS paved the way for TIC syndications to become a popular investment vehicle for part-time real estate investors wanting to sell their real estate holdings while deferring, possibly even eliminating, the capital gains tax that would otherwise result from such a sale. The fifteen factors of the Revenue Procedure are expounded in the paragraphs below.

Management Agreement

TIC co-owners enter into a management agreement, which must be renewable no less frequently than annually, with an agent, who may be the sponsor or a co-owner (or any person related to the sponsor or a co-owner), but who may not be a lessee. The management agreement may authorize the manager to maintain a common bank account for the collection and deposit of rents, and to offset expenses associated with the property against any revenues, before disbursing each co-owner's share of net revenues. In all events, the manager must disburse to the co-owners their shares of net revenues within three months from the date of receipt of those revenues. The management agreement may also authorize the manager to prepare statements for the co-owners, showing their share of revenue and costs from the property. In addition, the management agreement may authorize the manager to obtain or modify insurance on the property, and to negotiate modifications of the terms of any lease or any indebtedness encumbering the property, subject to the approval of the co-owners. The determination of any fees paid by the co-ownership to the manager must not depend in whole or in part on the income or profits derived by any person from the property, and may not exceed the fair market value of the manager's services. Any fee paid by the co-ownership to a broker must be comparable to fees paid by unrelated parties to brokers for similar services.

Tenancy in Common

Ownership requires each of the co-owners to hold title to the property (either directly or through a disregarded entity) as a tenant in common under local law. Thus, title to the property as a whole may not be held by an entity recognized under local law.

Number of Co-Owners

The number of co-owners must be limited to no more than thirty-five persons. For this purpose, a person is defined as in IRC 7701(a)(1), except that a husband and wife are treated as a single person, and all persons who acquire interests from a co-owner by inheritance are treated as a single person.

No Treatment of Co-Ownership as an Entity

The co-ownership may not file a partnership or corporate tax return, conduct business under a common name, execute an agreement identifying any or all the co-owners as partners, shareholders, or members of a business entity, or otherwise hold itself out as a partnership or other form of business entity (nor may the co-owners hold themselves out as partners, shareholders, or members of a business entity). The IRS generally will not issue a ruling under this revenue procedure if the co-owners held interests in the property through a partnership or corporation immediately prior to the formation of the co-ownership.

Co-Ownership Agreement

The co-owners may enter into a limited co-ownership agreement that may run with the land. For example, a co-ownership agreement may provide that a co-owner must offer the co-ownership interest for sale to the other co-owners, the sponsor, or the lessee at fair market value (determined as of the time the partition right is exercised) before exercising any right to partition; or that certain actions on behalf of the co-ownership require the vote of co-owners holding more than 50 percent of the undivided interests in the property.

Voting

The co-owners must retain the right to approve the hiring of any manager, the sale or other disposition of the property, any leases of a portion or all of the property, or the creation or modification of a blanket lien. Any sale, lease, or re-lease of a portion or all of the property, any negotiation or renegotiation of indebtedness secured by a blanket lien, the hiring of any manager, or the negotiation of any management contract (or any extension or renewal of such contract) must be by unanimous approval of the co-owners. For all other actions on behalf of the co-ownership, the co-owners may agree to be bound by the vote of those holding more than 50 percent of the undivided interests in the property.

Restrictions on Alienation

In general, each co-owner must have the rights to transfer, partition, and encumber the co-owner's undivided interest in the property without the agreement or approval of any person. However, restrictions on the right to transfer, partition, or encumber interests in the property that are required by a lender and that are consistent with customary commercial lending practices are not prohibited. Moreover, the co-owners, the sponsor, or the lessee may have a right of first offer (the right to have the first opportunity to offer to purchase the co-ownership interest) with respect to any co-owner's exercise of the right to transfer the co-ownership interest in the property. In addition, a co-owner may agree to offer the co-ownership interest for sale to the other co-owners, the sponsor, or the lessee at fair market value (determined as of the time the partition right is exercised) before exercising any right to partition.

Sharing Proceeds and Liabilities Upon Sale of Property

If the property is sold, any debt secured by a blanket lien must be satisfied, and the remaining sales proceeds must be distributed to the co-owners.

Proportionate Sharing of Profits and Losses

Each co-owner must share in all revenues generated by the property and all costs associated with the property in proportion to the co-owner's undivided interest in the property. Neither the other co-owners, nor the sponsor, nor the manager may advance funds to a co-owner to meet expenses associated with the co-ownership interest, unless the advance is recourse to the co-owner (and, where the co-owner is a disregarded entity, the owner of the co-owner) and is not for a period exceeding 31 days.

Proportionate Sharing of Debt

The co-owners must share in any indebtedness secured by a blanket lien in proportion to their undivided interests.

Options

A co-owner may issue an option to purchase the co-owner's undivided interest (call option), provided that the exercise price for the call option reflects the fair market value of the property determined as of the time the option is exercised. For this purpose, the fair market value of an undivided interest in the property is equal to the co-owner's percentage interest in the property multiplied by the fair market value of the property as a whole. A co-owner may not acquire an option to sell the co-owner's undivided interest (put option) to the sponsor, the lessee, another co-owner, or the lender, or any person related to the sponsor, the lessee, another co-owner, or the lender.

No Business Activities

The co-owners' activities must be limited to those customarily performed in connection with the maintenance and repair of rental real property (customary activities). Activities will be treated as customary activities for this purpose if the activities would not prevent an amount received by an organization from qualifying as rent under the regulations thereunder. In determining the co-owners' activities, all activities of the co-owners, their agents, and any persons related to the co-owners with respect to the property will be taken into account, whether or not those activities are performed by the co-owners in their capacities as co-owners. For example, if the sponsor or a lessee is a co-owner, then all the activities of the sponsor or lessee (or any person related to the sponsor or lessee) with respect to the property will be taken into account in determining whether the co-owners' activities are customary activities. However, activities of a co-owner or a related person with respect to the property (other than in the co-owner's capacity as a co-owner) will not be taken into account if the co-owner owns an undivided interest in the property for less than 6 months.

Leasing Agreements

All leasing arrangements must be bona fide leases for federal tax purposes. Rents paid by a lessee must reflect the fair market value for the use of the property. The determination of the amount of the rent must not depend, in whole or in part, on the income or profits derived by any person from the property leased (other than an amount based on a fixed percentage or percentages of receipts or sales). Thus, for example, the amount of rent paid by a lessee may not be based on a percentage of net income from the property, cash flow, increases in equity, or similar arrangements.

Loan Agreements

The lender with respect to any debt that encumbers the property, or with respect to any debt incurred to acquire an undivided interest in the property, may not be a related person to any co-owner, the sponsor, the manager, or any lessee of the property.

Payments to Sponsor

Except as otherwise provided by the revenue procedure, the amount of any payment to the sponsor for the acquisition of the co-ownership interest (and the amount of any fees paid to the sponsor for services) must reflect the fair market value of the acquired co-ownership interest (or the services rendered) and may not depend, in whole or in part, on the income or profits derived by any person from the property.

The Need of an LLC

The investor in a TIC has deeded title to the property, which would normally open up their personal assets to liability for the property owned in common. To limit this exposure, TIC investors typically set up a single purpose Limited Liability Corporation (LLC) for the purpose of TIC ownership, making them bankruptcy remote. The LLC is often registered in the State of Delaware due to its judicial precedent of maintaining the corporate veil.

Debt Structure under the TIC

Because each TIC investor holds title, there is often the requirement by a lender for the investors to sign "carve-outs" related to investor fraud and environmental issues. Traditionally, TIC offerings came with prearranged nonrecourse financing similar to DSTs. Due to stricter underwriting standards since the Great Recession, the recent trend has been to limit TIC offerings to all cash offerings with no mortgage debt.

TIC Advantages

If packaged as a security, TIC ownership carries with it all the advantages of securitized real estate. In addition, the main advantage of TIC ownership vis-à-vis DST ownership is that the TIC owner, who receives deeded title to the property, has greater say in the day-to-day operation of the property and its eventual sale. This arrangement may be preferred by the investor who is not fully comfortable with a DST structure, where the signatory trustee has authority to handle all the matters related to the property, or if the investor owns an especially large portion of a property and would like to retain a higher level of control.

TIC offerings are prepackaged with the structure put in place by the sponsor. The sponsor buys or arranges to buy the property. They arrange or obtain the mortgage financing. They prepare the offering documents and arrange for the closing of the property. The investor need only review and fill out subscription documents, complete their due diligence, and arrange for their equity to be delivered to escrow.

TIC offerings are structured to accommodate a variety of investors with different amounts of equity. While every offering has a minimum equity amount, an investor can invest any amount over the minimum (up to the maximum offering amount). This allows investors of various sizes to invest in an offering, and it allows an investor to divide their equity among two or more offerings, depending on the amount of equity that they have to invest. If any debt is placed on the property, it will be assumed on a pro-rata basis by the TIC investors.

Risks of Tenancy in Common

In addition to all the risks of investment real estate, owning real estate in common entails the risk of disagreement or conflict with the other tenants as to the management, financing or sale of the property. Unanimity among the tenants is required for all major decisions, and though there are usually provisions allowing the purchase of the interest of a dissenting tenant, this could prove difficult or time-consuming. If the property held in common is leveraged, there is the risk of being unable to refinance the program at the end of the loan term. Also, there is the risk of possible conflicts of interest with program sponsors, trustees, or property managers.

DST vs TIC Comparison

The following chart is a handy comparison of the major structural issues for DSTs and TICs.

DST Structure vs. TIC Structure

	DST Structure	TIC Structure
IRS Guidance:	Rev. Rul. 2004-86	Rev. Proc. 2002-22
Number of Investors:	Up to 499	Up to 35
Ownership:	Percentage of beneficial ownership in a DST that owns real property	Undivided tenant in common interest in real property
Investors receive property deed:	No	Yes
Investors form single member LLCs:	No	Yes (generally)
Major decision approval:	No voting rights	Equal voting rights and unanimous approval required
Number of borrowers:	One (the DST)	Up to 35
Bankruptcy remote:	Yes	No (Yes if using a single member LLC)

Chapter 22

The History of the TIC and DST Industry

The industry was effectively born in March of 2002, when the Internal Revenue Service issued Revenue Procedure 2002-22 giving formal guidance on how taxpayers could exchange their business or investment real property for a tenants-in-common (TIC) fractional ownership interest in like-kind property. Accordingly, the IRS played a key role in creating the fractional ownership industry and a significant role in its early development.

Tenants-in-common as a form of joint title to real estate was a British common law provision that has probably been around since soon after the signing of the Magna Carta by King John in 1215. In its traditional form, TIC ownership was between a small group of often related individuals. In the 1980's, several larger deals with greater numbers of unrelated investors were being put together. As the number of unrelated investors grew, so did the uncertainty as to whether the TIC replacement property would qualify for the tremendous tax advantages of the § 1031 tax deferral. As imaginative and creative property managers were putting more of these structures together, there was growing concern whether the investors were being exposed to the risk of having to pay capital gain tax and depreciation recapture on significant gains if the Service challenged the structure.

Early TIC sponsors had to request a private letter ruling to be certain that the IRS would honor their investors' exchange position. As these private letter rulings began to pile up, IRS officials determined to formally issue a ruling, that while not a safe harbor, would set forth the conditions under which the co-owners of real estate will not be considered partners in a partnership relative to § 1031.

In the early 2000's, William Passco and Tony Thompson were counseled by Darryl Steinhause, a prominent securities syndication attorney with then Luce Forward in San Diego (and more recently with DLA Piper), requesting a formal revenue procedure for their most current TIC deal. The three worked closely with the Internal Revenue Service for the better part of 2001 to modify the TIC structure in an effort to mitigate the concerns of the Service that the investment should be deemed to be a limited partnership, which is specifically disallowed by the statute. The result was the masterfully crafted IRS Revenue Procedure 2002-22.

It should be noted here that a Revenue Procedure, which specified the requirements for obtaining a Private Revenue Ruling, may only be relied upon by the taxpayer requesting and receiving the advice for the specific facts and circumstances of their unique transaction, unlike a Revenue Ruling which may be relied upon by other unrelated taxpayers. However, what gave the new industry life is that law firms could now use the provisions of Revenue Procedure 2002-22 to form a legal opinion as to whether a specific TIC deal meets the requirements outlined in the Revenue Procedure. Later, the industry's association organization, the Tenant-In-Common Association (TICA), would issue a best practice standard that, at a minimum, the legal opinion for a conforming TIC offering would be a "should" level or higher opinion.

The Revenue Procedure included fifteen factors to determine if a co-ownership arrangement such as a tenants-in-common format is likely to be treated as a partnership for income tax purposes, therefore not qualifying to enjoy the § 1031 exchange provisions. A full copy of the fifteen points of Revenue Procedure 2002-22 is included in Appendix B for your reference.

The IRS was present at many of the early TICA conferences. IRS representatives participated in round table discussions to answer questions, give guidance, and provide assurance that the Service was firmly behind the revenue procedure and the new industry that sprang from the procedure. In addition, the IRS issued several private letter rulings that were requested by various sponsors to make the TIC structure outlined by the Revenue Procedure more workable for managing real estate. One example was that many of the early sponsors were finding the Revenue Procedure provision that the property manager must be elected annually somewhat troublesome to implement, as all the TIC owners were required to actively elect the manager each year. However, many investors were not responding for the annual vote. The IRS ruled that the investment would still qualify for the § 1031 exchange if the annual vote to renew the management contract was conducted in the negative, meaning that if there were no objections, the management would automatically be elected each year.

As a side note, it may be said that Bill Passco, Tony Thompson, and Darryl Steinhause were the three founding fathers of the industry. Both Bill and Tony founded their separate TIC sponsors, each bearing their own name, with very different investment philosophies and each raising billions of dollars of investment equity into syndicated TIC and DST properties. Darryl Steinhause went on to help syndicate over $5 billion in TIC and DST offerings.

Development of an Industry

Thus, a new industry was born in America with a capital idea and a handful of free thinking and dedicated real estate, legal, and financial industry professionals. Their vision was to meet the cash flow and investment needs of the portion of the nation's population that had built wealth using real estate and "sweat equity" and now were looking to monetarize that equity into a truly passive cash flow stream to fund retirement or other activities.

Syndicated TIC industry sales for 2002, the first year of the new industry, were a modest $240,000 in 2002. However, the idea soon took hold and the sales dramatically increased year-after-year, to a record $3.6 billion only four years later in 2006. This remarkable growth was in spite of the fact that sponsors and broker-dealers were restricted in their advertising and marketing efforts by the private offering exemptions from the registration requirements of the Securities Act of 1933, including the prohibition on general solicitation. If it were not for the devastating effects of the Great Recession on real estate markets, the sales growth based on the trajectory over the first four years may have been astronomical.

What might have been? What might have been the reach and the height of this dynamic new industry if not for the artificial ceiling that capped sales in 2006 and then sent it plummeting in the following years from the 2006 precipice? See the 1031 market statistics graph in chapter 1.

Key Developments

Before analyzing the effects that the Great Recession had on the industry, we want to see some of the critical internal development that was transpiring during these initial four years of astronomical growth. One of the first advances was the creation of the new industry's association, the Tenant-in-Common Association or simply TICA. The TICA Foundation was established in 2003 as a nonprofit corporation for charitable and educational purposes. The TICA mission statement promoted the highest ethical standards to its members, as well as providing education and information to the entire TIC community. Furthermore, TICA's purpose was to protect the TIC industry by: (1) protecting the interests of investors; (2) promoting and protecting the common interests of members; (3) promoting the quality and integrity of offerings; (4) promoting high standards of professional conduct; and (5) providing members with quality education, information, resources, and networking opportunities.

The first TICA event in 2003 was held in South Jordan, UT at the Country Inn and Suites, with approximately 40-50 people. The next TICA event was at the Homestead Resort in Heber, Utah and had 85-100 people.[34] Cornerstone had entered the industry in the preceding year, but first attended the 2004 TICA conference at the beautiful Grand America Hotel. At its height, TICA had over 1,200 members from across the country in various TIC professions, including attorneys, CPAs, broker-dealers, sponsors, lenders, mortgage brokers, qualified intermediaries, real estate agents, registered investment advisors and registered representatives.

Central to its mission and the protections it attempted to afford investors was the development of a set of best practices. While taking real estate, securities, tax, and lender regulations into account, the TICA guide of best practices inform TIC professionals on how to properly structure, disclose, sell and manage TIC investments. Many of these best practices are still being used today, and include but are not limited to the following:

- The TIC offering private placement memorandum (PPM) to be provided to associated broker dealer due diligence departments;
- A timeline to ensure all associated parties have adequate time to review and assess the offering, namely a five-day broker-dealer due diligence cooling-off period;
- Guidelines for developing tables for the uses of equity and debt proceeds;
- Rules for a summary table to be included in the PPM with property name, location, projected and actual distribution rate, and projected and actual net operating income, and tables of appropriate track recording;
- Condition that each offering present a tax legal opinion at the "should level" as to whether the offering qualifies for IRC Section 1031 exchange;
- Sponsor procedures to ensure that the offered investment is appropriate for each investor in addition to being accredited, and including credit and background checks;
- Monthly distributions to be sent out promptly as set out in the TIC agreement, and investors notified immediately of any delays, with an explanation;
- Distributions varying by 10 percent of the projected amount should be accompanied by a detailed explanation of the reason by the sponsor;

- Quarterly reports to be distributed to investors to provide up-to-date information about the performance of the property;
- A detailed annual report on the property performance should be provided to the investors on an annual basis.

FINRA Notice to Members 05-18

Another major development for the young industry was the issuance by the Financial Industry Regulatory Authority (FINRA) of its Notice to Members 05-18 in March of 2005. This Notice reminded members that, when offering TIC interests that are securities to customers, members and their associated persons must comply with all applicable NASD rules, including those addressing

- suitability,
- due diligence,
- splitting commissions with unregistered individuals or firms,
- supervision, and
- recordkeeping.

The notice firstly confirmed that, for tax purposes, the TIC qualifies as real estate for IRC Section 1031 exchanges, while concurrently taking the position that TICs generally would constitute an investment contract and thus be a security under federal securities laws. It states that TICs (and similarly DSTs) are generally investment contracts because the tenants-in-common invest in an undivided fractional interest in the real property, by pooling their assets and sharing the risks and benefits of the enterprise, while obtaining profits derived predominantly from the efforts of others, such as through contracts concerning leasing, management, and operating of the acquired property. Furthermore, the Notice underlines the FINRA position that, while TIC interests are investment contracts under securities law, this fact does not inherently disqualify them as property that may be exchanged under Section 1031.

The Notice classified the TIC interest as a nonconventional interest, and the applicability of NASD Notice to Members 03-71. Specifically, that FINRA members are responsible to

- *conduct appropriate due diligence;*
- *perform reasonable-basis suitability analysis;*
- *perform customer-specific suitability analysis for recommended transactions;*
- *ensure the promotional materials used by the members are fair, accurate, and balanced;*
- *implement appropriate internal controls; and*
- *provide appropriate training to registered persons involved in the sale of these products.*

With respect to suitability and due diligence, the Notice states that, before recommending a TIC exchange, members must have a clear understanding of the investment goals and current financial status of the investor and consider asset concentrations and the risk of overconcentration against the benefits of tax deferral. Other risks that should be addressed are that of illiquidity, and that there is not a secondary market; that the TIC interests (not DST) may require unanimous consent to sell a TIC interest; and that fees charged could offset money saved through tax deferral. Given the importance of tax deferral, the member should obtain a "clean" legal opinion that a TIC "should" or "will" qualify for exchange under Section 1031.

Furthermore, the member should make reasonable investigations to ensure that the offering document does not contain false or misleading information. Such investigation should include background checks of sponsor's principals, review of agreements (e.g., property management, purchase and sale, lease and loan agreements), property inspection, and understanding the degree of likelihood that projections will occur.

The Notice prohibited a member broker-dealer from paying a fee to a real estate agent, or to split its brokerage commission with a real estate agent, as a violation of NASD Rule 2420, which prohibits the payment of commissions and fees to entities that operate as unregistered broker-dealers. This included indirect payment by reducing the member's commission so that the investor may pay the difference to a real estate agent. Accordingly, an associated person must be licensed to sell TIC interests by passing the appropriate qualifying examinations, namely either the Series 7 (General Securities Representative) or the Series 22 (Limited Representative—Direct Participation Program Securities) in addition to the state-required Series 63 (State Agents License). These representatives must be supervised by a General Securities Principal (Series 24) under a system of comprehensive written supervisory procedures designed to ensure compliance with applicable rules for suitability and sales practices.

Lastly, as a condition for qualifying under Regulation D for an exemption from registration under the 1933 Securities Act, the Notice prohibits general solicitation or general advertising. No issuer or any person acting on its behalf may offer or sell securities based on a general solicitation, including communications published in any newspaper or similar media, or any seminar or meeting whose attendees have been invited by any general solicitation or advertising. In short, the representative must first have an adequate preexisting relationship with the TIC offeree, so that the member representative may evaluate the potential TIC investor's sophistication and financial circumstances.

Real Estate vs. Securities

The Notice to Members 05-18 put to bed a long-standing debate in the early industry, whether a TIC interest should be sold as real estate by licensed real estate professionals or as securities to be sold by FINRA members and representatives. Real estate professionals argued that, since the investment was in real estate, it required experience and training in real estate matters such as appraisals, markets, leases, and loan covenants, and that securities professionals who traditionally sell stocks and bonds lacked these critical skills and knowledge. Several states championed the argument and passed legislation on the state level that a real estate professional had to be involved in the transaction. Securities professionals countered with the argument that real estate professionals where not competent in such issues as assessing investor suitability and concentration risk. Many conscientious advisors, such as Cornerstone, obtained licenses and competencies in both real estate and securities to better serve their clients.

Ultimately, the Notice to Members 05-18, while only having authority over registered securities representatives, warned those paying fees to real estate agents to carefully review SEC and NASD precedent and, if necessary, consult an attorney with experience in these matters. The Tenant-in-Common Association allowed membership to real estate TIC sponsors but took the position that most TICs should be sold as securities per the FINRA Notice to Members.

The permitted exception was based on a 1946 US Supreme Court[35] definition of an investment contract. It defined as a security any investment contract in which profits were to be derived solely from the efforts of others. Accordingly, if the TIC sponsor only structured the initial investment and did not service the debt, manage the property, or help facilitate the ultimate sale of the property, then it might be considered a real estate offering. Metaphorically, the TIC sponsor could help the investors get into the boat but had to let them sail off together alone without the sponsor towards the horizon, presumably with a nonrelated third-party asset manager as captain. Practically, this would prove difficult to structure as a truly passive investment, and nearly all TIC sponsors conformed to the securities model.

The DBSI Debacle

One TIC sponsor that sold TIC interest as real estate was DBSI based in Boise, Idaho. DBSI tried to accommodate both the real estate professionals, with their seemingly unlimited referral source of the real estate agents throughout the county through their FOR1031 division, and the securities professionals, with their high-net-worth accredited investor clients through their affiliated securities broker-dealers.

DBSI used a blanket master lease, funded by income from all its TIC properties, to pay monthly cash flow to all its investors. Accordingly, cash flow shortages from poorly performing properties were being supported by the cash flow from the better performing properties. Interestingly, many of the more astute securities broker-dealers, required by the Notice to Members to perform more detailed due diligence, withdrew selling agreements under a requirement that each property should stand on its own and support its own cash flow projections. Real estate agents without the due diligence requirements continued to sell the properties. Over time, and as the national economy slipped into recession, the poorly performing properties outnumbered those with surplus cash flow, and the whole house of cards fell. DBSI soon defaulted on its master lease that they had previously used as a marketing tool—advertising to investors that they had never defaulted on their master lease payment over a 50-year operating history. Investors who were happy to invest through their real estate agents were all too happy to sue the Idaho-based sponsor for securities law violations.

The losses and law suit were well publicized in the media, which did not make a distinction between real estate TICs and the majority of TIC sponsors selling standalone properties under the proper securities laws with due diligence. Unfortunately, the entire industry suffered a major hit to its reputation due to the noncompliance of one rogue and reprobate sponsor.

Seeking Higher Cash Flow

Another disturbing trend that manifested itself as the industry grew and developed was the desire for ever-higher cash flows. Many well-structured offerings with sound real estate fundamentals and conservative cash flow projections were passed over by investors looking for TIC offerings with ever higher cash flow projections.

Solid asset classes such as single-tenant retail with strong credit tenants under long-term leases and cash flows in the 6 percent range were passed over for hospitality assets with daily leases and cash flow projections in the 8 percent range. While the TIC risk-to-return ratio was not efficiently priced, higher cash flow typically meant lower credit worthiness of the tenant, shorter lease terms, and/or more tertiary markets. Investors gained the impression, maybe because the offerings were sold as securities, that the TIC interest was a bond-like investment with a certainty of future cash flow, rather than the normal flow of monthly rent revenues through operating expenses to net operating income with all its uncertainties. Accordingly, investors and their representatives often overlooked the property fundamentals, viewed all TIC offerings as fungible, and shopped for the highest cash flow on the market. Consequently, the higher-cash-flow offerings would sell out in a matter of days, if not hours, while lower-cash-flow TIC offerings languished for months. Sponsors looking for faster deal turnover would ether make aggressive rent growth and vacancy estimates for higher cash flow projections, or use financial engineering (e.g., excessive interest-only financing with higher loan-to-value levels) to offer higher projected yields. The economic and market pressures of the coming Great Recession would soon test these misguided practices, as well as be a kind of natural selection, to use a science analogy, to eliminate sponsors and broker-dealers who were either too aggressive or lacked the technical experience to survive the downturn.

The Great Recession

Just as the industry was beginning to spread its wings and soar, it was met with the devastating headwinds of the Great Recession. According to the US National Bureau of Economic Research, the recession began in December 2007 and ended in June 2009, thus extending over nineteen months. The International Monetary Fund concluded that it was the worst global recession since the 1930s. The Great Recession was related to the financial crisis of 2007–2008 and the US subprime mortgage crisis of 2007–2009. The Great Recession resulted in the scarcity of valuable assets in the market economy and the collapse of the financial sector in the world economy.

The Great Recession was particularly severe in several aspects. Real gross domestic product (GDP) fell 4.3 percent from its peak in 2007 Q4 to its trough in 2009 Q2, the largest decline in the postwar era (based on data from October 2013). The unemployment rate, which was 5 percent in December 2007, rose to 9.5 percent in June 2009, and peaked at 10 percent in October 2009. The financial effects of the Great Recession were similarly massive: home prices fell approximately 30 percent, on average, from their mid-2006 peak to mid-2009, while the S&P 500 index fell 57 percent from its October 2007 peak to its trough in March 2009. The net worth of US households and nonprofit organizations fell from a peak of approximately $69 trillion in 2007 to a trough of $55 trillion in 2009.[36]

Interestingly, the default rate for commercial real estate loans prerecession was as low as 0.58 percent in the first half of 2006, and had solid economic projections to remain low, had it not been for the fiasco in the residential real estate debt market created by improper underwriting of home mortgages and the greed of mortgage default swap obligations. By comparison, the home mortgage default rate in the fourth quarter of 2006 was 1.91 percent, or more than triple that of the default rate for commercial mortgages. Home mortgage defaults peaked in the first quarter of 2010 at an astounding 11.53 percent.[37] By June 2010, the mortgage delinquency rate for commercial real estate rose to 4.17 percent of commercial loans defaulted in the first quarter of 2010[38]. In real dollar terms, that is $45.5 billion in bank-held loans. Thus, at the height of the recession, home mortgage default rates were 2¾ times those of the commercial real estate debt.

It may be extrapolated from the data that commercial debt underwriting was significantly superior to home mortgage underwriting standards before the recession, which together with the fact that commercial owners typically have greater resources, resulted in significantly fewer defaults during the recession years. So it was the residential and not the commercial real estate market that was to blame for the great recession, with the commercial real estate market being victim to the residential markets. Accordingly, a compelling argument can be made for exchanging from residential rental property to commercial property investments.

The commercial real estate market constitutes about $6 trillion of real estate value in the United States, and encompasses the following asset classes:

- Apartment complexes (although for residential use, these properties are commercial real estate. There are around 33 million square feet of apartment rental space, worth about $1.44 trillion.);
- Hotels (including motels, luxury resorts and business hotels. There are roughly 4.4 million hotel rooms worth $1.92 trillion.);
- Industrial (properties used to distribute or warehouse a product. There are 13 billion square feet of industrial property worth around $240 billion.);
- Retail (including indoor shopping malls, outdoor strip malls, and big box retailers. It also includes grocery stores and restaurants. Its value is around $2.1 trillion, or 36 percent of the total value of commercial real estate and consists of at least 9.5 billion square feet of shopping center space.);
- Office buildings (including everything from Manhattan skyscrapers to your lawyer's office. There are roughly 4 billion square feet of office space, worth around $1.7 trillion, or 29 percent of the total.); and
- Any other properties used for business purposes.

Commercial real estate is a cyclical industry, whose performance is directly related to the rise and fall of the economy. In times of growth, property owners enjoy a massive demand for office space and a steady stream of rental income. Consumers also tend to spend more, boosting demand for retail space. Inversely, when economic conditions are tight, businesses reduce their demand for office space. This equals significant vacancy rates and decreasing rents for property owners. Those with retail space also suffer as consumers reduce spending on nonnecessary goods and services.

When the Great Recession hit in late 2007, the $6-trillion US commercial real estate market was pummeled, although a less serious beating than the residential market. The TIC and DST industry is mainly fueled by built-up equity in the exchange investor's individual rental residential properties. When the recession erased approximately 30 percent of that equity, there was little to no equity that needed to be exchanged, particularly as investors who still had equity were holding properties for a better future market. Consequently, the TIC industry equity investment declined from $3.6 billion in 2006 to just over $100 million by 2010.

Before the recession, most TIC sponsors were conservatively projecting rent growth at a standard 3 percent rate—just above inflation. However, over the recession years, actual rent growth was negative for most asset classes. Vacancy rates soared. Demand for office space took a nosedive, as employers were forced to trim their payrolls in the thick of the economic turmoil. US office vacancy rates soared to 17.4 percent in the second quarter of 2010, with the market losing 1.8 million square feet of occupied space—the highest level since 1993. A building is considered vacant when less than 31 percent of its square footage is leased.[39]

Needless to say, these unforeseen economic realities resulted in missed or overprojected cash flow projections. Many multifamily residential TIC properties were forced to cut rents to sustain occupancy, and therefore were forced to cut cash flows by two hundred to eight hundred basis points. Likewise, multitenant retail TIC properties also had to cut cash flow projections by nearly half, due to vacancies caused by smaller mom-and-pop and other lower-credit tenants. The hardest hit asset class was hospitality with its twenty-four-hour leases, due to the loss in business travel customers, and multitenant office with its three- to five-year leases. In most cases, these cash flows, which had been projected on the higher end of the spectrum, were slashed down to zero for months or even years. In a few worst cases, debt service could not be maintained, and the properties were foreclosed on by the lender. This was especially true for hotels and office buildings that had taken on higher leverage of 70 percent to 80 percent loan-to-value.

The superstar asset class during the recession was that of single-tenant retail with long-term leases and large national credit tenants. TIC investors in these assets did not feel the effects of the recession as the rent check came in month by month per the lease agreements. With longer-term leases, investors were able to wait out the effects of the recession and its aftermath and sell into the up market at a profitable CAP rate.

Consolidation Period

During this period of recession and consolidation, the stronger and better-capitalized TIC sponsors began to assume the asset management contracts for many of the TIC properties that were orphaned by sponsors who were forced into bankruptcy, or who simply exited the industry due to the loss of revenue. For TIC properties with good fundamentals, some of these stronger sponsors help to raise additional capital for TIC owners who were either unable to or unwilling to make capital calls. The capital was typically raised in funds using private placement offering with an LLC fund structure that would purchase TIC interests at a significant discount. The additional equity and more prudent management helped to reposition assets for success and rescue the earlier TIC investors from a possible foreclosure, albeit with a haircut to their equity positions. We view this development as an additional advantage of syndicated fractional ownership over traditional single ownership, as more capital and human resources were able to be deployed in the TIC industry than in other segments of the commercial real estate industry, to save troubled TIC properties.

With a standard management fee of 3 percent of gross revenues, those TIC sponsors who survived the recession and assumed multiple management contracts enjoyed a significant revenue stream once those assets were stabilized, in addition to and apart from syndication fees for new offerings. As is the case with adversity in its many forms, what did not kill these 16 to 20 remaining TIC sponsors only made them stronger. Likewise, broker-dealers and registered representatives who had developed larger client bases were able to substitute revenue from TIC sales with the sales of private REITs and real estate investment funds. Clients intuitively knew that the recession years were the time to acquire real estate. While most investors did not have the larger equity amounts to invest due to shrinkage in the equity of their real estate holdings, they did have some savings and retirement funds to invest, with minimum investments as low as $2,500. Those investors blessed with liquidity during the recession did very well with their recession-syndicated investments.

By the time of the recession, lending banks and at least four of the twelve major commercial backed securities (CBS) lenders had grown comfortable with the TIC structure and were able to sell off the packaged loans to their B-piece buyers. However, after the recession and under pressure from the Fed's, these lenders developed more stringent underwriting standards, and would not lend to the TIC structure with typically twenty to thirty investors on title. This was a major dilemma that was nearly a death sentence for the industry, had it not been for a brilliant attorney named Arnold Harrison back in 2004 and the advent of the DST.

DSTs and Revenue Ruling 2004-86

With the new realities post-Great Recession, a little-noticed Revenue Ruling from 2004 came back into focus. The Revenue Ruling and the DST structure were championed within the TIC Association by attorney Arnold Harrison in May of 2004—at a time when TIC sales were going through the roof and with very little appetite or need for an alternative investment structure. At that time, Arnold S. Harrison was an attorney and partner in Jenner & Block's Chicago office, where he chaired the real estate securities practice, and cochaired both the tax and tax controversy practices. The TICA conference breakout session introducing DST's was probably one of the poorest attended—although Cornerstone was in attendance.

Phoenix from the Ashes

The Delaware statutory trust structure was fully developed in the previous chapters, but here we would like to point out that the DST not only gave new life to the industry but provided a far superior investment structure. Chief among these was that the DST, unlike the TIC, did not paralyze the sponsor with the requirement to obtain a unanimous vote from the owners in order to react to problematic market and financial situations. Under a DST structure, the trustee could make unilateral decisions on issues like sale or refinance (assuming a springing LLC), while the master lessee could make decisions on re-leasing and property management. In addition, banks and many CMBS lenders favored the DST over the TIC structure, as only the trust was on title, and the lender did not have to underwrite multiple individual investors. So offerings were able to obtain favorable debt financing again by utilizing the financial strength and credit of the sponsor trustees. In addition, more conservative lender underwriting also translated into lower, more conservative leverage, less interest-only financing, and greater mortgage amortization over the hold period. Post-recession, CAP rates, due to lower sales prices, were much higher, and provided not only better chances for the return of capital, but also for appreciation. Stricter lender underwriting of DST retail properties also required more national retailer tenants with investment-grade credit ratings or better.

In the wake of the recession, the industry has begun to rebound, with over $1 billion in equity placed into DST properties for 2105 and 2016. If this trend of industry growth continues, the vision of those original industry founders is still in focus: to provide the smaller individual real estate investor with passive institutional-grade real estate, while preserving wealth on a tax-deferred basis, and funding retirement and other cash flow needs. Through the adversity of the Great Recession, the DST as the instrument to make that vision a reality has been tried, tested, and perfected: an instrument that should serve the real estate investor well for years and decades to come.

Direct Investments (Non-1031)

Chapter 23

Private Real Estate Investment Trusts

A Real Estate Investment Trust (REIT) is a corporation that invests in real estate directly, either through properties or mortgages, and which is sold as a security. REITs typically raise $1 to 2 billion in capital and purchase a portfolio of properties over a period of several years, with the intention that these properties produce rental income and appreciation. REITs are commonly offered privately to accredited or other suitable investors as part of their initial raise. In this phase, these REITs are essentially illiquid. Commonly, the goal of these private REITs is to eventually be offered publicly through an initial public offering or to be purchased entirely by a larger REIT. These outcomes, however, cannot be predicted with certainty, and depend upon the performance of the particular properties in the REIT as well as trends in the real estate market as a whole.

Because of the risk of illiquidity, their smaller relative size, and the risks of investing in the early period of the life cycle of the REIT, private REITs will have aggregate capitalization rates significantly higher than publicly traded REITs. This means that an investment in a private REIT can potentially realize significant appreciation simply by the process of becoming publicly traded. Together with the positive characteristics of illiquid investments, this potential appreciation through transition to public trading is one of the most attractive features of private REITs.

The purpose of this chapter is not to discuss the specific real estate or asset class characteristics common among REITs, but rather to touch on the structural issues and general characteristics of REITs. Regarding the real estate assets held in a REIT, most of the same criteria considered in chapter 11, "Choosing a Property," can be applied to the selection of a REIT.

REIT Guidelines

A company must meet the following requirements to be qualified as a REIT:

- Invest at least 75 percent of its total assets in real estate, cash or US Treasuries;
- Receive a minimum of 75 percent of its gross income from rents from real property, interest on mortgages financing real property, or from sales of real estate;
- Be an entity that is taxable as a corporation;
- Be managed by a board of directors or trustees;
- Have a minimum of one hundred 100 shareholders;
- Have no more than 50 percent of its shares held by five or fewer individuals.

A REIT must abide by particular rules and restrictions so that it is not required to pay corporate income taxes. Specifically, it must distribute at least 90 percent of its taxable income to shareholders annually in the form of dividends. As a result, all dividend distributions made by the REIT to its investors are taxed only at the investor level, thereby avoiding any double taxation.

Tax Advantages and the 2017 Tax Cuts and Jobs Act

A new advantage to REIT investing is that the REIT dividend will qualify for the 20 percent Qualified Business Income Deduction per the 2017 Tax Cuts and Jobs Act. In addition, dividend income will be sheltered by depreciation. Similar to real estate funds, but distinct from DSTs, REITs typically offer a preferred return with a waterfall profit split on the back end, effectively at the time of IPO or sale. Please see chapter 24 for a discussion of how such a preferred return with waterfall profit split works at the time of disposition.

Private vs. Public REITs

Individuals can invest in REITs either by purchasing their shares directly on an open exchange, or by investing in a mutual fund that specializes in public real estate. Some REITs are SEC-registered and public but not listed on an exchange; others are private.

REITs can either be publicly traded, offered to suitable investors based upon the 250 70/70 standard (see below), or offered as private placement investments to accredited investors. Nonpublicly traded REITs are illiquid investments with a typical projected hold period of five to seven years, similar to DSTs, LPs and LLCs. Illiquidity is correctly identified as a risk, in particular because an investor is limited in their ability to access their equity prior to the conclusion of an illiquid investment, but this same illiquidity is conversely a significant hedge against the very real risk of market volatility.

Practically, this means that the performance of the nonmarket-correlated REIT depends much more directly upon the performance of the assets held by the REIT than upon various market trends, most of which will have little or nothing to do with the actual assets held. While private REITs are basically illiquid, most will have some element of liquidity in the form of limited redemption polices (typically 5 percent per year). But it is important to keep in mind that, while such a limited redemption policy may be able to accommodate the occasional investor who needs liquidity unrelated to the performance of the REIT itself, it will quickly be exhausted if a large number of investors seek to exit the investment due to its performance. Therefore, it should not be relied upon as a sure liquidity option.

Investment Timing

Because a private REIT will be available for a fixed price over the initial raise period, there are certain advantages to investing towards the end of the raise rather than at the beginning. Typically, sponsors will raise a minority of the capital over a majority of the raise period, and then raise the bulk of the capital at the very end just prior to closing. This is because the success of the REIT in the initial phase is uncertain, and only a few, if any, assets have been acquired. In this sense, it is really a blind pool investment. However, after the raise has picked up momentum and a good number of assets have been acquired, the eventual success of the REIT, at least in terms of being able to achieve the targeted raise, will be clearer. Then the investor will be able to look at the assets that have already been acquired. To clarify this point, a hundred-dollar investment will acquire the same share value, or percentage interest of the REIT, throughout the raise period. Investors who invest at the very end will acquire the same percentage for the same price as those who entered at the beginning. The earlier investors will accrue cash flow over a longer period of time, but the advantages of investing later will typically outweigh the early cash flow, resulting in the somewhat imbalanced raise rate and schedule of most private REITs.

Lower Accreditation Standards

As REITs are registered with the SEC (unlike a DST, TIC or Fund), nonpublicly traded private REITs often have lower suitability standards, and thus are available to certain nonaccredited investors. While the suitability standards will vary from state to state and will be detailed in the PPM, many REITs can be invested in by investors with either $250,000 total net worth, or $70,000 total net worth *and* $70,000 average annual income, informally known as the 250 70/70 suitability standard.

REIT Diversification

REITS are an excellent way for investors to achieve tremendous diversification across the real estate market. Many REITs invest specifically in one area of real estate. For example, one REIT may concentrate investments in shopping malls, while another may concentrate investments in multifamily. Some REITs may concentrate on a specific region, state or country; others are more diversified. Most REITs raise in excess of a billion dollars of equity and may ultimately hold hundreds of properties. With minimum investments as low as $2,500, investors can easily invest in a cross section of REITs, achieving diversification across properties, asset classes, and geographically. Individual REIT assets will typically be institutional quality, professionally managed, large properties, often recently constructed, in growing markets, similar to DSTs and real estate funds.

Types of REITs

Equity REITs invest in and own real property and are measured by the equity or value of their real estate assets. Their revenues come principally from their properties' rents. Mortgage REITs invest in and own property mortgages, loaning mortgage money to owners of real estate, or purchase existing mortgages or mortgage-backed securities. Their revenues are generated primarily by the interest earned on the mortgage loans. Hybrid REITs combine the investment strategies of equity REITs and mortgage REITs by investing in both properties and mortgages. The advantages and disadvantages of mortgage-based REITs versus equity-based REITs are similar to those of debt-based versus equity-based securities. Mortgage REITs should be considered as more conservative in principle, while equity REITs have greater appreciation potential, albeit with greater risk. However, different from most equity-based securities, equity-based REITs have a strong cash flow component, often ranging from 5 to 6 percent of equity invested, usually distributed monthly.

Conclusion

While not the focus of this book, due the fact that they are not considered viable like-kind property for the purposes of 1031 exchange, REIT investments can be an attractive choice for investors seeking to diversify into real estate-backed securities. REITs provide excellent diversification across properties, asset classes, and geographically, either within one REIT or by investing in multiple REITs. REIT investments provide both the benefits and risks of real estate investments, such as rent-based cash flow, depreciation, and appreciation potential. While market-traded REITs offer liquidity and often larger size, nonpublicly traded REITs are nonmarket correlated, hedging against market volatility, though they do typically require a multiyear hold period with limited exit options during the hold. These nontraded REITs can be either private placement securities for accredited investors, or available to suitable investors who meet the 250 70/70 financial qualifications, thus providing an option to invest in nonpublicly traded real estate securities to nonaccredited investors.

Chapter 24

Real Estate and Other Funds

Real Estate Funds are a type of investment vehicle that is composed of a pool of capital raised from a group of investors for the purpose of investing in real estate. These funds seek to generate income and/or capital gains for the fund's investors through a variety of investment strategies. Real Estate Funds are structured either as a Limited Partnership (LP) or as a Limited Liability Company (LLC), and are typically larger than DSTs but smaller than REITs. Funds often seek to raise $100 million or more in capital, which is then used to purchase income-producing real estate assets. Beyond the capital raised through investor participation, many funds will make use of leverage to increase their purchasing power and projected returns. An investment into a real estate fund is not considered to be an interest in real estate, thus this type of investment is not eligible for 1031 exchange, but can be an excellent addition to a diversified investment portfolio.

Real Estate Funds are illiquid investments offered to accredited investors, or other suitable investors, and are often put forth as a private placement security. The accreditation standards for funds do limit who may invest similar to the standards for DSTs and other private placement offerings. For an individual, an accredited investor is any investor with a net worth of $1,000,000 or more, not including the equity in the investor's primary residence. Alternatively, the individual investor may qualify with an income level of $200,000 ($300,000 if married) for the prior two years, and an expectation of the same for the current year. Please see chapter 5 for a detailed discussion on accreditation standards for entities and trusts.

Real estate funds often focus on four main types of investment opportunities:

- Distressed Assets
- Debt
- Development
- Oil and Gas

Distressed Asset Funds

Distressed asset funds seek to purchase real estate that has fallen into distress for various reasons, such as running out of money during the construction phase or failing to keep up with mortgage payments. While the reasons that any property would find itself in this financial situation are varied, the opportunity that they offer is that of a purchase price at a significant discount. The discounted price serves to provide the seller with much-need cash, while also expediting the timing of the transaction by enticing buyers to consider the purchase opportunity. Additionally, funds that seize these opportunities at the discounted price are able to provide high returns to their investors through the growth of their invested capital when the properties are ultimately sold. During the past Great Recession many investors used these distressed asset funds to invest in undervalued properties. Investors did not have large amounts of built up equity to exchange as the value of their real estate holdings were also depressed. However, many had some limited liquidity and knew intuitively that the recession years were the best time to invest. By using these distressed asset funds with lower minimum investment requirements they were able to pool investments with other like-minded investors and take advantage of some real buying opportunities. These opportunities were especially acute with funds that were acquiring foreclosed assets from the banks and CMBS lenders. Distressed asset funds can provide investors with both cash flow during the hold period and additional growth of principal when the investment goes full cycle.

Debt Funds

Debt funds pool capital from investors with the objective of originating senior real estate collateralized loans for qualified borrowers. Unlike funds that seek to purchase distress assets, debt funds make their money through the interest rates and fees that they charge to the borrowers. These fees include items such as original fees, early termination fees, exit fees, etc., and serve to increase the total return to fund investors. Taking a debt position is a hedge against risk by requiring that the loan be backed by a hard asset as collateral. Many investors prefer this type of investment strategy due to long-term and anticipatory nature of the cash flow that will be paid by the borrowers. Debt funds provide investors with consistent cash flow during the hold period but offer limited growth of their principal at the end of the investment.

Development Funds

Development funds focus on purchasing either raw land or an infill parcel of land and then working to construct new assets on that site. Development projects not only serve to provide for new assets in a growing market, but also play a vital role in the revitalization of communities across the United States. Recognizing the shortage of a particular asset class in a local community, such as multifamily, retail, senior assisted living, or hospitality central to the strategy of development funds. Additionally, as these acquired properties are developed to reach their highest and best use, the value they possess increases significantly as well.

As one might expect, the construction and/or development phase of these projects is not able to provide any cash flow to investor due to the reality that the assets are not operational stabilized. With this in view, investors in development funds should anticipate the majority of their return coming in the form of growth of principal at the exit when the property is eventually sold. While cash flow may begin to be generated during the hold period of the investment, this cash flow is limited in nature, thus development funds are considered a growth investment and are more suited for investors seeking growth rather than cash flow.

Oil and Gas Funds

As of the time of writing, the world continues to rely on oil and natural gas to meets its current energy needs. While other forms of energy continue to make advancements in their effectiveness and efficiency, they have not progressed to the point that oil and natural gas are no longer a critical part of every life. Oil and gas funds seek to leverage the strong global demand for these products and to provide investors with higher levels of return through investing in various oil drilling programs, saltwater disposal programs, and royalty programs.

The potential for high returns does not come without a price, and for these types of funds, the price to be paid is risk. The price of oil changes almost daily, thus, oil and gas funds are subject to greater volatility than that of the other funds previously discussed. This volatility and risk are mitigated by both the potential for higher returns and by the tax advantages that come with oil drilling programs.

While providing much needed capital to these types of energy operations and receiving the potential return on that investment, investors can benefit greatly due to the tax advantages related to oil exploration. As these types of investments help our nation in its effort to become and continue as energy independent, they often qualify for a tax write-off for a portion of the cash used by the operator for Intangible Drilling Costs (or IDC). When investing into a drilling program as a General Partner, investors receive the benefit of being able to write off between approximately 80 percent to 90 percent of their investment as a tax deduction due to the IDCs that are associated with the program. Once the IDC was captured then investors revert to a limited partnership interest to protect their noninvested assets from partnership liabilities such as in the unlikely event of environmental contamination. Apart from any returns that the fund may ultimately provide, this deduction can provide investors with a significant opportunity to offset their taxable income and reduce their tax obligation in any given tax year. As such, investors can utilize these funds not only as a means to generate income or grow their principal, but also as mechanism to manage their overall tax obligation.

Blind Pools

Even though each fund has its own investment strategy and provides potential investors with as much information as possible, it is important to note that funds are usually operated as blind pools wherein the investors will not know at the time of investment every asset that the fund will ultimately purchase. Because investors will not usually have a comprehensive list of every future asset that will purchased by the fund, it is important that they understand the strategy and criteria that the fund will employ when it selects assets to acquire as part of its business model.

Due to the fact that funds are blind pools, investors are investing more in the strategy that is set forth by the fund, and the ability of the fund's management team to execute that strategy than they are in the underlying real estate itself. To this end, investors should take the time to thoroughly understand the nature of a fund by reading through its Private Placement Memorandum (PPM) prior to making an investment decision. Studying the details of any offering and the sponsor's prior success will ensure that investors have visibility and understanding required to gain the confidence that a fund is a suitable investment for their individual investment needs.

Sample Returns

Real estate funds provide higher projected returns than DSTs, due to the nature of their structure and the upside potential of the real estate in which they invest. Additionally, these funds often provide a preferred return to investors. A preferred return means that investors will be the first to receive returns up to a predetermined level. Upon reaching this level of return, the remaining profits are split according to the negotiated rate. The preferred return is also premised upon the full return of the original principal investment to the investor.

In the way of illustration, let us consider an example of real estate fund that offers a 7 percent preferred return with a seventy-five/twenty-five split in effect above and beyond the 7 percent preferred return. Let's assume that the investor initially contributed one hundred dollars and that the property cash flowed an average of 6 percent annually over the five-year hold period. Not taking into account any compounding of the return (which would depend upon the contract terms of the purchase agreement of the offering), the sponsor would need to distribute $135 to the investor (one hundred dollars of principal plus thirty-five dollars due to the 7 percent annual rate and the five-year hold) over the course of the investment to achieve the preferred return. Thirty dollars was already distributed over the hold period in the form of cash flow.

Let us assume further that the investor's interest in the property is sold for $125 after closing costs. The sponsor would then distribute to the investor the full original principal amount of $100, plus the remaining five dollars to reach the preferred return total of $135. At this point the seventy-five/twenty-five profit split is applied to the remaining twenty dollars, with fifteen dollars being distributed to the investor, and five dollars to the sponsor. Thus, in total the investor would invest one hundred dollars and receive a total of $150 on the back-end for a noncompounded IRR of 10 percent. The sponsor, in addition to certain asset management or other fees, would receive five dollars. Note, this is only an example to illustrate the way a preferred return structure works at the time of the disposition of the property and close of the investment. All such investments entail significant risks which have been highlighted in earlier chapters. It is possible for such investments to incur loss to principal, or a total loss of principal. Likewise, cash flow over the hold is not guaranteed.

For those who are more visually oriented, the same sample return is presented below in a more concise manner.

SAMPLE INVESTMENT RETURN

Original Principal Placed:	$100
Preferred Return:	7 percent
Projected Cash Flow:	6 percent
Hold Period:	5 Years
Anticipated Preferred Return over 5 Year hold period:	$35
Preferred Return paid via Cash Flow during Hold:	$30 ($6 per year for 5 years)
Preferred Return paid at property sale:	$5
Total Preferred Return:	$35
Additional Return paid to investors per profit split:	$15
Total Return to Investors:	$150 (principal + Pref + Split)

Conclusion

Even though these funds have the potential for higher returns and diversification opportunity, they are not for everyone and there are significant elements of risk that should be evaluated by an investor prior to purchase. Additionally, because there is not a strong secondary market for these types of interests, these funds should be considered illiquid investments.

If one were to list the best investment strategy for investors to follow in only one word, that one word would be *diversification*. We all know the risk of placing all our eggs into only one basket, and a properly balanced investment portfolio will combine more aggressive investment strategies with more secure investment strategies. Real estate funds provide investors with the potential to receive much higher returns and greater tax advantages as compared to other investment options, and as such could play an important role of providing additional diversification to an investment portfolio.

Appendix A

Revenue Ruling 2004-86

Classification of a Delaware statutory trust. This ruling explains how a Delaware statutory trust described in the ruling will be classified for federal tax purposes and whether a taxpayer may acquire an interest in the Delaware statutory trust without recognition of gain or loss under § 1031 of the Code. Rev. Ruls. 78-371 and 92-105 distinguished.

Issue(s)

(1) In the situation described below, how is a Delaware statutory trust, described in Del. Code Ann. title 12, §§ 3801-3824, classified for federal tax purposes? (2) In the situation described below, may a taxpayer exchange real property for an interest in a Delaware statutory trust without recognition of gain or loss under § 1031 of the Internal Revenue Code?

Facts

On January 1, 2005, A, an individual, borrows money from BK, a bank, and signs a 10-year note bearing adequate stated interest, within the meaning of § 483. On January 1, 2005, A uses the proceeds of the loan to purchase Blackacre, rental real property. The note is secured by Blackacre and is nonrecourse to A. Immediately following A's purchase of Blackacre, A enters into a net lease with Z for a term of 10 years. Under the terms of the lease, Z is to pay all taxes, assessments, fees, or other charges imposed on Blackacre by federal, state, or local authorities. In addition, Z is to pay all insurance, maintenance, ordinary repairs, and utilities relating to Blackacre. Z may sublease Blackacre. Z's rent is a fixed amount that may be adjusted by a formula described in the lease agreement that is based upon a fixed rate or an objective index, such as an escalator clause based upon the Consumer Price Index, but adjustments to the rate or index are not within the control of any of the parties to the lease. Z's rent is not contingent on Z's ability to lease the property or on Z's gross sales or net profits derived from the property.

Also, on January 1, 2005, A forms DST, a Delaware statutory trust described in the Delaware Statutory Trust Act, Del. Code Ann. title 12, §§ 3801-3824, to hold property for investment. A contributes Blackacre to DST. Upon contribution, DST assumes A's rights and obligations under the note with BK and the lease with Z. In accordance with the terms of the note, neither DST nor any of its beneficial owners are personally liable to BK on the note, which continues to be secured by Blackacre. The trust agreement provides that interests in DST are freely transferable. However, DST interests are not publicly traded on an established securities market. DST will terminate on the earlier of 10 years from the date of its creation or the disposition of Blackacre, but will not terminate on the bankruptcy, death, or incapacity of any owner or on the transfer of any right, title, or interest of the owners. The trust agreement further provides that interests in DST will be of a single class, representing undivided beneficial interests in the assets of DST.

Under the trust agreement, the trustee is authorized to establish a reasonable reserve for expenses associated with holding Blackacre that may be payable out of trust funds. The trustee is required to distribute all available cash less reserves quarterly to each beneficial owner in proportion to their respective interests in DST. The trustee is required to invest cash received from Blackacre between each quarterly distribution and all cash held in reserve in short-term obligations of (or guaranteed by) the United States, or any agency or instrumentality thereof, and in certificates of deposit of any bank or trust company having a minimum stated surplus and capital. The trustee is permitted to invest only in obligations maturing prior to the next distribution date and is required to hold such obligations until maturity. In addition to the right to a quarterly distribution of cash, each beneficial owner has the right to an in-kind distribution of its proportionate share of trust property.

The trust agreement provides that the trustee's activities are limited to the collection and distribution of income. The trustee may not exchange Blackacre for other property, purchase assets other than the short-term investments described above, or accept additional contributions of assets (including money) to DST. The trustee may not renegotiate the terms of the debt used to acquire Blackacre and may not renegotiate the lease with Z or enter into leases with tenants other than Z, except in the case of Z's bankruptcy or insolvency. In addition, the trustee may make only minor nonstructural modifications to Blackacre, unless otherwise required by law. The trust agreement further provides that the trustee may engage in ministerial activities to the extent required to maintain and operate DST under local law.

On January 3, 2005, B and C exchange Whiteacre and Greenacre, respectively, for all of A's interests in DST through a qualified intermediary, within the meaning of § 1.1031(k)-1(g). A does not engage in a § 1031 exchange. Whiteacre and Greenacre were held for investment and are of like kind to Blackacre, within the meaning of § 1031. Neither DST nor its trustee enters into a written agreement with A, B, or C, creating an agency relationship. In dealings with third parties, neither DST nor its trustee is represented as an agent of A, B, or C. BK is not related to A, B, C, DST's trustee or Z within the meaning of § 267(b) or § 707(b). Z is not related to B, C, or DST's trustee within the meaning of § 267(b) or § 707(b).

Law

Delaware law provides that a Delaware statutory trust is an unincorporated association recognized as an entity separate from its owners. A Delaware statutory trust is created by executing a governing instrument and filing an executed certificate of trust. Creditors of the beneficial owners of a Delaware statutory trust may not assert claims directly against the property in the trust. A Delaware statutory trust may sue or be sued, and property held in a Delaware statutory trust is subject to attachment or execution as if the trust were a corporation. Beneficial owners of a Delaware statutory trust are entitled to the same limitation on personal liability because of actions of the Delaware statutory trust that is extended to stockholders of Delaware corporations. A Delaware statutory trust may merge or consolidate with or into one or more statutory entities or other business entities. § 671 provides that, where the grantor or another person is treated as the owner of any portion of a trust (commonly referred to as a "grantor trust"), there shall be included in computing the taxable income and credits of the grantor or the other person those items of income, deductions, and credits against tax of the trust which are attributable to that portion of the trust to the extent that the items would be taken into account under chapter 1 in computing taxable income or credits against the tax of an individual.

§ 1.671-2(e)(1) of the Income Tax Regulations provides that, for purposes of subchapter J, a grantor includes any person to the extent such person either creates a trust or directly or indirectly makes a gratuitous transfer of property to a trust. Under § 1.671-2(e)(3), the term "grantor" includes any person who acquires an interest in a trust from a grantor of the trust if the interest acquired is an interest in certain investment trusts described in § 301.7701-4(c).

Under § 677(a), the grantor is treated as the owner of any portion of a trust whose income without the approval or consent of any adverse party is, or, in the discretion of the grantor or a nonadverse party, or both, may be distributed, or held or accumulated for future distribution, to the grantor or the grantor's spouse. A person that is treated as the owner of an undivided fractional interest of a trust under subpart E of part I, subchapter J of the Code (§§ 671 and following), is considered to own the trust assets attributable to that undivided fractional interest of the trust for federal income tax purposes. See Rev. Rul. 88-103, 1988-2 C.B. 304; Rev. Rul. 85-45,

1985-1 C.B. 183; and Rev. Rul. 85-13, 1985-1 C.B. 184. See also § 1.1001-2(c), Example 5. § 761(a) provides that the term "partnership" includes a syndicate, group, pool, joint venture, or other unincorporated organization through or by means of which any business, financial operation, or venture is carried on, and that is not a corporation or a trust or estate. Under regulations the Secretary may, at the election of all the members of the unincorporated organization, exclude such organization from the application of all or part of subchapter K, if the income of the members of the organization may be adequately determined without the computation of partnership taxable income and the organization is availed of (1) for investment purposes only and not for the active conduct of a business, (2) for the joint production, extraction, or use of property, but not for the purpose of selling services or property produced or extracted, or (3) by dealers in securities for a short period for the purpose of underwriting, selling, or distributing a particular issue of securities.

§ 1.761-2(a)(2) provides the requirements that must be satisfied for participants in the joint purchase, retention, sale, or exchange of investment property to elect to be excluded from the application of the provisions of subchapter K. One of these requirements is that the participants own the property as co-owners. § 1031(a)(1) provides that no gain or loss is recognized on the exchange of property held for productive use in a trade or business or for investment if such property is exchanged solely for property of like kind that is to be held either for productive use in a trade or business or for investment.

§ 1031(a)(2) provides that § 1031(a) does not apply to any exchange of stocks, bonds or notes, other securities or evidences of indebtedness or interest, interests in a partnership, or certificates of trust or beneficial interests. It further provides that an interest in a partnership that has in effect a valid election under § 761(a) to be excluded from the application of all of subchapter K shall be treated as an interest in each of the assets of the partnership and not as an interest in a partnership.

Under § 301.7701-1(a)(1) of the Procedure and Administration Regulations, whether an organization is an entity separate from its owners for federal tax purposes is a matter of federal tax law and does not depend on whether the organization is recognized as an entity under local law. Generally, when participants in a venture form a state law entity and avail themselves of the benefits of that entity for a valid business purpose, such as investment or profit, and not for tax avoidance, the entity will be recognized for federal tax purposes. See Moline Properties, Inc. v. Comm'r, 319 US 436 (1943); Zmuda v. Comm'r, 731 F.2d 1417 (9th Cir. 1984); Boca Investerings P'ship v. United States, 314 F.3d 625 (D.C. Cir. 2003); Saba P'ship v. Comm'r, 273 F.3d 1135 (D.C. Cir. 2001); ASA Investerings P'ship v. Comm'r, 201 F.3d 505 (D.C. Cir. 2000); Markosian v. Comm'r, 73 T.C. 1235 (1980).

§ 301.7701-2(a) defines the term "business entity" as any entity recognized for federal tax purposes (including an entity with a single owner that may be disregarded as an entity separate from its owner under § 301.7701-3) that is not properly classified as a trust under § 301.7701-4 or otherwise subject to special treatment under the Code. A business entity with two or more owners is classified for federal tax purposes as either a corporation or a partnership. A business entity with only one owner is classified as a corporation or is disregarded.

§ 301.7701-3(a) provides that an eligible entity can elect its classification for federal tax purposes. Under § 301.7701-3(b)(1), unless the entity elects otherwise, a domestic eligible entity is a partnership if it has two or more owners or is disregarded as an entity separate from its owner if it has a single owner.

§ 301.7701-4(a) provides that the term "trust" refers to an arrangement created either by will or by an inter vivos declaration whereby trustees take title to property for the purpose of protecting and conserving it for the beneficiaries. Usually the beneficiaries of a trust do no more than accept the benefits thereof and are not voluntary planners or creators of the trust arrangement. However, the beneficiaries of a trust may be the persons who create it, and it will be recognized as a trust if it was created for the purpose of protecting and conserving the trust property for beneficiaries who stand in the same relation to the trust as they would if the trust had been created by others for them. § 301.7701-4(b) provides that there are other arrangements known as trusts because the legal title to property is conveyed to trustees for the benefit of beneficiaries, but that are not classified as trusts for federal tax purposes because they are not simply arrangements to protect or conserve the property for the beneficiaries. These trusts, which are often known as business or commercial trusts, generally are created by the beneficiaries simply as a device to carry on a profit-making business that normally would have been carried on through business organizations that are classified as corporations or partnerships.

§ 301.7701-4(c)(1) provides that an "investment" trust will not be classified as a trust if there is a power under the trust agreement to vary the investment of the certificate holders. See Comm'r v. North American Bond Trust, 122 F.2d 545 (2d Cir. 1941), cert. denied, 314 US 701 (1942). An investment trust with a single class of ownership interests, representing undivided beneficial interests in the assets of the trust, will be classified as a trust if there is no power to vary the investment of the certificate holders.

A power to vary the investment of the certificate holders exists where there is a managerial power, under the trust instrument, that enables a trust to take advantage of variations in the market to improve the investment of the investors. See Comm'r v. North American Bond Trust, 122 F.2d at 546. Rev. Rul. 75-192, 1975-1 C.B. 384, discusses the situation where a provision in the trust agreement requires the trustee to invest cash on hand between the quarterly distribution dates. The trustee is required to invest the money in short-term obligations of (or guaranteed by) the United States, or any agency or instrumentality thereof, and in certificates of deposit of any bank or trust company having a minimum stated surplus and capital. The trustee is permitted to invest only in obligations maturing prior to the next distribution date and is required to hold such obligations until maturity. Rev. Rul. 75-192 concludes that, because the restrictions on the types of permitted investments limit the trustee to a fixed return similar to that earned on a bank account and eliminate any opportunity to profit from market fluctuations, the power to invest in the specified kinds of short-term investments is not a power to vary the trust's investment.

Rev. Rul. 78-371, 1978-2 C.B. 344, concludes that a trust established by the heirs of a number of contiguous parcels of real estate is an association taxable as a corporation for federal tax purposes where the trustees have the power to purchase and sell contiguous or adjacent real estate, accept or retain contributions of contiguous or adjacent real estate, raze or erect any building or structure, make any improvements to the land originally contributed, borrow money, and mortgage or lease the property. Compare Rev. Rul. 79-77, 1979-1 C.B. 448 (concluding that a trust formed by three parties to hold a single parcel of real estate is classified as a trust for federal income tax purposes when the trustee has limited powers that do not evidence an intent to carry on a profitmaking business).

Rev. Rul. 92-105, 1992-2 C.B. 204, addresses the transfer of a taxpayer's interest in an Illinois land trust under § 1031. Under the facts of the ruling, a single taxpayer created an Illinois land trust and named a domestic corporation as trustee. Under the deed of trust, the taxpayer transferred legal and equitable title to real property to the trust, subject to the provisions of an accompanying land trust agreement. The land trust agreement provided that the taxpayer retained exclusive control of the management, operation, renting, and selling of the real property, together with an exclusive right to the earnings and proceeds from the real property. Under the agreement, the taxpayer was required to file all tax returns, pay all taxes, and satisfy any other liabilities with respect to the real property.

Rev. Rul, 92-105 concludes that, because the trustee's only responsibility was to hold and transfer title at the direction of the taxpayer, a trust, as defined in § 301.7701-4(a), was not established. Moreover, there were no other arrangements between the taxpayer and the trustee (or between the taxpayer and any other person) that would cause the overall arrangement to be classified as a partnership (or any other type of entity). Instead, the trustee was a mere agent for the holding and transfer of title to real property, and the taxpayer retained direct ownership of the real property for federal income tax purposes.

Analysis

Under Delaware law, a DST is an entity that is recognized as separate from its owners. Creditors of the beneficial owners of a DST may not assert claims directly against Blackacre. A DST may sue or be sued, and the property of a DST is subject to attachment and execution as if it were a corporation. The beneficial owners of a DST are entitled to the same limitation on personal liability because of actions of a DST that is extended to stockholders of Delaware corporations. A DST may merge or consolidate with or into one or more statutory entities or other business entities. A DST is formed for investment purposes. Thus, a DST is an entity for federal tax purposes.

Whether DST or its trustee is an agent of DST's beneficial owners depends upon the arrangement between the parties. The beneficiaries of DST do not enter into an agency agreement with DST or its trustee. Further, neither DST nor its trustee acts as an agent for A, B, or C in dealings with third parties. Thus, neither DST nor its trustee is the agent of DST's beneficial owners. Cf. Comm'r v. Bollinger, 485 US 340 (1988). This situation is distinguishable from Rev. Rul. 92-105. First, in Rev. Rul. 92-105, the beneficiary retained the direct obligation to pay liabilities and taxes relating to the property. DST, in contrast, assumed A's obligations on the lease with Z and on the loan with BK, and Delaware law provides the beneficial owners of DST with the same limitation on personal liability extended to shareholders of Delaware corporations.

Second, unlike A, the beneficiary in Rev. Rul. 92-105 retained the right to manage and control the trust property.

Issue 1. Classification of Delaware Statutory Trust

Because DST is an entity separate from its owner, DST is either a trust or a business entity for federal tax purposes. To determine whether DST is a trust or a business entity for federal tax purposes, it is necessary, under § 301.7701-4(c)(1), to determine whether there is a power under the trust agreement to vary the investment of the certificate holders.

Prior to, but on the same date as, the transfer of Blackacre to DST, A entered into a 10-year nonrecourse loan secured by Blackacre. A also entered into the ten-year net lease agreement with Z. A's rights and obligations under the loan and lease were assumed by DST. Because the duration of DST is 10 years (unless Blackacre is disposed of prior to that time), the financing and leasing arrangements related to Blackacre that were made prior to the inception of DST are fixed for the entire life of DST. Further, the trustee may only invest in short-term obligations that mature prior to the next distribution date and is required to hold these obligations until maturity. Because the trust agreement requires that any cash from Blackacre, and any cash earned on short-term obligations held by DST between distribution dates, be distributed quarterly, and because the disposition of Blackacre results in the termination of DST, no reinvestment of such monies is possible.

The trust agreement provides that the trustee's activities are limited to the collection and distribution of income. The trustee may not exchange Blackacre for other property, purchase assets other than the short-term investments described above, or accept additional contributions of assets (including money) to DST. The trustee may not renegotiate the terms of the debt used to acquire Blackacre and may not renegotiate the lease with Z or enter into leases with tenants other than Z, except in the case of Z's bankruptcy or insolvency. In addition, the trustee may make only minor nonstructural modifications to Blackacre, unless otherwise required by law.

This situation is distinguishable from Rev. Rul. 78-371, because DST's trustee has none of the powers described in Rev. Rul. 78-371, which evidence an intent to carry on a profitmaking business. Because all the interests in DST are of a single class representing undivided beneficial interests in the assets of DST and DST's trustee has no power to vary the investment of the certificate holders to benefit from variations in the market, DST is an investment trust that will be classified as a trust under § 301.7701-4(c)(1).

Issue 2. Exchange of Real Property for Interests under § 1031

B and C are treated as grantors of the trust under § 1.671-2(e)(3) when they acquire their interests in the trust from A. Because they have the right to distributions of all trust income attributable to their undivided fractional interests in the trust, B and C are each treated, by reason of § 677, as the owner of an aliquot portion of the trust and all income, deductions, and credits attributable to that portion are includible by B and C under § 671 in computing their taxable income. Because the owner of an undivided fractional interest of a trust is considered to own the trust assets attributable to that interest for federal income tax purposes, B and C are each considered to own an undivided fractional interest in Blackacre for federal income tax purposes. See Rev. Rul. 85-13. Accordingly, the exchange of real property by B and C for an interest in DST through a qualified intermediary is the exchange of real property for an interest in Blackacre, and not the exchange of real property for a certificate of trust or beneficial interest under § 1031(a)(2)(E). Because Whiteacre and Greenacre are of like kind to Blackacre and provided the other requirements of § 1031 are satisfied, the exchange of real property for an interest in DST by B and C will qualify for nonrecognition of gain or loss under § 1031. Moreover, because DST is a grantor trust, the outcome to the parties will remain the same, even if A transfers interests in Blackacre directly to B and C, and B and C immediately form DST by contributing their interests in Blackacre.

Under the facts of this case, if DST's trustee has additional powers under the trust agreement such as the power to do one or more of the following: (i) dispose of Blackacre and acquire new property; (ii) renegotiate the lease with Z or enter into leases with tenants other than Z; (iii) renegotiate or refinance the obligation used to purchase Blackacre; (iv) invest cash received to profit from market fluctuations; or (v) make more than minor nonstructural modifications to Blackacre not required by law, DST will be a business entity which, if it has two or more owners, will be classified as a partnership for federal tax purposes, unless it is treated as a corporation under §

7704 or elects to be classified as a corporation under § 301.7701-3. In addition, because the assets of DST will not be owned by the beneficiaries as co-owners under state law, DST will not be able to elect to be excluded from the application of subchapter K. See § 1.761-2(a)(2)(i).

Holdings

(1) The Delaware statutory trust described above is an investment trust, under § 301.7701-4(c), that will be classified as a trust for federal tax purposes.
(2) A taxpayer may exchange real property for an interest in the Delaware statutory trust described above without recognition of gain or loss under § 1031, if the other requirements of § 1031 are satisfied.

EFFECT ON OTHER REVENUE RULINGS

Rev. Rul. 78-371 and Rev. Rul. 92-105 are distinguished.

Appendix B

Revenue Procedure 2002-22

Conditions for Obtaining Rulings

The IRS ordinarily will not consider a request for a ruling under this revenue procedure unless the conditions described below are satisfied. Nevertheless, where the conditions described below are not satisfied, the IRS may consider a request for a ruling under this revenue procedure where the facts and circumstances clearly establish that such a ruling is appropriate.

1. Tenancy in Common Ownership

Each of the co-owners must hold title to the property (either directly or through a disregarded entity) as a tenant in common under local law. Thus, title to the property as a whole may not be held by an entity recognized under local law.

2. Number of Co-Owners

The number of co-owners must be limited to no more than thirty-five persons. For this purpose, a person is defined as in 7701(a)(1), except that a husband and wife are treated as a single person and all persons who acquire interests from a co-owner by inheritance are treated as a single person.

3. No Treatment of Co-Ownership as an Entity

The co-ownership may not file a partnership or corporate tax return, conduct business under a common name, execute an agreement identifying any or all the co-owners as partners, shareholders, or members of a business entity, or otherwise hold itself out as a partnership or other form of business entity (nor may the co-owners hold themselves out as partners, shareholders, or members of a business entity). The IRS generally will not issue a ruling under this revenue procedure if the co-owners held interests in the property through a partnership or corporation immediately prior to the formation of the co-ownership.

4. Co-Ownership Agreement

The co-owners may enter into a limited co-ownership agreement that may run with the land. For example, a co-ownership agreement may provide that a co-owner must offer the co-ownership interest for sale to the other co-owners, the sponsor, or the lessee at fair market value (determined as of the time the partition right is exercised) before exercising any right to partition (see section 6.06 of this revenue procedure for conditions relating to restrictions on alienation); or that certain actions on behalf of the co-ownership require the vote of co-owners holding more than 50 percent of the undivided interests in the property (see section 6.05 of this revenue procedure for conditions relating to voting).

5. Voting

The co-owners must retain the right to approve the hiring of any manager, the sale or other disposition of the property, any leases of a portion or all of the property, or the creation or modification of a blanket lien. Any sale, lease, or re-lease of a portion or all of the property, any negotiation or renegotiation of indebtedness secured by a blanket lien, the hiring of any manager, or the negotiation of any management contract (or any extension or renewal of such contract) must be by unanimous approval of the co-owners. For all other actions on behalf of the co-ownership, the co-owners may agree to be bound by the vote of those holding more than 50 percent of the undivided interests in the property. A co-owner who has consented to an action in conformance with this section 6.05 may provide the manager or other person a power of attorney to execute a specific document with respect to that action but may not provide the manager or other person with a global power of attorney.

6. *Restrictions on Alienation*

In general, each co-owner must have the rights to transfer, partition, and encumber the co-owner's undivided interest in the property without the agreement or approval of any person. However, restrictions on the right to transfer, partition, or encumber interests in the property that are required by a lender and that are consistent with customary commercial lending practices are not prohibited. See section 6.14 of this revenue procedure for restrictions on who may be a lender. Moreover, the co-owners, the sponsor, or the lessee may have a right of first offer (the right to have the first opportunity to offer to purchase the co-ownership interest) with respect to any co-owner's exercise of the right to transfer the co-ownership interest.

In addition, a co-owner may agree to offer the co-ownership interest for sale to the other co-owners, the sponsor, or the lessee at fair market value (determined as of the time the partition right is exercised) before exercising any right to partition.

7. *Sharing Proceeds and Liabilities upon Sale of Property*

If the property is sold, any debt secured by a blanket lien must be satisfied, and the remaining sales proceeds must be distributed to the co-owners.

8. *Proportionate Sharing of Profits and Losses*

Each co-owner must share in all revenues generated by the property and all costs associated with the property in proportion to the co-owner's undivided interest in the property. Neither the other co-owners, nor the sponsor, nor the manager may advance funds to a co-owner to meet expenses associated with the co-ownership interest, unless the advance is recourse to the co-owner (and, where the co-owner is a disregarded entity, the owner of the co-owner) and is not for a period exceeding 31 days.

9. Proportionate Sharing of Debt

The co-owners must share in any indebtedness secured by a blanket lien in proportion to their undivided interests.

10. Options

A co-owner may issue an option to purchase the co-owner's undivided interest (call option), provided that the exercise price for the call option reflects the fair market value of the property determined as of the time the option is exercised. For this purpose, the fair market value of an undivided interest in the property is equal to the co-owner's percentage interest in the property multiplied by the fair market value of the property as a whole. A co-owner may not acquire an option to sell the co-owner's undivided interest (put option) to the sponsor, the lessee, another co-owner, or the lender, or any person related to the sponsor, the lessee, another co-owner, or the lender.

11. No Business Activities

The co-owners' activities must be limited to those customarily performed in connection with the maintenance and repair of rental real property (customary activities). See Revenue Ruling 75-374, 1975-2 C.B. 261. Activities will be treated as customary activities for this purpose if the activities would not prevent an amount received by an organization described in 511(a)(2) from qualifying as rent under 512(b)(3)(A) and the regulations thereunder. In determining the co-owners' activities, all activities of the co-owners, their agents, and any persons related to the co-owners with respect to the property will be taken into account, whether or not those activities are performed by the co-owners in their capacities as co-owners. For example, if the sponsor or a lessee is a co-owner, then all the activities of the sponsor or lessee (or any person related to the sponsor or lessee) with respect to the property will be taken into account in determining whether the co-owners' activities are customary activities. However, activities of a co-owner or a related person with respect to the property (other than in the co-owner's capacity as a co-owner) will not be taken into account if the co-owner owns an undivided interest in the property for less than six months.

12. Management and Brokerage Agreements

The co-owners may enter into management or brokerage agreements, which must be renewable no less frequently than annually, with an agent, who may be the sponsor or a co-owner (or any person related to the sponsor or a co-owner), but who may not be a lessee. The management agreement may authorize the manager to maintain a common bank account for the collection and deposit of rents and to offset expenses associated with the property against any revenues before disbursing each co-owner's share of net revenues. In all events, however, the manager must disburse to the co-owners their shares of net revenues within three months from the date of receipt of those revenues. The management agreement may also authorize the manager to prepare statements for the co-owners showing their shares of revenue and costs from the property. In addition, the management agreement may authorize the manager to obtain or modify insurance on the property, and to negotiate modifications of the terms of any lease or any indebtedness encumbering the property, subject to the approval of the co-owners. (See section 6.05 of the revenue procedure for conditions relating to the approval of lease and debt modifications.) The determination of any fees paid by the co-ownership to the manager must not depend in whole or in part on the income or profits derived by any person from the property and may not exceed the fair market value of the manager's services. Any fee paid by the co-ownership to a broker must be comparable to fees paid by unrelated parties to brokers for similar services.

13. Leasing Agreements

All leasing arrangements must be bona fide leases for federal tax purposes. Rents paid by a lessee must reflect the fair market value for the use of the property. The determination of the amount of the rent must not depend, in whole or in part, on the income or profits derived by any person from the property leased (other than an amount based on a fixed percentage or percentages of receipts or sales). See section 856(d)(2)(A) and the regulations thereunder. Thus, for example, the amount of rent paid by a lessee may not be based on a percentage of net income from the property, cash flow, increases in equity, or similar arrangements.

14. Loan Agreements

The lender with respect to any debt that encumbers the property or with respect to any debt incurred to acquire an undivided interest in the property may not be a related person to any co-owner, the sponsor, the manager, or any lessee of the property.

15. Payments to Sponsor

Except as otherwise provided in this revenue procedure, the amount of any payment to the sponsor for the acquisition of the co-ownership interest (and the amount of any fees paid to the sponsor for services) must reflect the fair market value of the acquired co-ownership interest (or the services rendered) and may not depend, in whole or in part, on the income or profits derived by any person from the property.

Endnotes

1. Revenue Ruling 78-371.
2. IRC Section 301.7701-4(c)(1).
3. IRC Section 677; Revenue Ruling 85-13.
4. Revenue Ruling 2004-86.
5. US Census Bureau.
6. What is a Delaware Statutory Trusts by Rich Bell.
7. A Short History of the Court of Chancery by William T. Quillen and Manrahan.
8. Article VI, Section 14 of the Second Delaware Constitution adopted in 1792.
9. Common Law Trusts—Delaware's Statutory Advantage by Richard, Layton & Finger.
10. Delaware Business Trusts by Larry D. Sullivan, Esquire.
11. A Delaware Statutory Trust as an Alternative Borrower for Tenant-in-Common Programs by Arnold S. Harrison, Esq.
12. IRS Private Letter Ruling 90-63.
13. *Gregory v. Helvering*, 293 US 465 (1935).
14. A Delaware Statutory Trust as an Alternative Borrower for Tenant-in-Common Programs by Arnold S. Harrison, Esq.
15. See Section 1202(e)(3)(A).
16. See Section 1202(e)(3)(A).
17. Under Secs. 162(a) and 62(a)(1).
18. Groetzinger, 480 US 23, 35 (1987).
19. (See also Higgins, 312 US 212 (1941); Stanton, 399 F.2d 326 (5th Cir. 1968); and Dagres, 136 T.C. 263 (2011).
20. Section 108(a)(1)(D).
21. A trust under Section 301.7701-4(c).
22. See powers described in Rev. Rul. 78-371.
23. Section 301.7701-2(a).

24 Joint Explanatory Statement of the Committee of Conference.
25 Federal Reserve Statistical Relaease, Z.1 Financial Accounts of the United States, Flow of Funds, Balance Sheets, and Integrated Macroeconomic Accounts, Fourth Quarter 2016.
26 2016 Ling and Petrova Study "the Economic Impact of Repealing or Limiting Section 1031 Like-Kind Exchanges in Real Estate."
27 Starker v. United States, 1979, retrieved 2007-07-04 ; Starker v. United States, 602 F. 2d 1341—Court of Appeals, 9th Circuit 1979.
28 Treasury Regulation §1.1031(k)-1(g)(7).
29 Long & Vrbanac, supra. note 2, § 4:06; Treas. Reg. §§ 1.1031(b)-1(c), 1.1031(d)-2, Example (2); Rev. Rul. 79-44, 1979-1 CB 265.
30 Section 12 of the 1933; see also FDIC v. Clark.
31 NASD, Special Report: Due Diligence Seminars (July 1981), p. 5.
32 See also Escott v. BarChris Construction Corporation.
33 AMERICAN LAW § 6.1, at 3.
34 Information provided by Taylor Garrett of Orchard Securities.
35 SEC v. W.J. Howey Company, the US Supreme Court.
36 Federal Reserve History.
37 Board of Governors of the Federal Reserve System (US).
38 Per Real Capital Analytics.
39 Zurichna Whitepaper, Lingering Recession Effects Real Estate.

CPSIA information can be obtained
at www.ICGtesting.com
Printed in the USA
LVHW091733020820
662196LV00001B/54